Georgia's Vintage
Coca-Cola Wall Signs

Delicious and Refreshing

By Robert Willson

MOUNTAIN PAGE PRESS
Hendersonville, NC

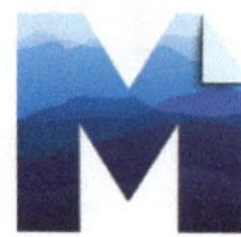

In memory of my father, Dr. Allan Edmond Willson, VP Coca-Cola
Director of Horticultural Research

Dad was my best friend.
His life was a living witness for Jesus Christ.

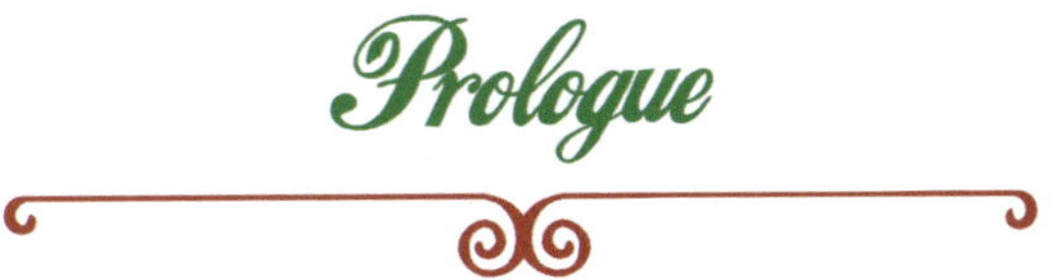

Painted Coca-Cola wall signs bring back memories of the days when life was slower and less complicated, and people were engaging with each other. This was the time before cell phones, mass media, and the internet. I asked why, where, and when these signs were painted, and as I asked these questions, I discovered an unexpected part of our American heritage.

Read on, but be careful! You might become another obsessed wall sign hunter, enjoying the thrill of discovery in every town you pass through.

Table of Contents

My fascination with Coca-Cola wall signs began years ago when my wife, Diane, and I were traveling the back roads of Georgia to visit our daughter, Lauren, at Auburn University. While traveling along U.S. 82, we noticed an old brick building on Main St. in the turn-of-the-century town of Sasser, Georgia. The antique stores, the old brick buildings, and the fading Coca-Cola wall sign painted over a Ballard's Obelisk Flour sign caught my interest.

I always carry my camera, so the fading Coca-Cola sign was a picture I had to take. Years later, while I was reviewing old pictures, the Sasser Coca-Cola sign caught my interest once again. What was the history behind the fading sign on an old brick building? I discovered that these disappearing, fading wall signs are an important part of American history.

I take no responsibility if after reading this you can no longer pass through a town without trying to find a wall sign, and discover the secret history it might hold.

My father worked for Coca-Cola, and like many boys, growing up I had the opportunity to work with my dad one very hot summer day in South Florida. We walked all day in dusty orange groves and had lunch at Yeehaw Junction. Years later I can still remember holding the iconic shape of an ice cold bottle of Coke. I lifted it to my lips and experienced the cold, bubbly liquid filling my mouth with a tingly, never-to-be-forgotten taste. I am sure Coca-Cola planned the "Delicious and Refreshing" taste experience to be remembered every time a Coca-Cola sign is seen!

The famous Coca-Cola wall signs painted on brick buildings were the forerunners of billboard advertising seen on trucks, stores, and highways all over the world. I began my Coca-Cola wall sign documentary project in Georgia for two main reasons: the Coca-Cola corporate headquarters and museum are located in Atlanta, Georgia, and in 1886, John Pemberton crafted the iconic drink in Columbus, Georgia.

Coca-Cola's Company Archives Department was very helpful and went beyond what I expected in providing information and help with this documentary. It was their information that made the discovery of Coca-Cola wall signs and their place in American history possible.

Some of the Coca-Cola signs pictured in this book may no longer exist, or soon will disappear forever. These fading signs are sometimes referred to as "ghost signs." I believe the history associated with these signs, buildings, and individual memories is an American treasure that should be preserved.

Coca-Cola wall signs were first painted in 1894, when Coca-Cola salesman and sign painter James Couden arrived in Cartersville, Georgia. Wanting to increase sales, he painted what is considered the first Coca-Cola wall sign, on a brick building that was home to Young and Mary's Drug Store.

James chose the location near the railroad tracks intentionally. Hot and thirsty departing passengers would know where to buy a refreshing Coca-Cola. The popularity of this advertising increased Coca-Cola sales and resulted in the birth of wall advertising.

Since the population traveled mainly by rail from the 1890s to the mid-1940s, many older Coca-Cola wall signs are located near train depots and railroad tracks. The early wall sign painters rapidly increased in number, and soon became known as "wall dogs."

In the 1920s and 1930s Coca-Cola began to realize the power of wall advertising, and for the first time needed to address brand conformity.

The company developed full-sized stencils with perforated holes, solving the uniformity problem.

Sign painters would start a sign by bouncing a cheesecloth bag filled with chalk over the stencil. Once painters removed the stencil, proper proportions could easily be painted in. The early stencils were called pounce patterns, and the cheesecloth bags were called pounce bags.

The iconic Coca-Cola silhouette girl was introduced in 1938, during this time.

Between the 1940s and 1960s, the traveling public would leave the train and transition to the more convenient automobile. Commuting to and from towns on the improving road system became the norm.

This change in travel pattern changed wall sign placement in several ways. Wall signs now appeared in city centers, with uniform color and script at eye level, easily seen from blocks away.

To address changing travel patterns, the Coca-Cola Company published the confidential booklet *Coca-Cola Outdoor Paint*. Coca-Cola colors were now standardized with mixing formulas, or could be purchased premixed directly from Sherwin Williams.

- Coca-Cola Red: No. Rx 20555
- Privilege Green: No. Rx 227-D
- Coca-Cola Border: No. Rx 22063
- Coca-Cola Yellow: No. Rx 213-L
- Black in Oil: No. Rx 102
- Pure White Lead in boiled Linseed Oil

During this time, the Coca-Cola Company wanted the public to use the name "Coca-Cola." The Sprite Boy pointing to a Coca-Cola bottle came on the scene around 1942. The slogan at the time was "The Only Thing Like Coca-Cola is Coca-Cola Itself."

Similar cola products were arriving on the market and the public was calling all of them Coke. Calling all drinks a Coke could potentially endanger Coca-Cola's identity and brand name.

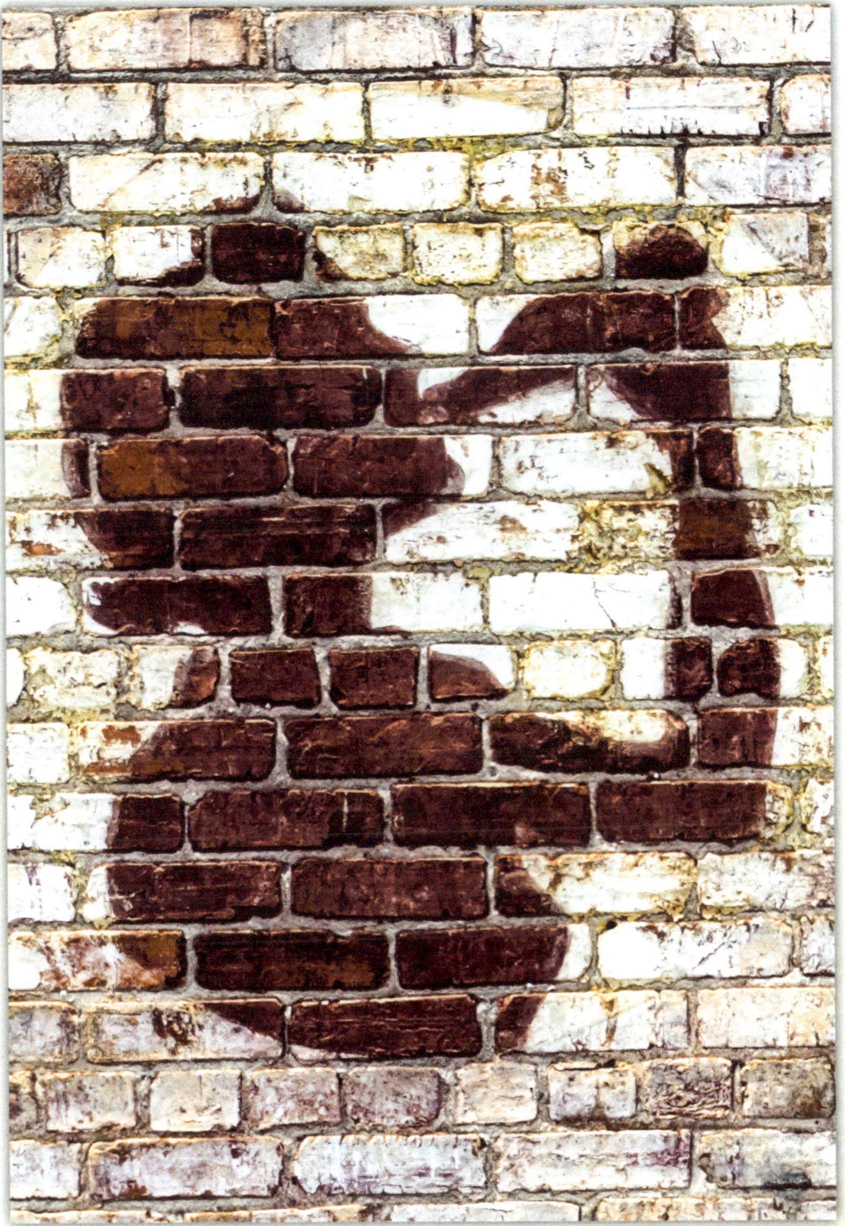

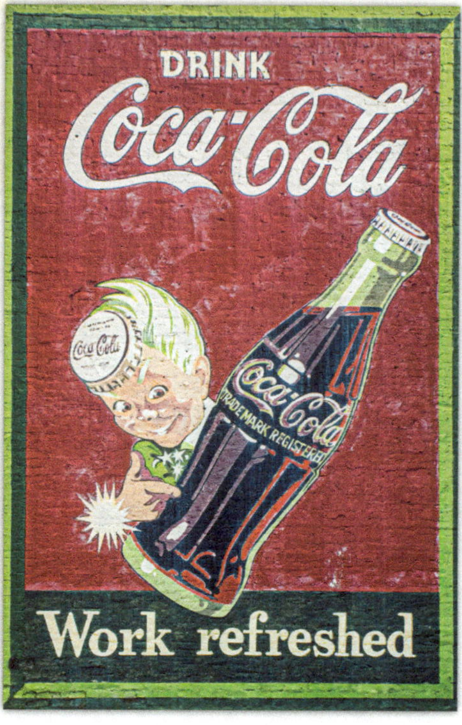

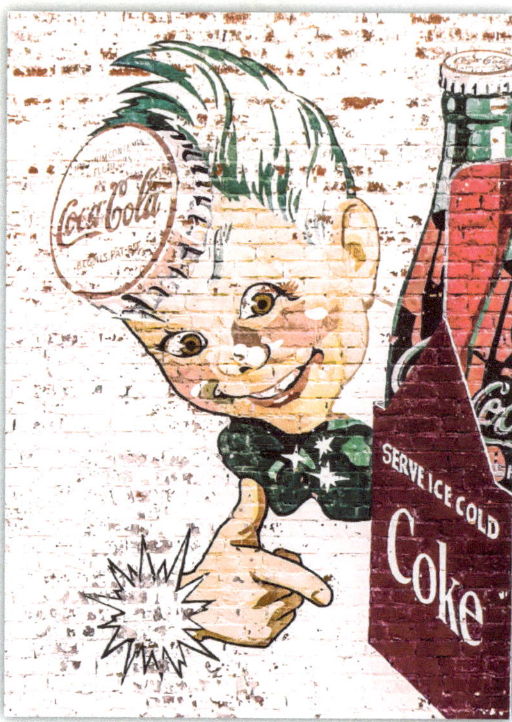

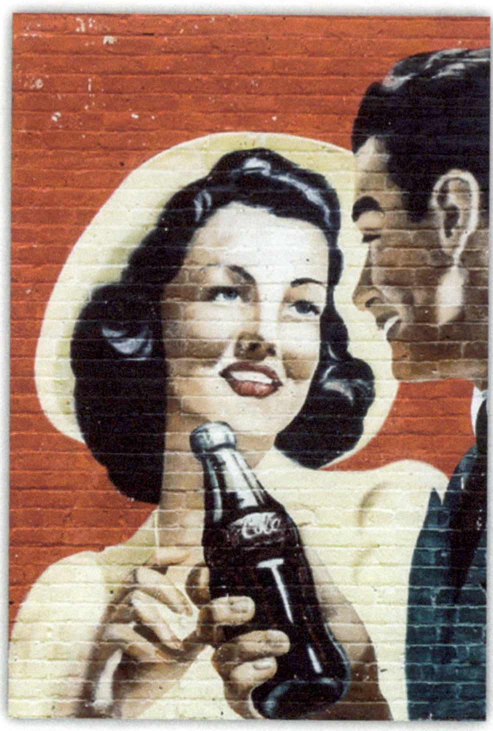

Coca-Cola had resigned itself to the fact that the public would use the names "Coke" and "Coca-Cola" for the same product. The Sprite Boy below is now pointing at a case of Coke.

In the 1950s, the Sprite Boy acquired a family of men, women, and a policeman, all holding bottles of Coke.

From the 1960s onward, the interstate system was developing. Cities were relocated or bypassed as the public started traveling on the interstate highways. In many cases cities were declining, so new wall signs were seldom painted.

Today, few of the old wall signs remain as they fade away, are painted over, or the building is demolished. The exceptions are signs saved and repainted as part of city renovation and revitalization projects.

I was able to find many remaining Coca-Cola wall signs with the help of Google Earth. I followed railroad tracks and went to historic city centers throughout Georgia, and soon discovered many towns had signs, but no one had any idea when they might have been painted.

Two very important pieces of information helped to determine with greater accuracy when a wall sign might have been painted. The first critical piece of information was the year a Coca-Cola slogan came into use. If the slogan was painted on the sign, it had to be painted that year or sometime later.

The list on the next page covers slogans through 2000, but few new wall signs were painted after 1982. If you are like me, reading the list of slogans brings back fond memories. How far back do you remember the slogans and what memories do you have?

Delicious and Refreshing

Coca-Cola Slogans Throughout the Years

1886	Drink Coca-Cola
1904	Delicious and Refreshing
1905	Coca-Cola Revives and Sustains
1906	The Great National Temperance Beverage
1917	Three Million a Day
1921	Thirst Knows No Season
1923	Enjoy Thirst
1924	Refresh Yourself
1925	Six Million a Day
1926	It Had to Be Good to Get Where It Is
1927	Pure as Sunlight
1927	Around the Corner from Everywhere
1932	Ice Cold Sunshine
1936	The Pause that Refreshes
1938	The Best Friend Thirst Ever Had
1939	Thirst Asks Nothing More
1942	The Only Thing Like Coca-Cola is Coca-Cola Itself
1948	Where There's Coke There's Hospitality
1949	Along the Highway to Anywhere
1952	What You Want is a Coke
1956	Coca-Cola…Makes Good Things Taste Better
1957	Sign of Good Taste
1958	The Cold, Crisp Taste of Coke
1959	Be Really Refreshed
1963	Things Go Better With Coke
1969	It's the Real Thing
1971	I'd Like to Buy the World a Coke
1975	Look Up America
1976	Coke Adds Life
1979	Have a Coke and a Smile
1982	Coke Is It!
1993	Always Coca-Cola
2000	Coca-Cola. Enjoy

The second piece of critical information is how the trademark is placed in the Coca-Cola wall sign. When John Stith Pemberton developed the now-famous Coca-Cola formula, he needed a name for his new product. His bookkeeper and associate at the time was Frank Mason Robinson, and it is Frank who receives credit for the famous name and original idea for the script lettering.

The lettering has changed and evolved through the years. Early lettering from the 1880s through about 1891 used various scripts with diamond variations and unusual script styles.

Between 1887 and 1890 the now familiar Coca-Cola script came into use. The familiar sweeping tail of the "C" under "Coca" and over "Cola," passing through the "L," was the evolving standard.

In the late 1890s, the United States patent office for the first time required trademarks to be registered and displayed. The appearance of the Coca-Cola script and the placement of the required trademark information helps determine when the wall sign might have been painted.

The crude Coca-Cola script was used from 1894 to 1903. The word "trade-mark" appeared in the tail of the "C" in Coca, or not at all. The first painted wall sign in Cartersville, Georgia, was painted around this time.

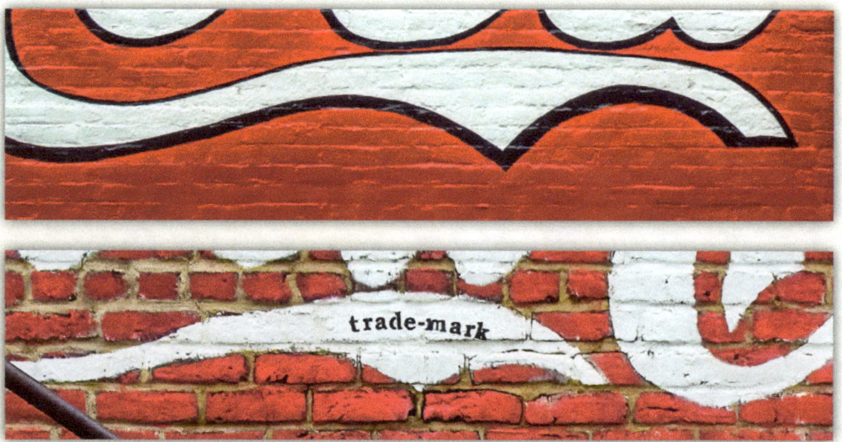

Between 1903 and 1931, Coca-Cola standardized the crude font to the now-familiar script we see today. "Trade-mark" was still displayed inside the tail of the "C" in Coca. The word REG or REGISTERED was added and started to show up.

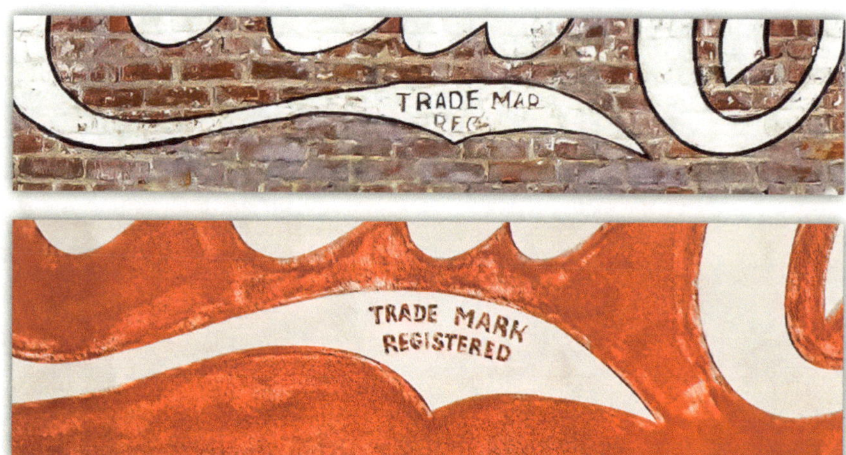

The United States patent office changed its mind once again between 1930 and 1941. The trademark information was still displayed inside the tail of the "C" in Coca, and the patented abbreviation "PAT." was now added to REGISTERED under TRADE MARK. The variation REG. U.S. PAT. OFF. was also used.

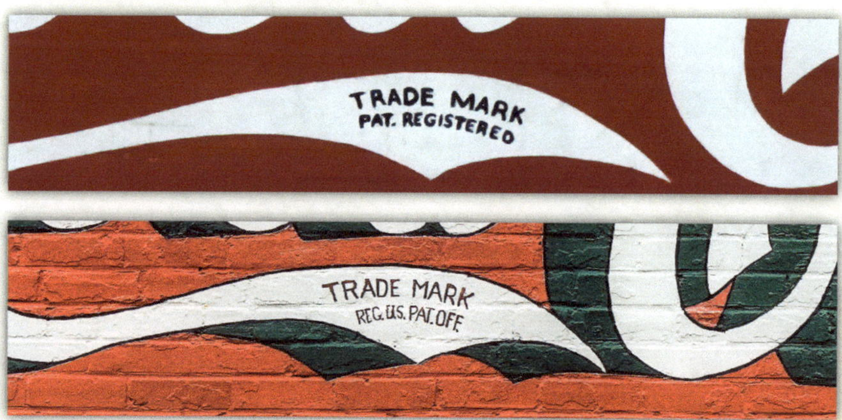

From 1940 to 1962, for the first time the trademark information moved outside of the tail of the "C" in Coca, appearing below the Coca-Cola name. The trademark information style also changed once again.

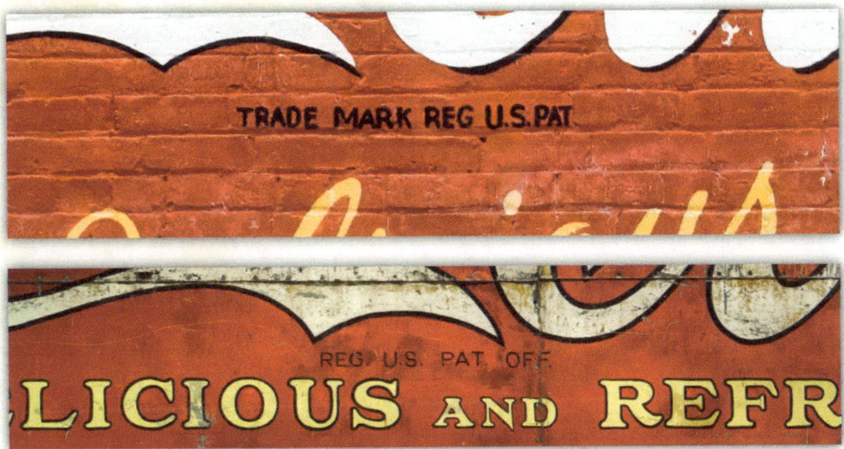

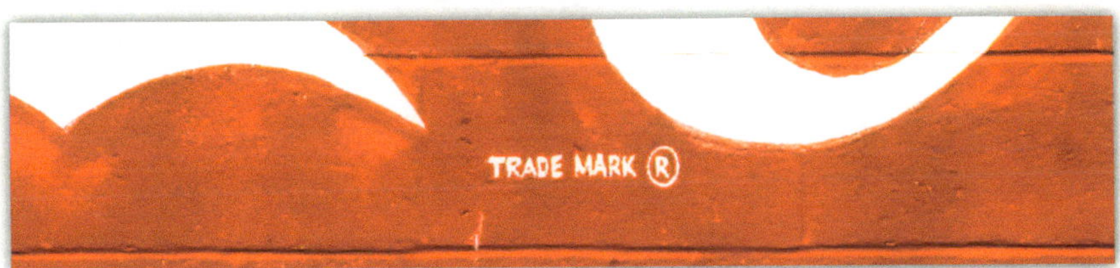

The trademark information would remain outside of the tail and below Coca-Cola from the 1950s to the present. Currently, the trademark information is simplified to the word "Trademark" with the ®, or simply the ® by itself.

It was in 1969 that the dynamic ribbon called the wave was introduced; it is still in use today. Trademark information is still located below the Coca-Cola name, and above the dynamic ribbon.

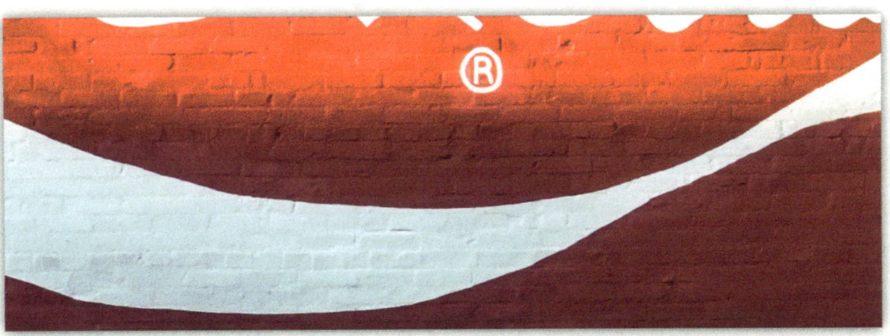

A condensed version of all the wall sign dating information can be found in the Appendix.

The fading Coca-Cola wall signs represent a time in our history when hometown businesses were an integral part of our lives, families were closely connected, and a nation was still being built. Since this documentary project started in 2015, I have talked with individuals, mayors, historians, business owners, building owners, and city employees. It is their stories and memories in the following pages that reveal the hidden magic of the Coca-Cola wall sign.

Acworth

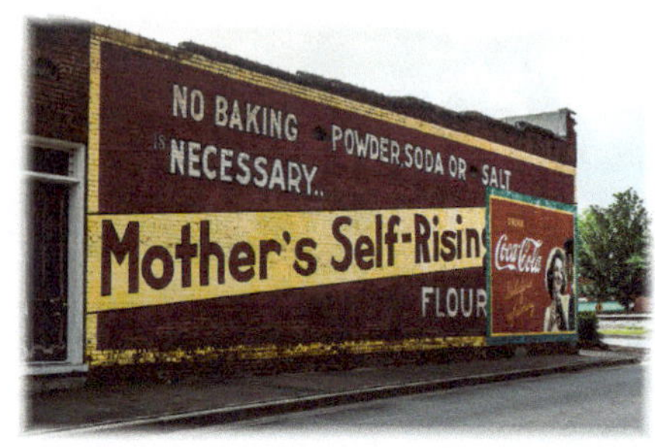

Southside Drive and Pedestrian Mall
GPS 34°3'58" N 84°40'40" W

The Acworth Coca-Cola sign on Cherokee St. was likely painted over the self-rising flour sign in the 1940s.
This Coke sign was restored in 2003 by Dianna Love Snell and Karl Snell of Art Productions, Inc.

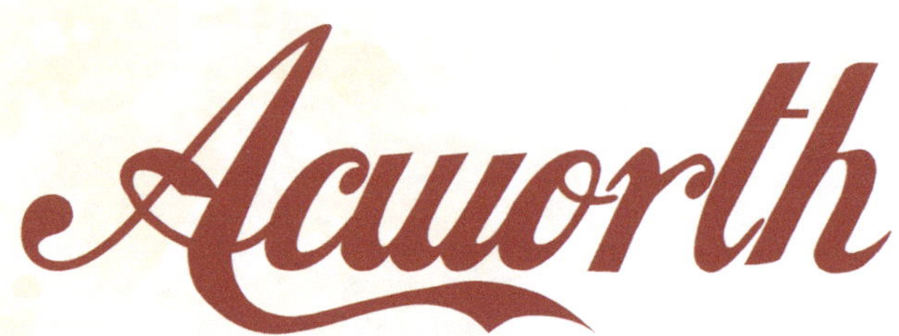

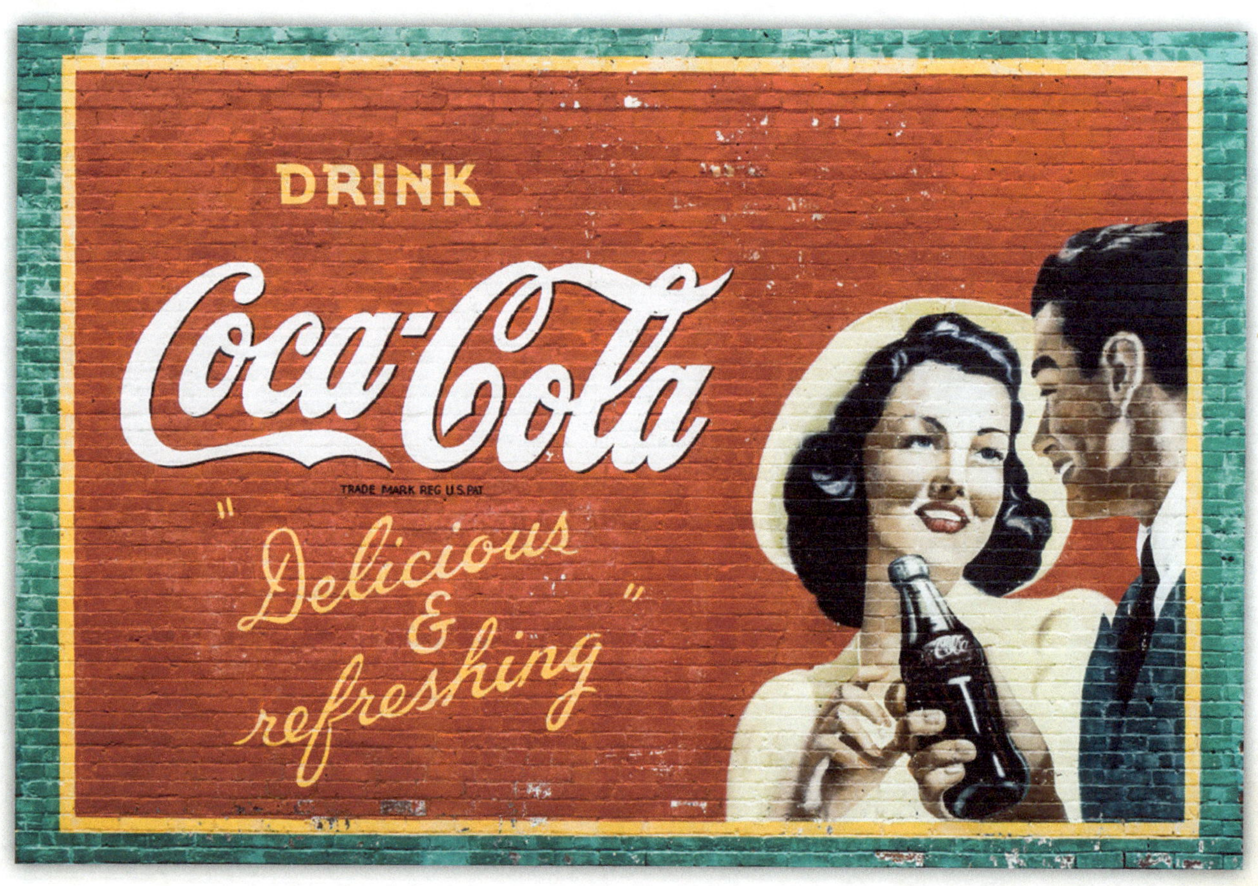

Delicious and Refreshing

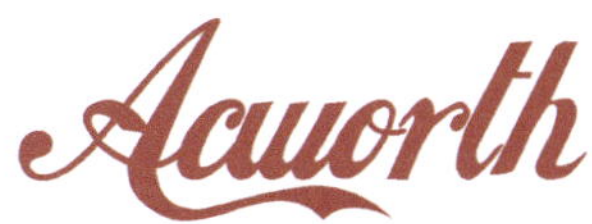

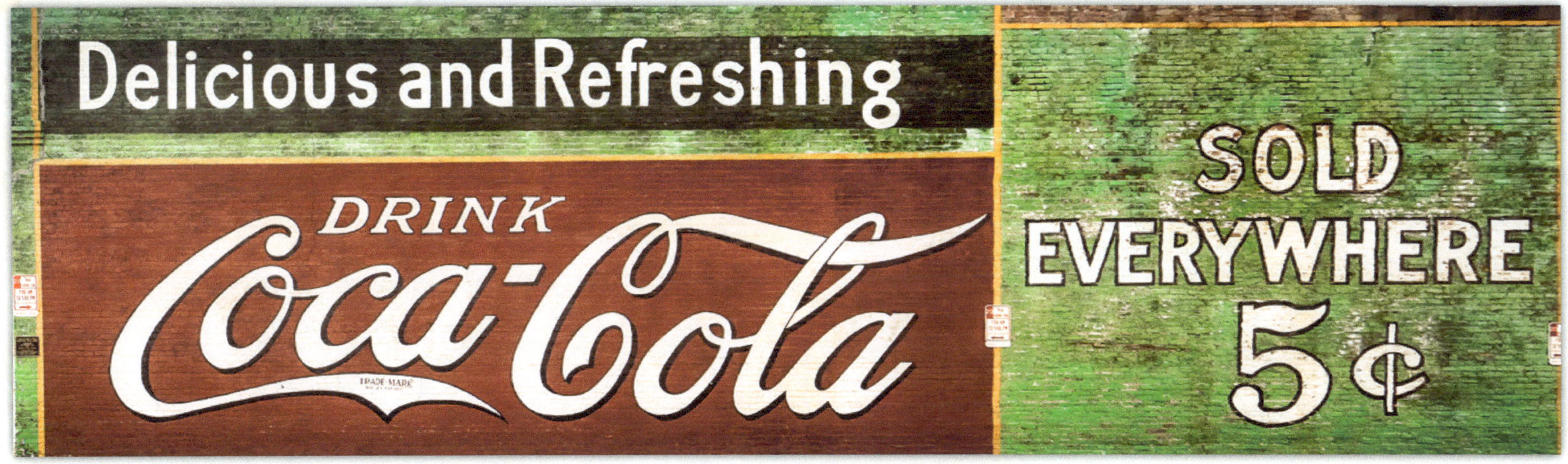

Corner of South Main St/Old Highway 41 NW and Dallas Street
GPS 34°3'60" N 84°40'39" W

Jeff Chase shared the details of the discovery of the Dallas St. Coca-Cola sign. This old sign was found as the wall was being prepared for a mural by the owner of Lacey Drug Co.

The owner of Lacey Drug Co. restored the original 1920s Coca-Cola sign in 2002; the work was done by Mark and Allan Lemon. The building's original business was dry goods, as indicated on a 1921 Sanborn map. Dianna Love Snell and Karl Snell of Art Productions, Inc. restored this sign to its original 2003 look.

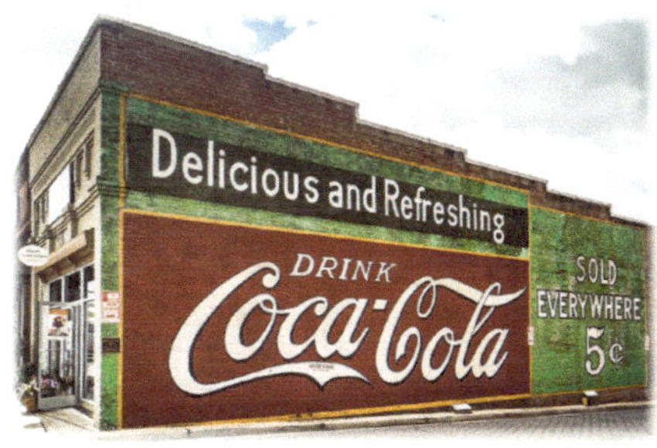

Allentoun

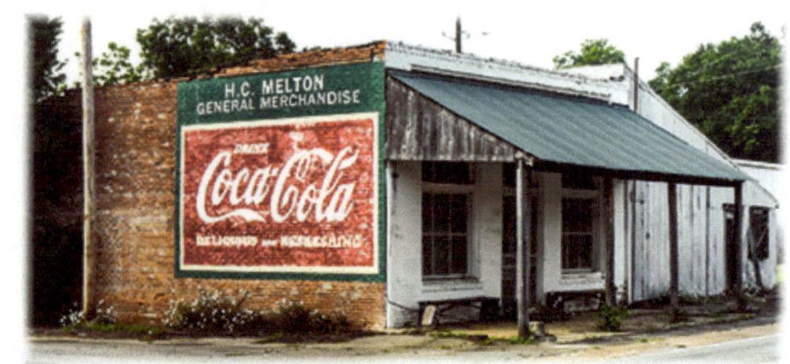

Corner of Balls Ferry Road and Allen Avenue
GPS 32°35'34" N 83°13'33" W

Mayor Robert Davidson remembers this building was built by Issac Adams for Henry Melton in 1900, and always had the sign. Growing up, Mayor Davidson remembers buying a 5-cent Coke from Mr. Melton. If he was a penny short, Melton "took care of it."

Henry Melton's wife was blind and helped him in the store. This sign was restored in 2007 by Casey Adams, "exactly as it originally appeared."

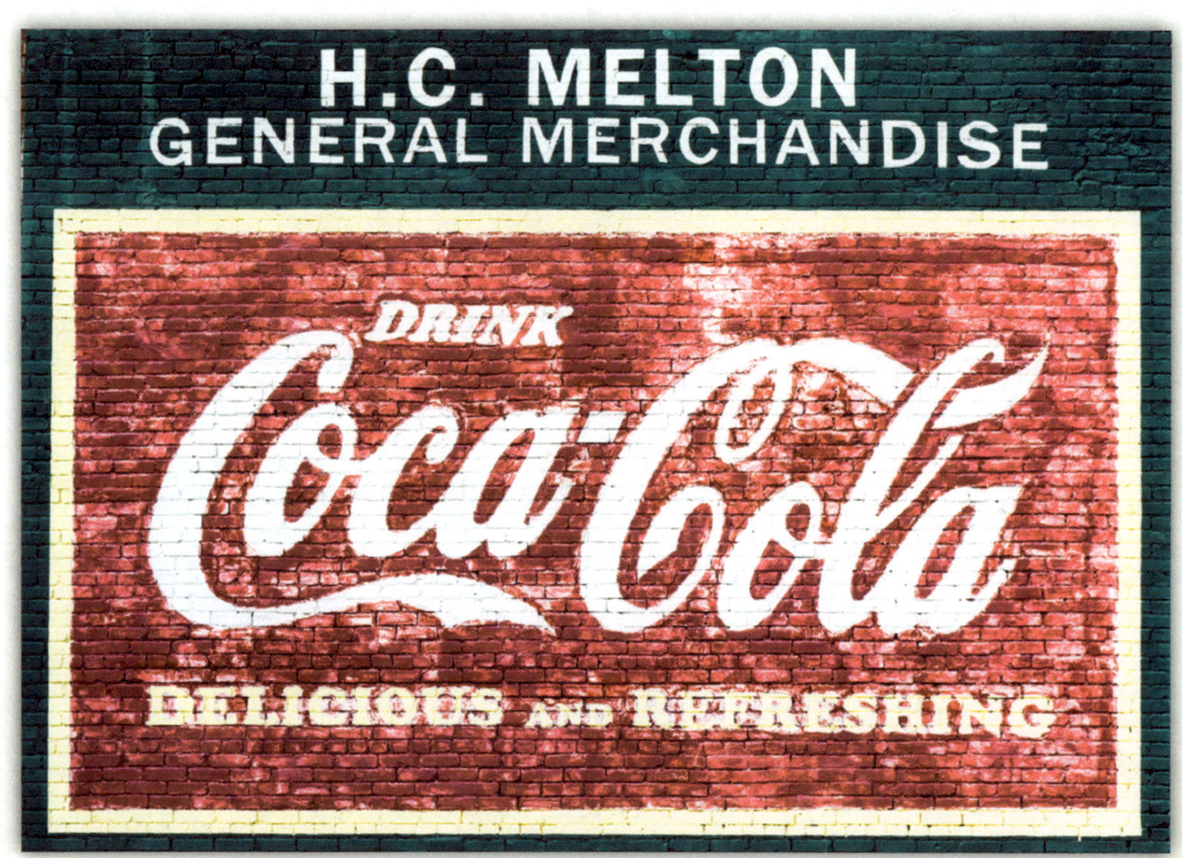

Delicious and Refreshing

Appling

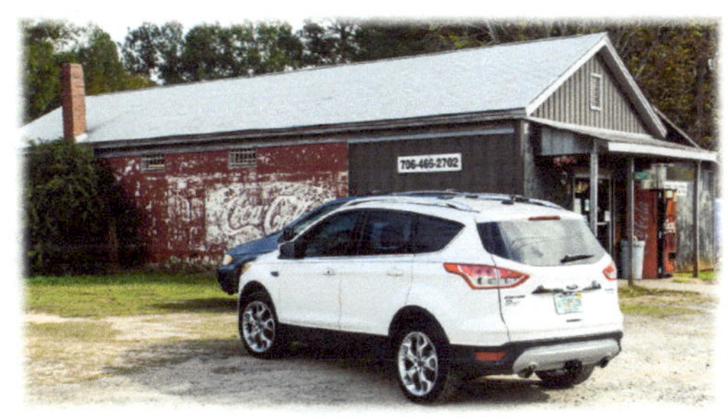

Cobbham Road near Mt. Carmel Church
GPS 33°24'27" N 82°39'45" W

According to resident David Bodie, the neighborhood grocery store was built by Ralph Dozier in 1942, but "when the sign was painted is unknown."

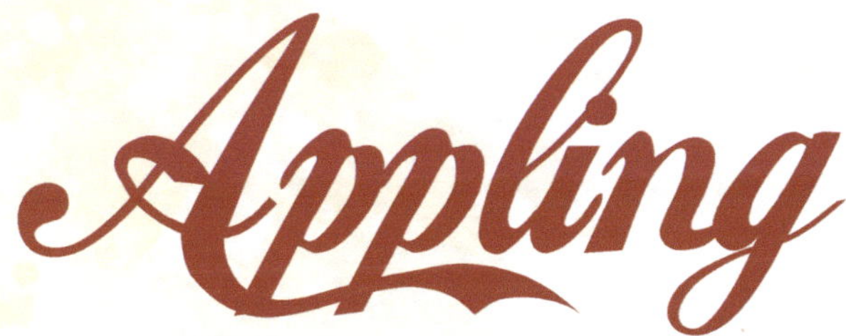

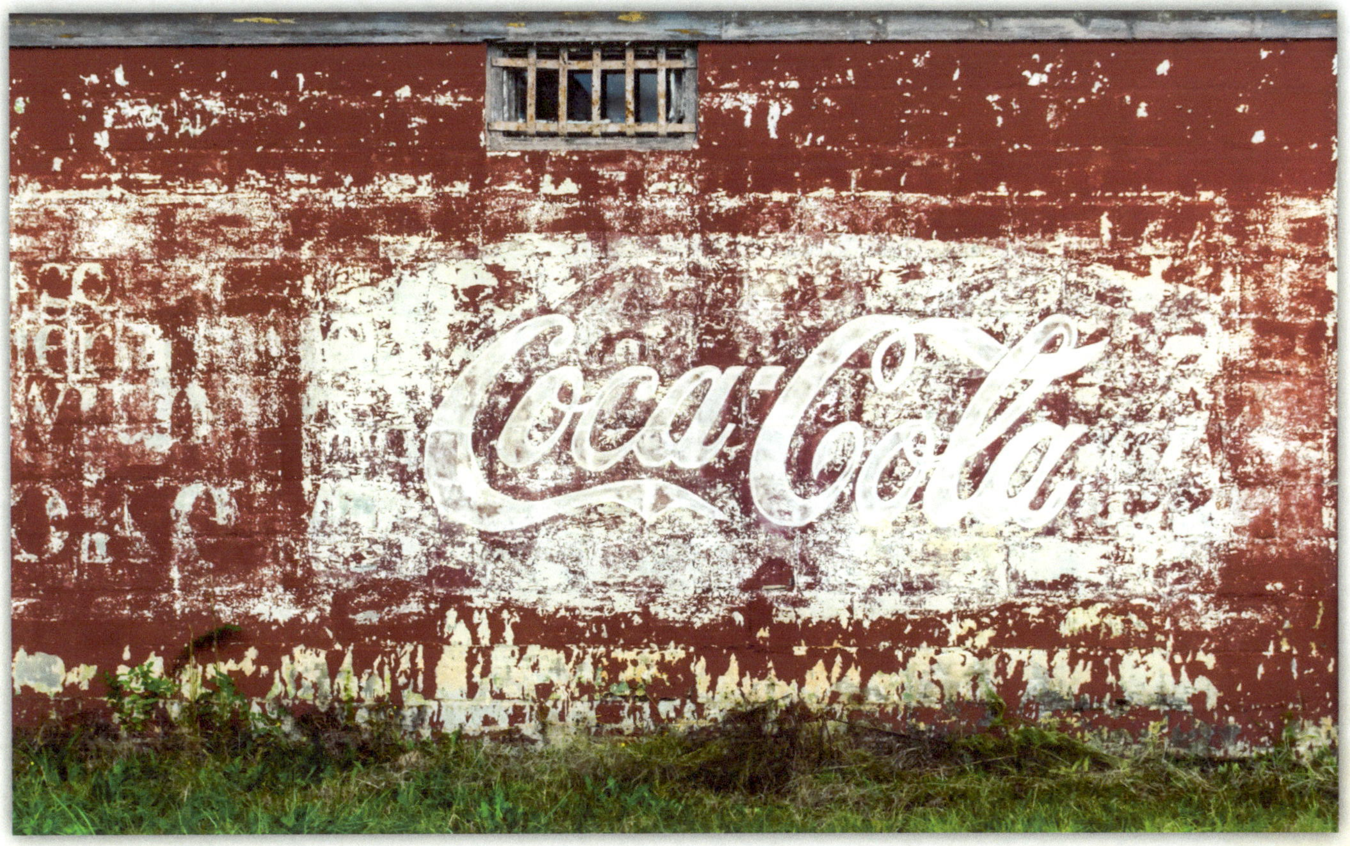

Corner of Meigs Street and N Newton Street

GPS 33°57'36" N 83°22'57" W

Steve Brown and Theresa Flynn of the Athens Historical Society determined the building was remodeled as a bottleworks between the late 1930s and the 1950s. Since the Coca-Cola wave, which came into use after 1962, is visible, it is likely this wall sign was painted around that time.

An older ghost sign visible underneath might date back to the building's bottleworks days.

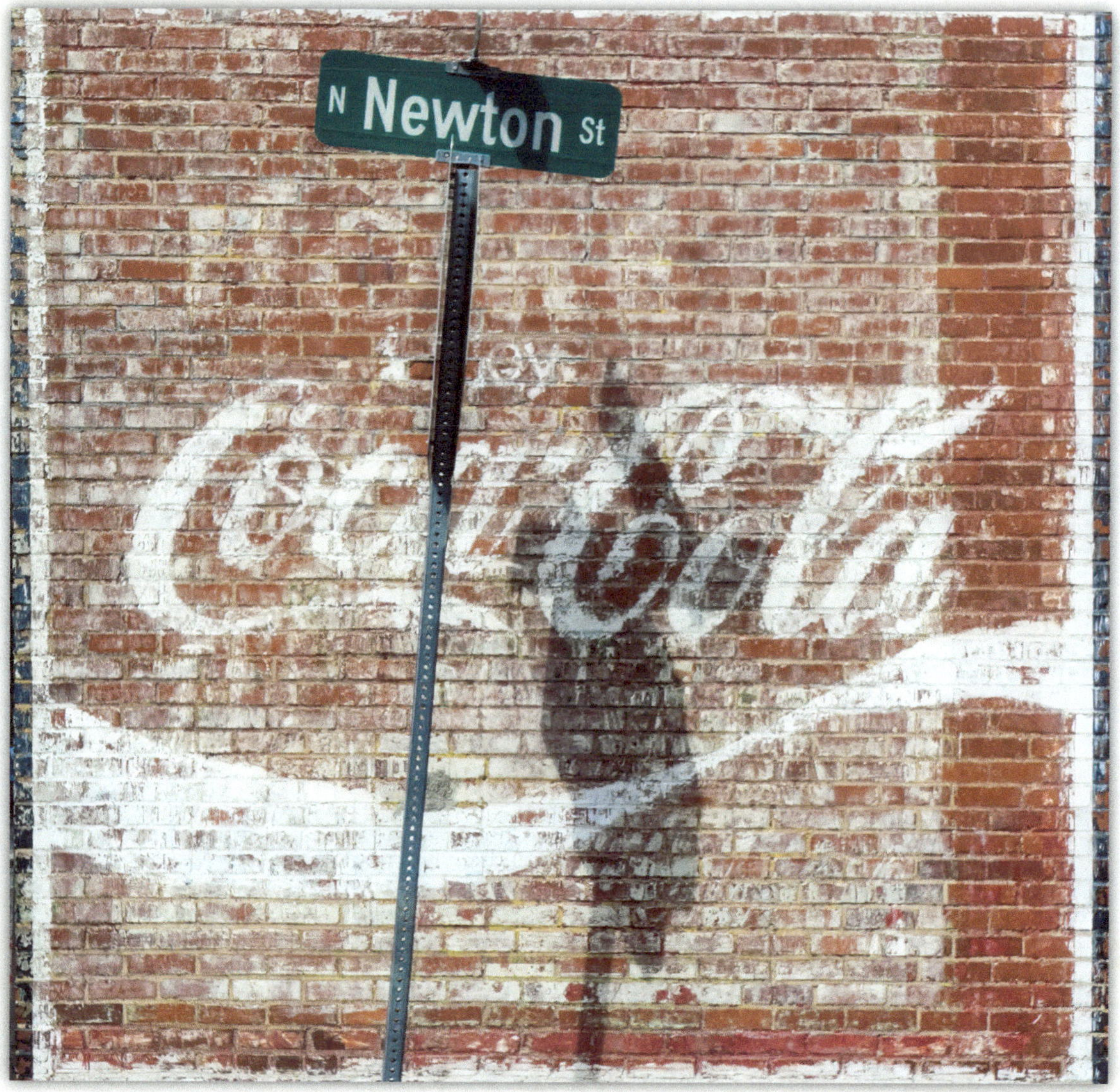

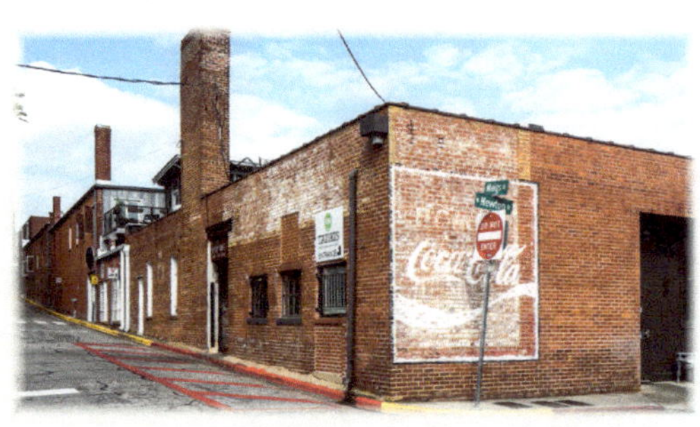

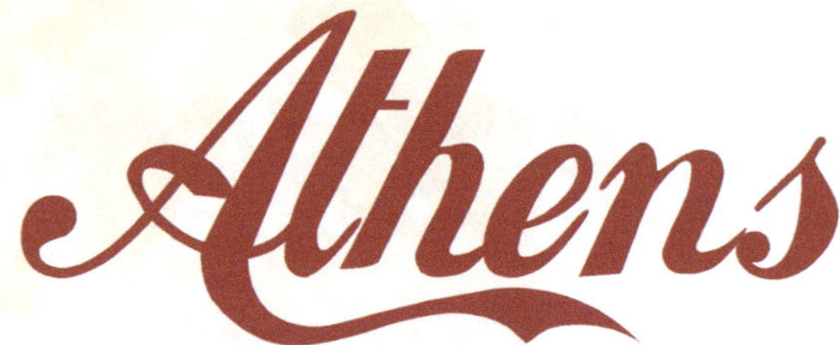

Atlanta

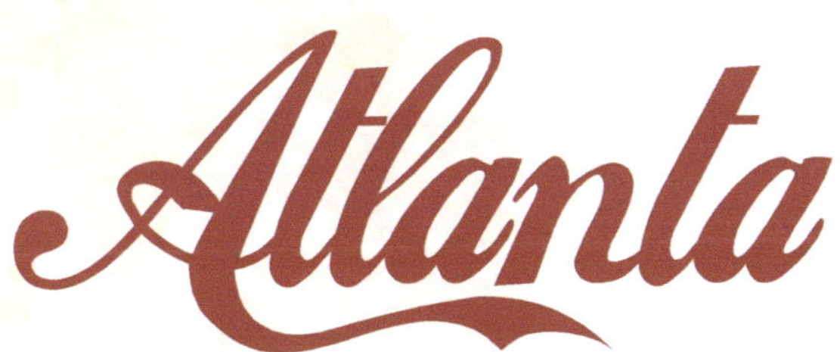

Mary Mac's - Corner of
Ponce DeLeon Avenue and Myrtle Street
GPS 33°46'21" N 84°22'48" W

Mary Mac's Tea Room is the last of 16 tea rooms that once were in this Atlanta area. Mary Mac established this tea room in 1945. It was passed down to Margaret Lupo, then to John Ferrell.

Matt Thompson, the current owner, shared that John and the retired chief executive officer of Coca-Cola Douglas Ivester were good friends, and Mary Mac's was Doug's favorite place to eat.

Doug had this sign painted and designed by Dianna Love Snell and Karl Snell of Art Productions, Inc., in 1997. The Snells have recently repainted it.

The 2011 Georgia House of Representatives voted Mary Mac's as "Atlanta's Dining Room." Many famous people have dined at Mary Mac's, including Jimmy Carter, Hillary Clinton, Joe Biden, and the 14th Dalai Lama.

Enjoy some great food, as I have done, and see the Coca-Cola sign.

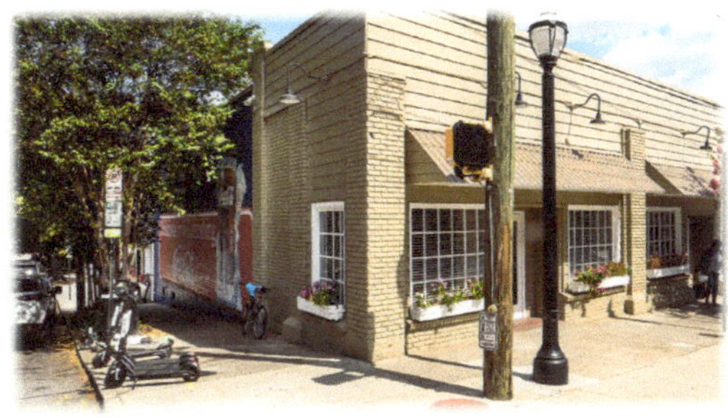

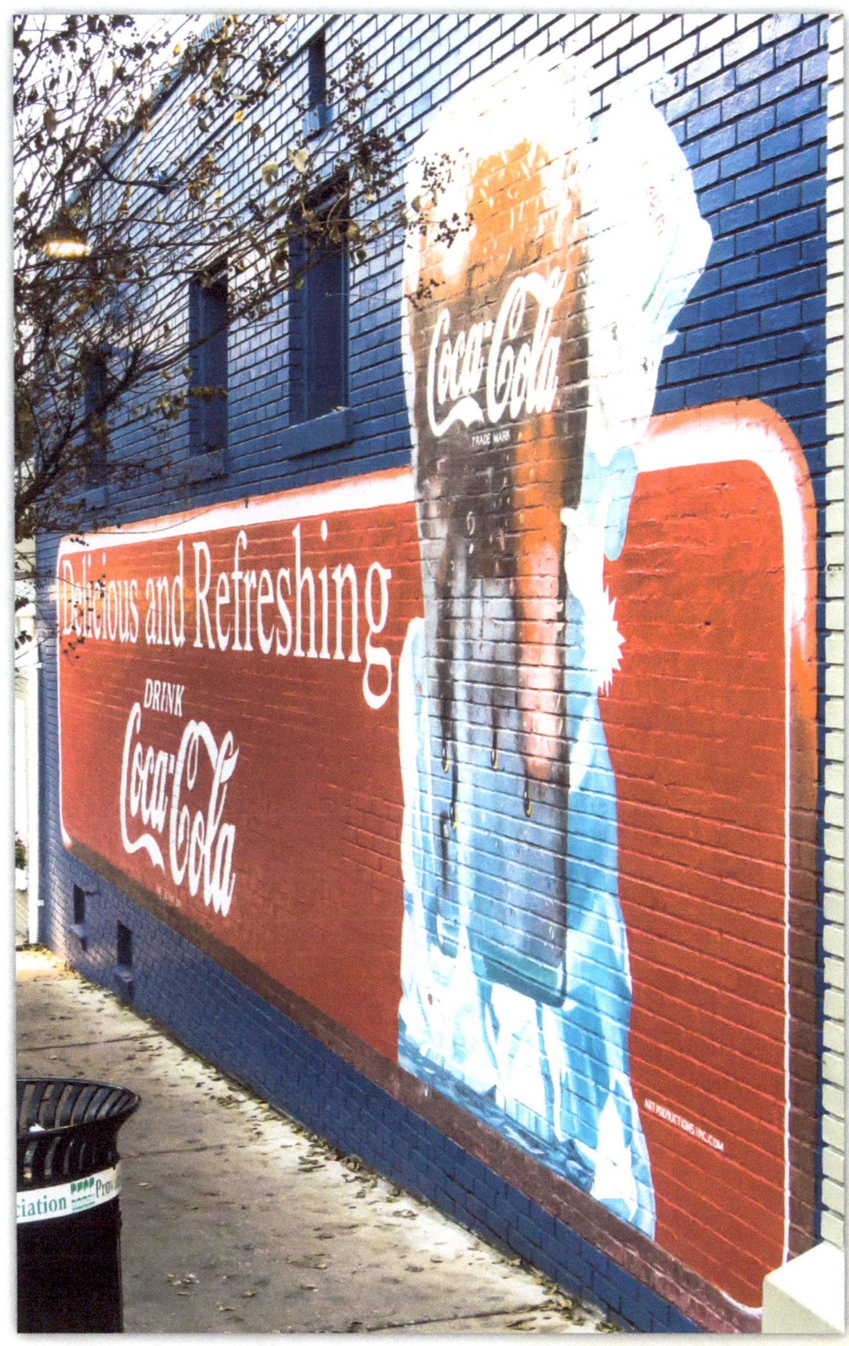

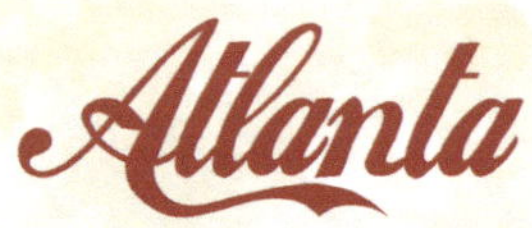

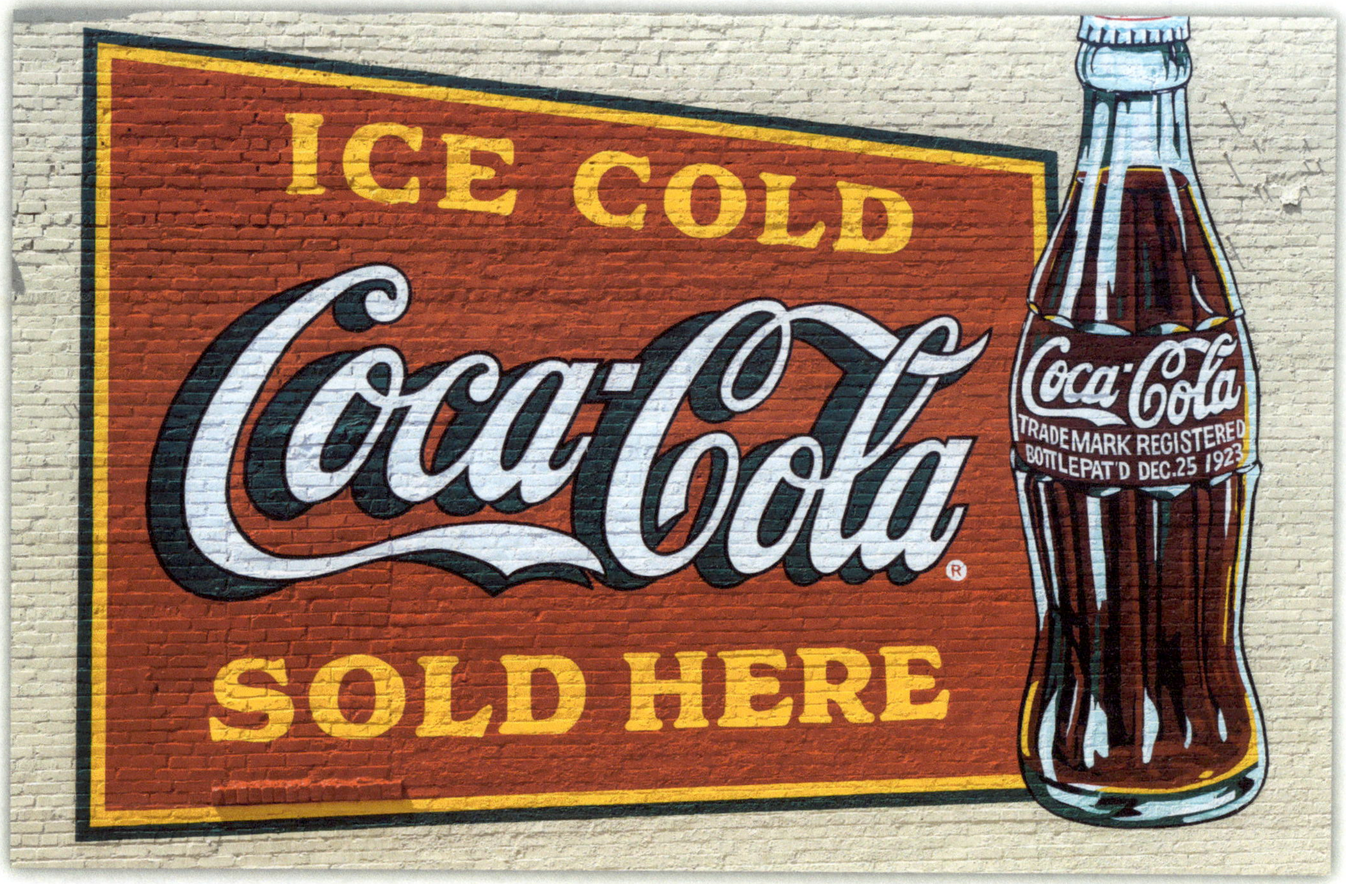

Manuel's Tavern - Corner of N. Highland Avenue NE and Williams Mill Road NE
GPS 33°46'14" N 84°21'10" W

Tavern owner Brian Maloof remembers seeing this Coke sign while growing up here in the 1980s. It has been repainted many times by Dianna Love Snell and Karl Snell of Art Productions, Inc., and later by Jack Fralin and Bill Johnson for the 1996 Atlanta Olympic Games.

This wall sign has been featured in the Coca-Cola Company's annual report, and as a backdrop for many images featuring U.S. presidents, celebrities, and local legislators.

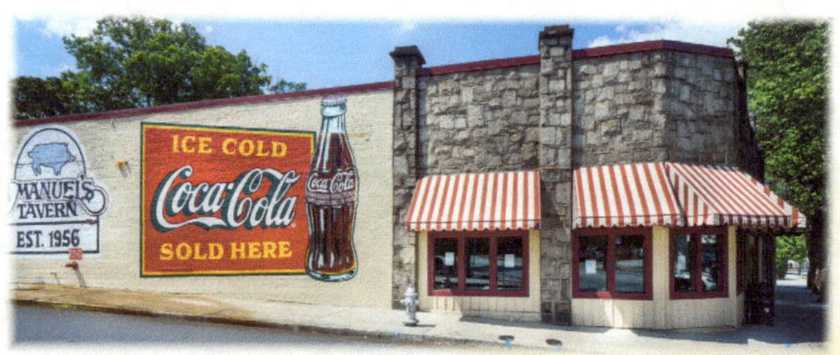

Delicious and Refreshing

Grant Park Coffee -
Corner of Augusta Avenue SE and Cherokee Avenue SE
GPS 33°44'1" N 84°22'25" W

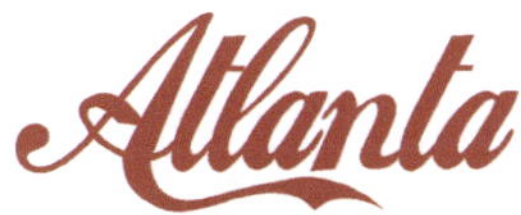

The Coca-Cola sign on the Grant Park Coffeehouse building is located in Atlanta's historic Grant Park area, across the street from the zoo.

The coffeehouse today is run by Rahel Pafari, and is a center for community gatherings and a place to enjoy a good cup of coffee and tasty treats. The wave is visible, so this wall sign was painted after 1969.

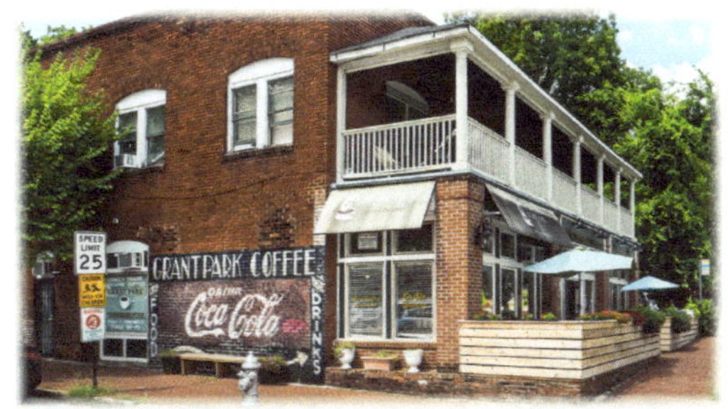

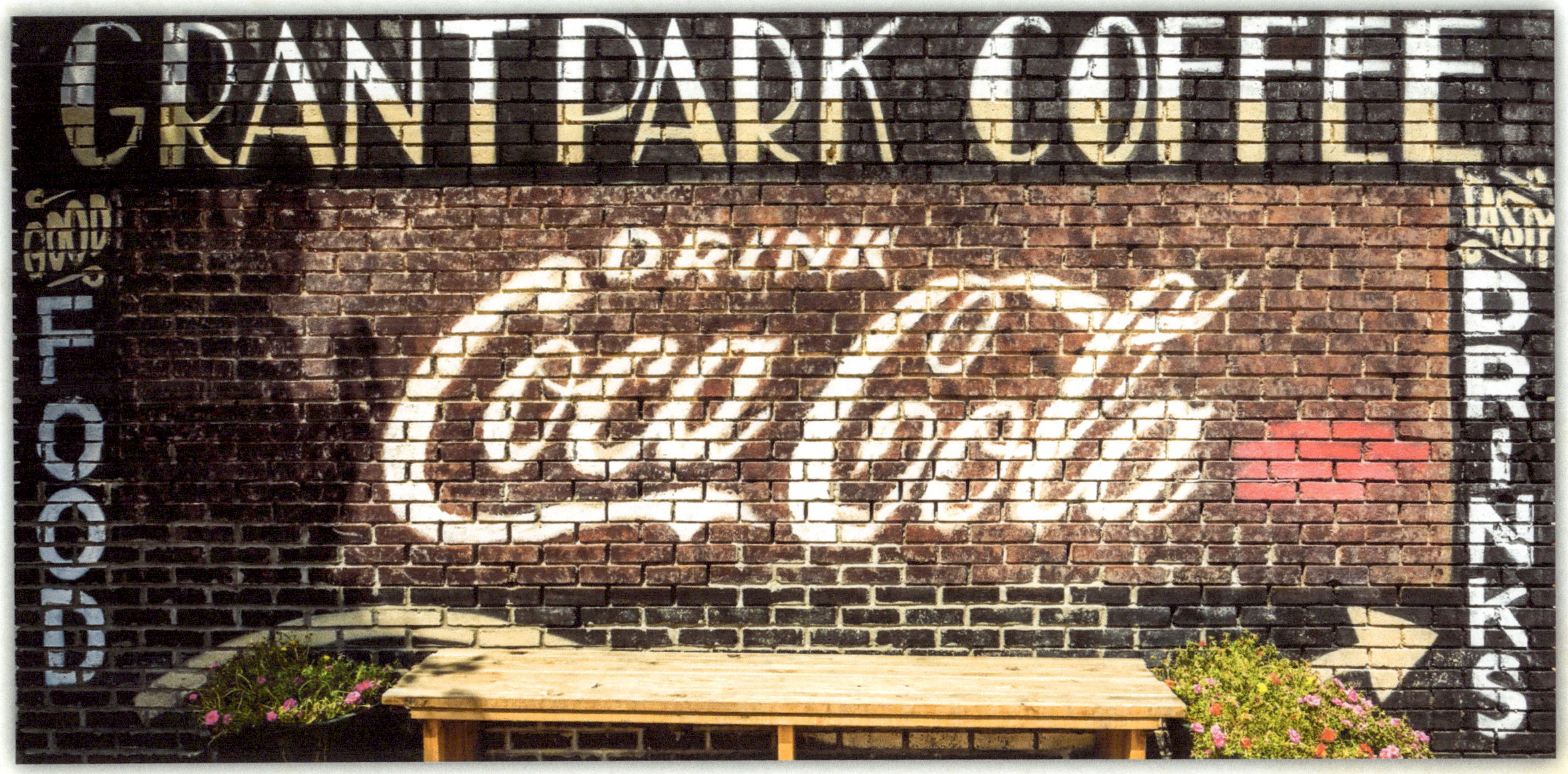

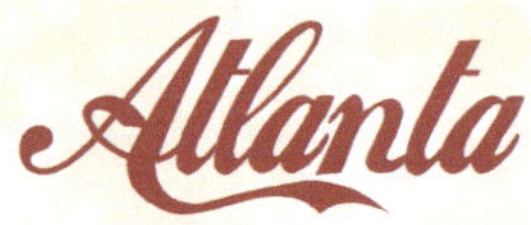

Underground Atlanta, Upper Alabama Street
GPS 33°45'8" N 84°23'25" W

This building was constructed by Frank E. Block for his candy factory located on the upper floors. In 1921, the downstairs tenant was the Carlos Soda Company, which had the Coca-Cola wall sign painted.

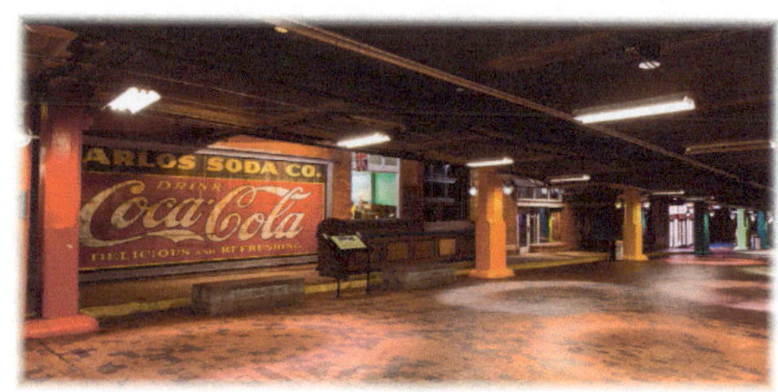

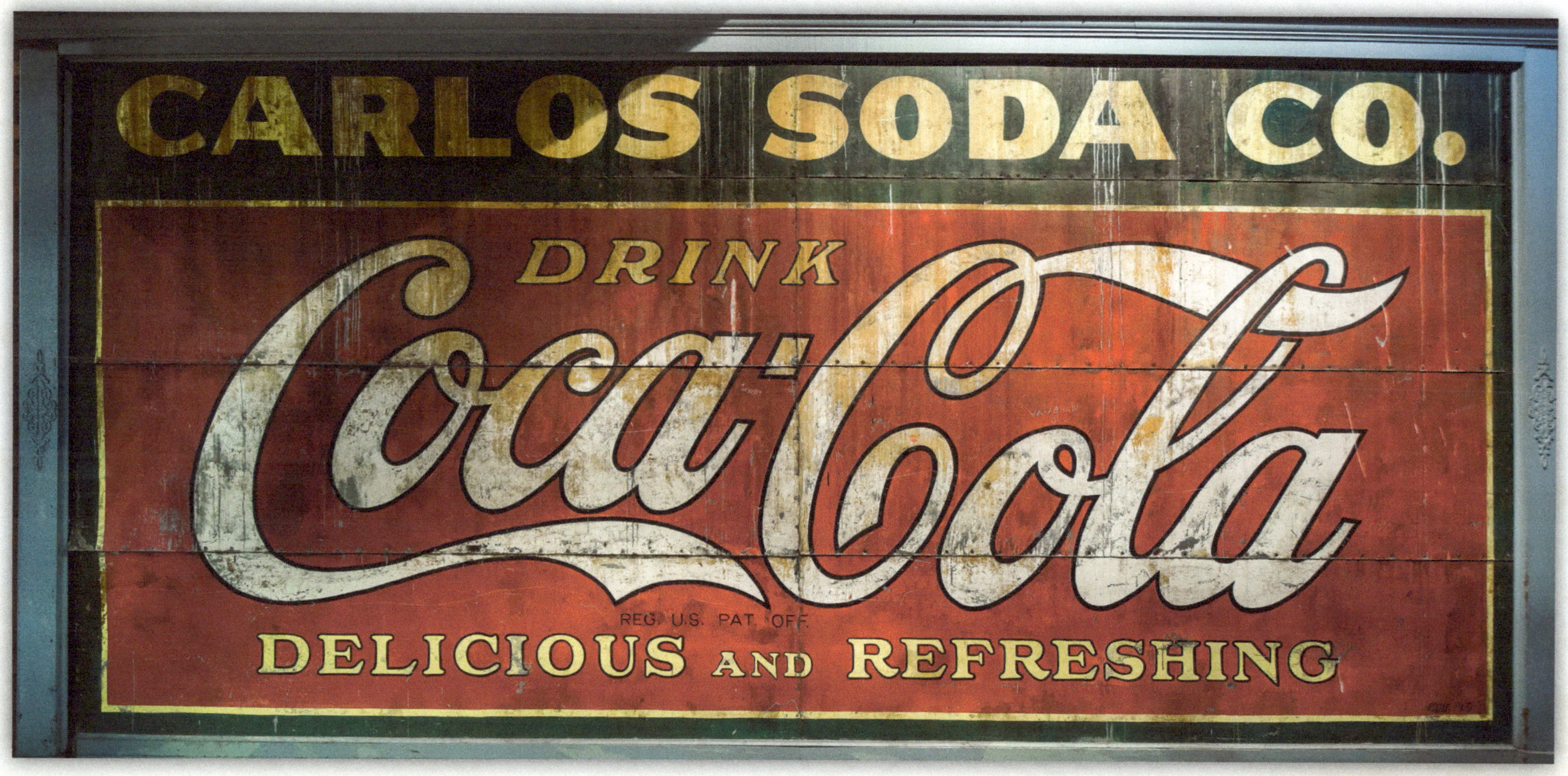

Delicious and Refreshing

Attapulgus

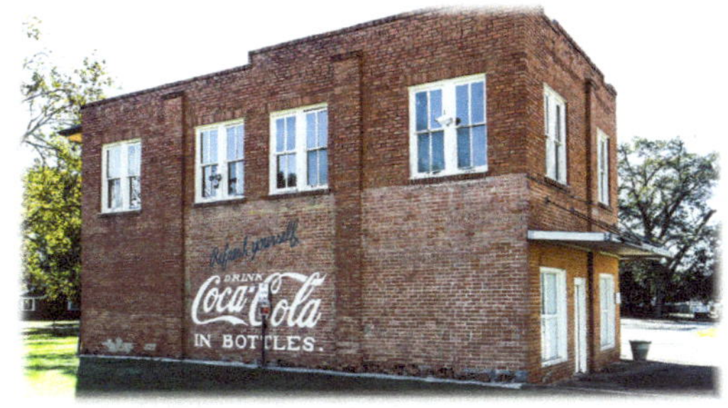

Near the corner of Church Street and E Griffin Avenue
GPS 30°44'56" N 84°29'3" W

This sign was painted around 1941 on the general store and post office, where Doris Gay remembers going for a 5-cent Coke and to meet her friends.

The building was donated to the town by Dr. Charles R. Hatcher Jr., and is now the Attapulgus Community Club.

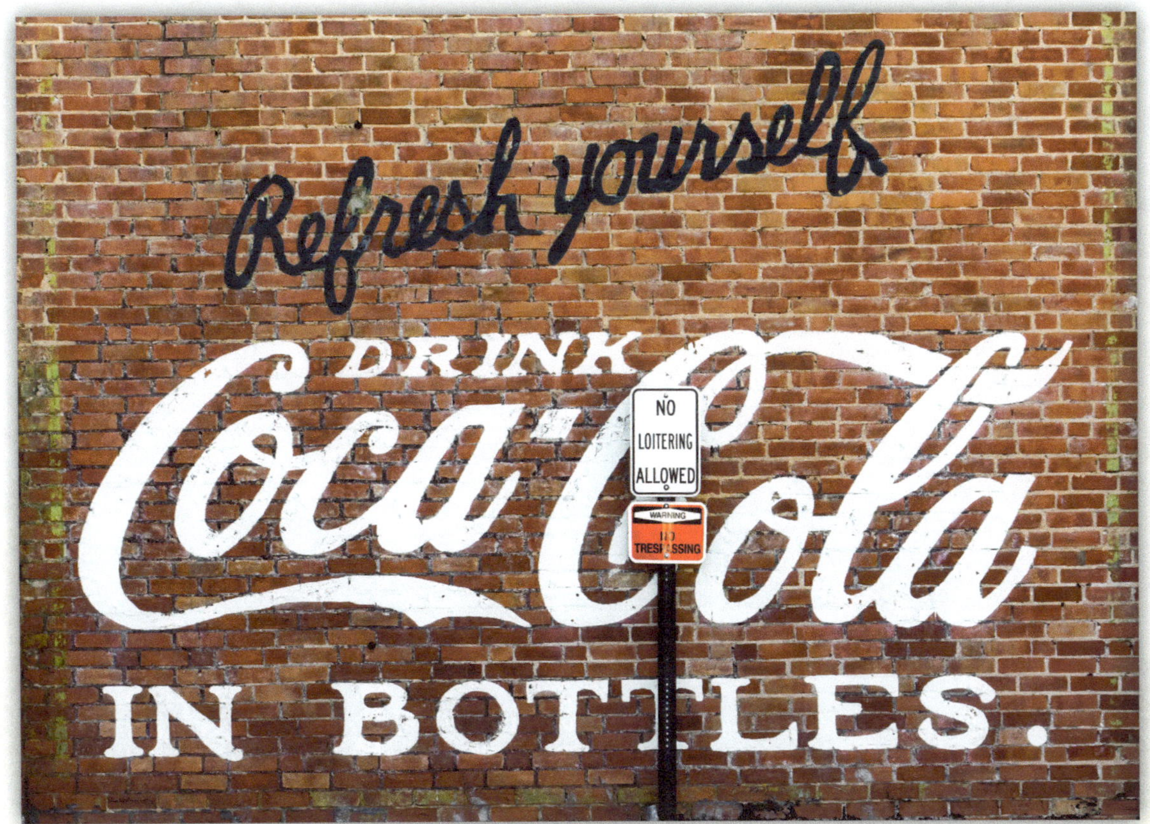

Austell

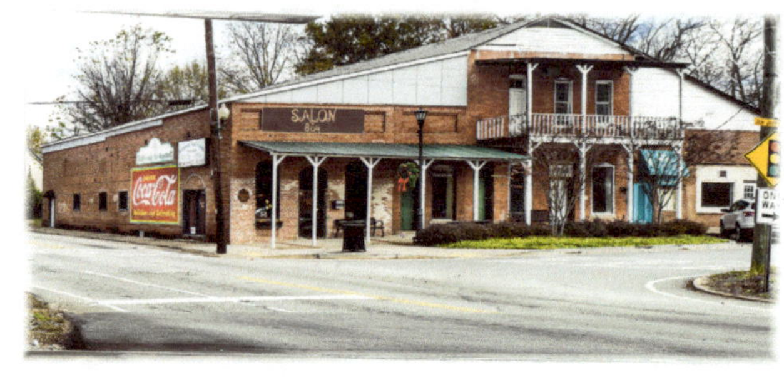

Corner of Powder Springs Road and Broad Street
GPS 33°48'48" N 84°38'5" W

This Coca-Cola wall sign is a newly painted original. Jeff Cross, who has been painting wall signs since 1982,
thought the town needed the sign, so he painted it in 2012. The building, once the Salt Springs Hotel, is the oldest building in town.

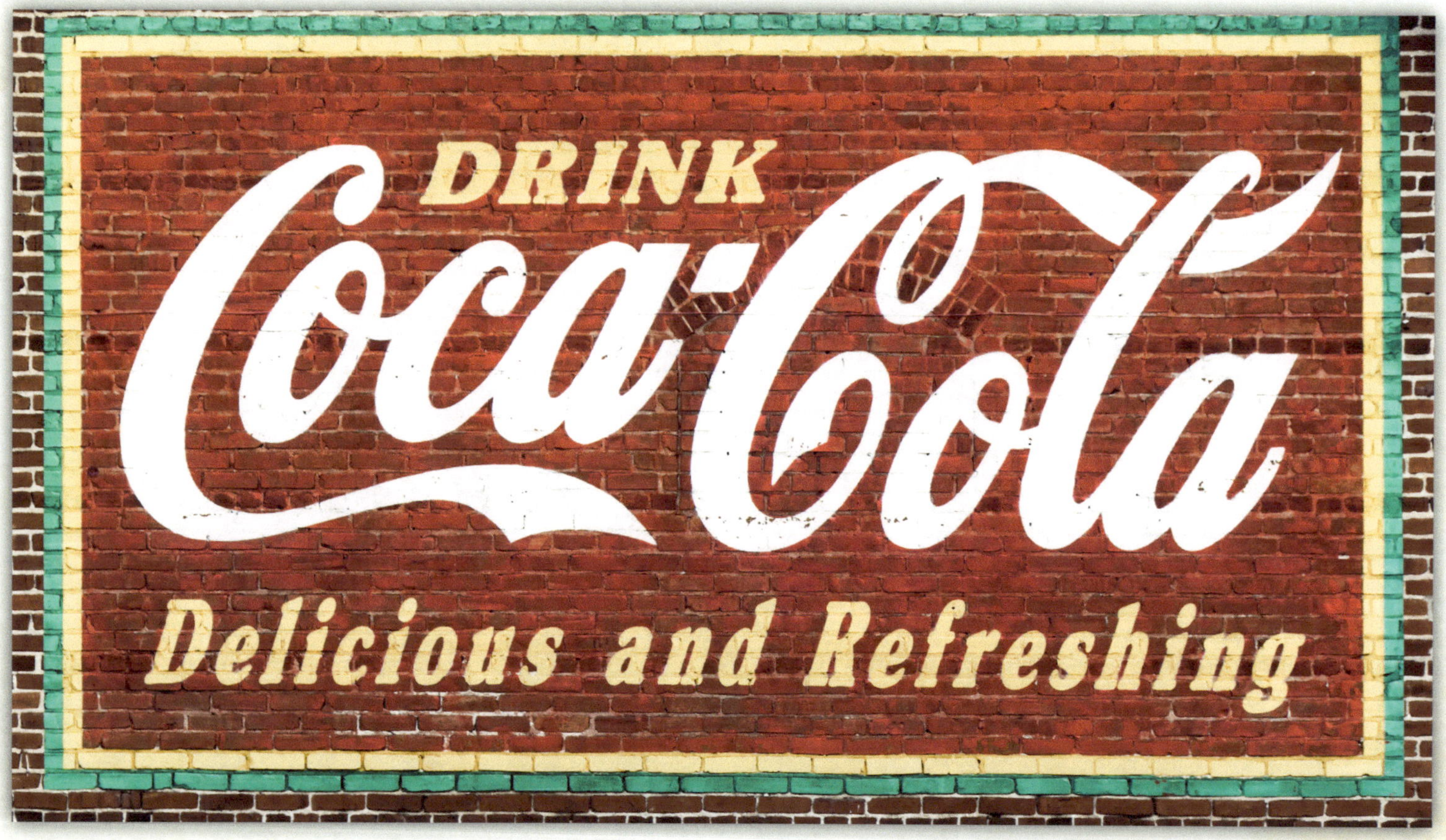

Delicious and Refreshing

Baxley

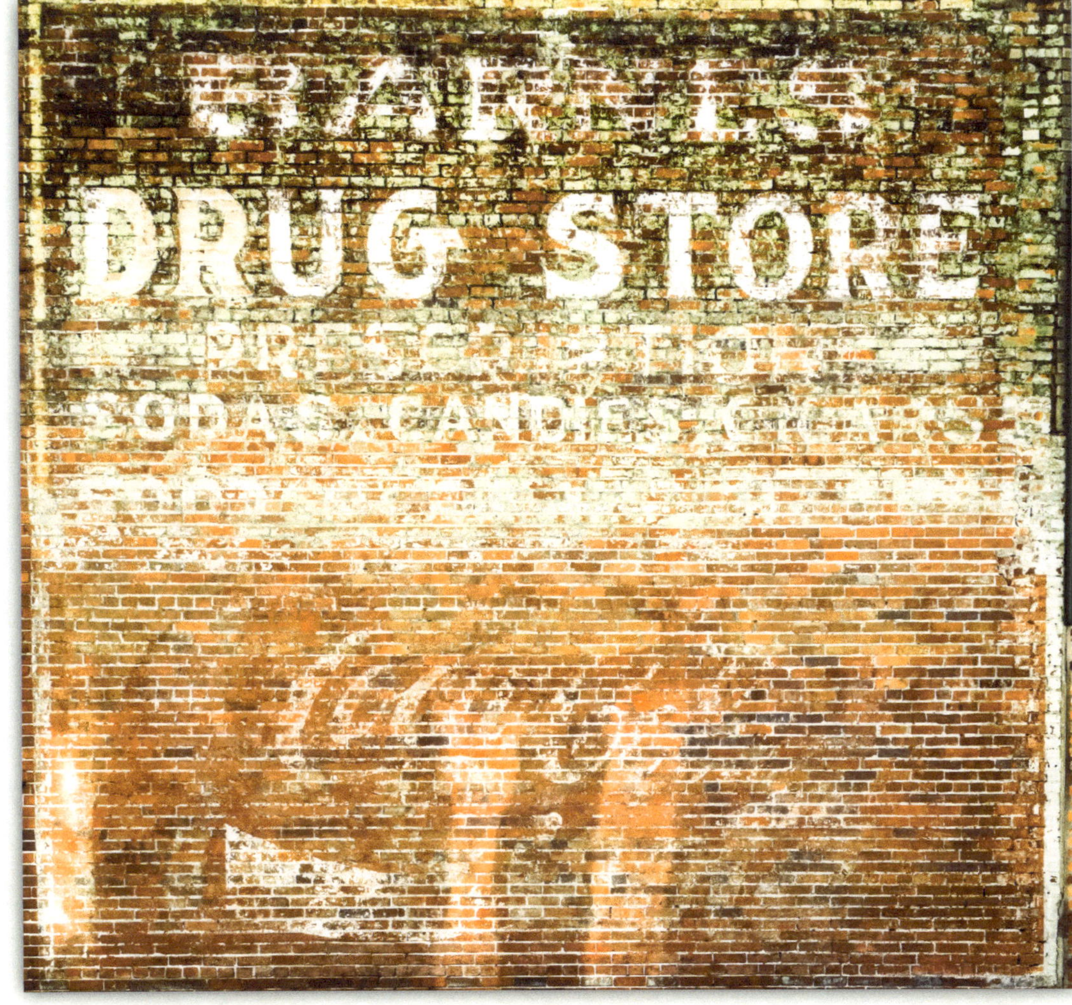

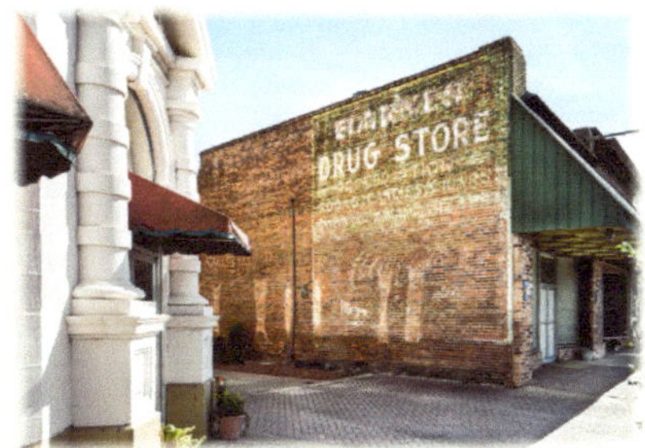

Between NE Park Avenue and Washington Street on N Main Street/U.S. Highway 1 N

GPS 31°46'39" N 82°20'56" W

This wall sign was painted in the 1930s or early 1940s on the Barnes Pharmacy building. Mark Barnes, a third-generation pharmacy owner, shared that his great-grandfather, Thomas Jefferson Barnes, acquired the pharmacy from Dr. Goodman in 1928.

In 1921, Dr. Goodman's pharmacy was the first business in Baxley.

The pharmacy's soda fountain existed from 1930 to 1961. It was at this soda fountain that Caroline Miller wrote the novel *Lamb in His Bosom* in 1933. Caroline was the first Georgian to win the Pulitzer Prize for fiction and, in 1934, France's Prix Femina.

Mark also shared that the original soda fountain can still be seen today in Atlanta's Coke museum.

Bremen

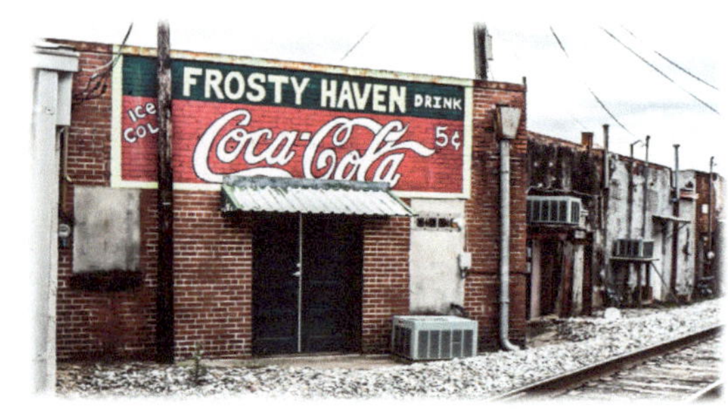

Buchanan Street in the Parking Lot

GPS 33°43'17" N 85°8'50" W

The Bremen Coca-Cola wall sign was painted in the late 1950s or early 1960s on the popular gathering place known as Hamburger Haven. Randall Redding has fond memories of going to the restaurant with his grandfather for a "burger and Coke."

No one seems to know why the sign was painted on the back of the building.

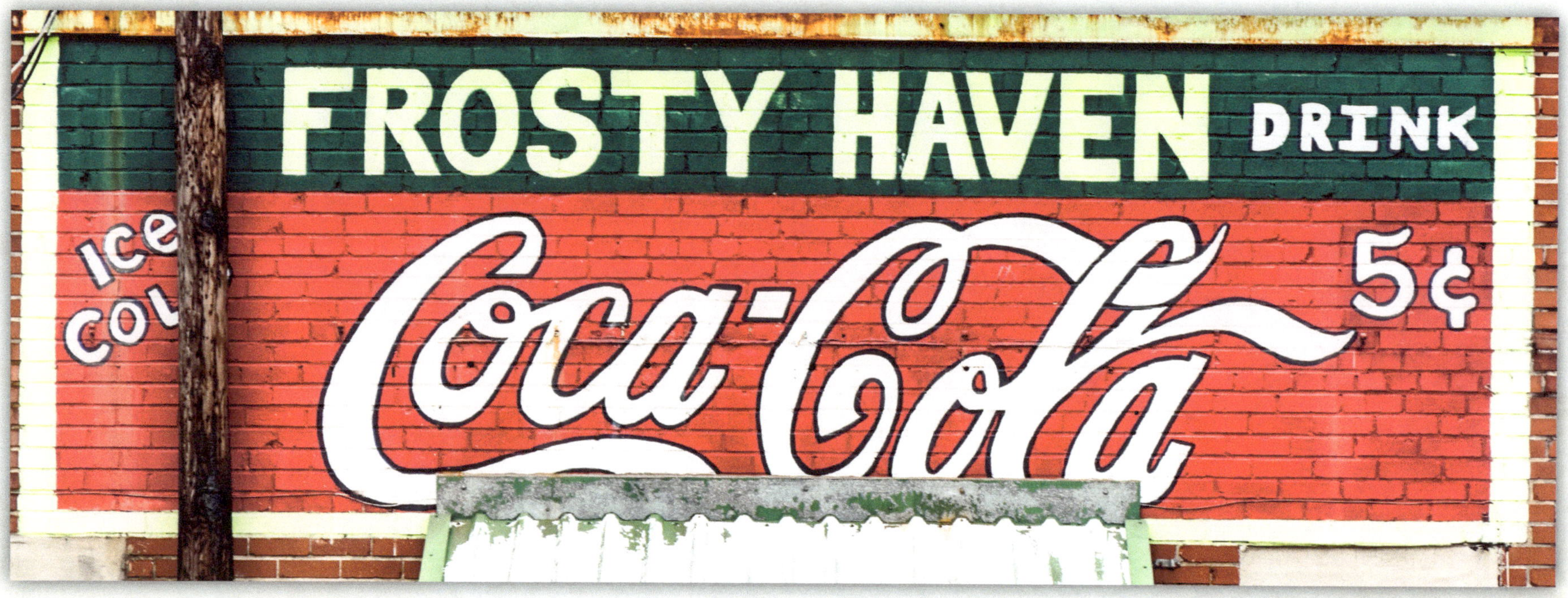

Delicious and Refreshing

Buchanan

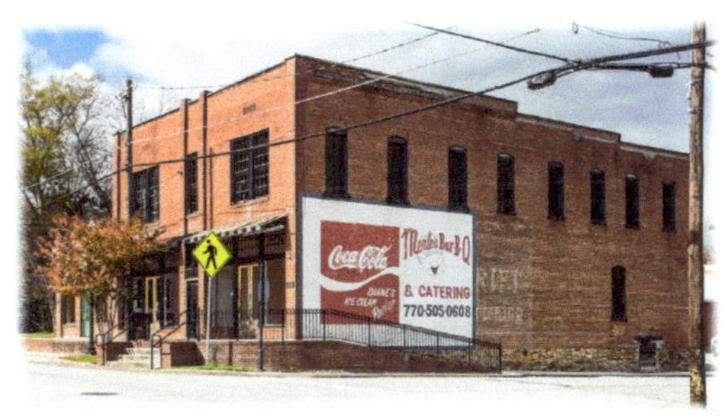

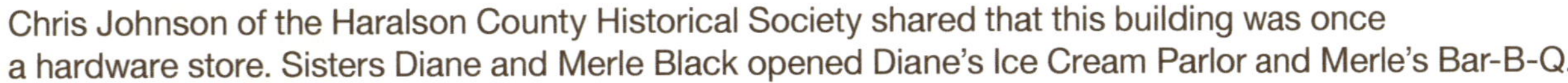

Corner of Tallapoosa Road and Van Wert Street
GPS 33°48'8" N 85°11'21" W

Chris Johnson of the Haralson County Historical Society shared that this building was once a hardware store. Sisters Diane and Merle Black opened Diane's Ice Cream Parlor and Merle's Bar-B-Q.

This Coca-Cola wall sign was painted in 2009, but no one is sure if the 2009 sign is the original, or if an earlier sign existed underneath.

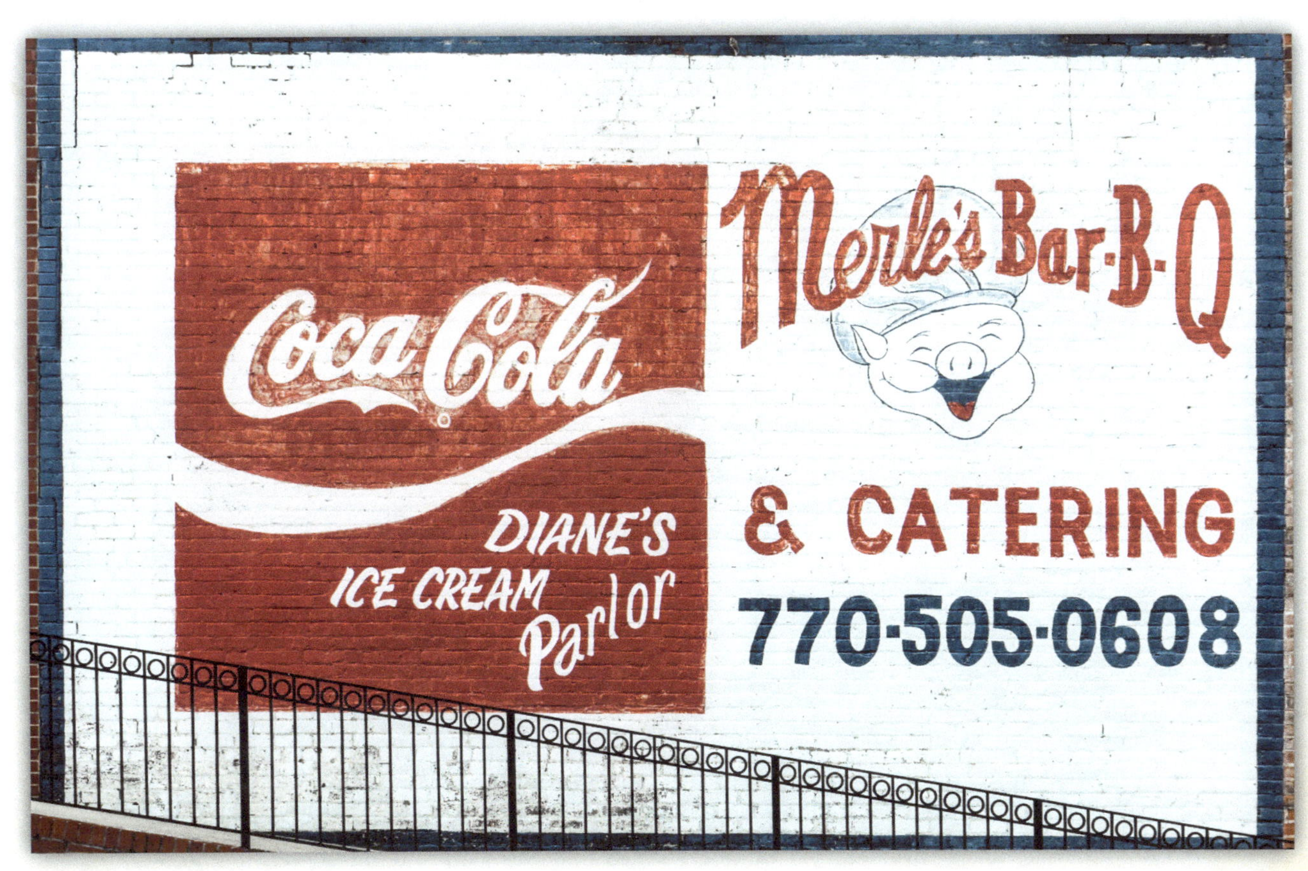

Buena Vista

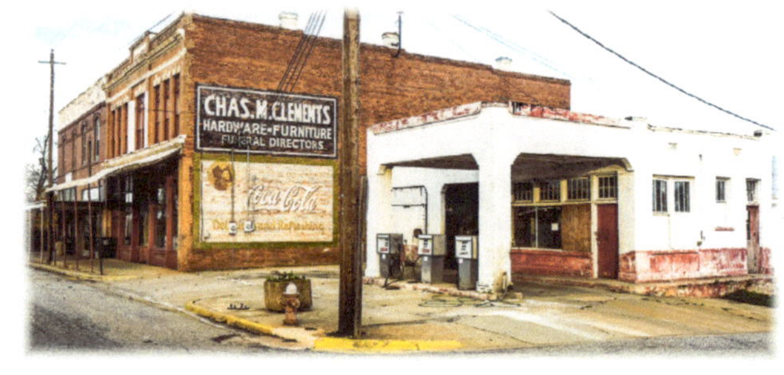

Corner of Forsyth Street and 4th Avenue
GPS 32°19'9" N 84°31'4" W

Britt Moon, owner of both the building and Swamp Fox Distilling Company, confirmed the building was built in 1903 and was the city hardware store.

Little is known about this sign or when it was painted. The "Delicious and Refreshing" slogan came out in 1904 and was used on many signs. With no obvious trademark information inside the tail of the "C" and the presence of the silhouette girl as clues, my guess is this sign was painted sometime after 1938.

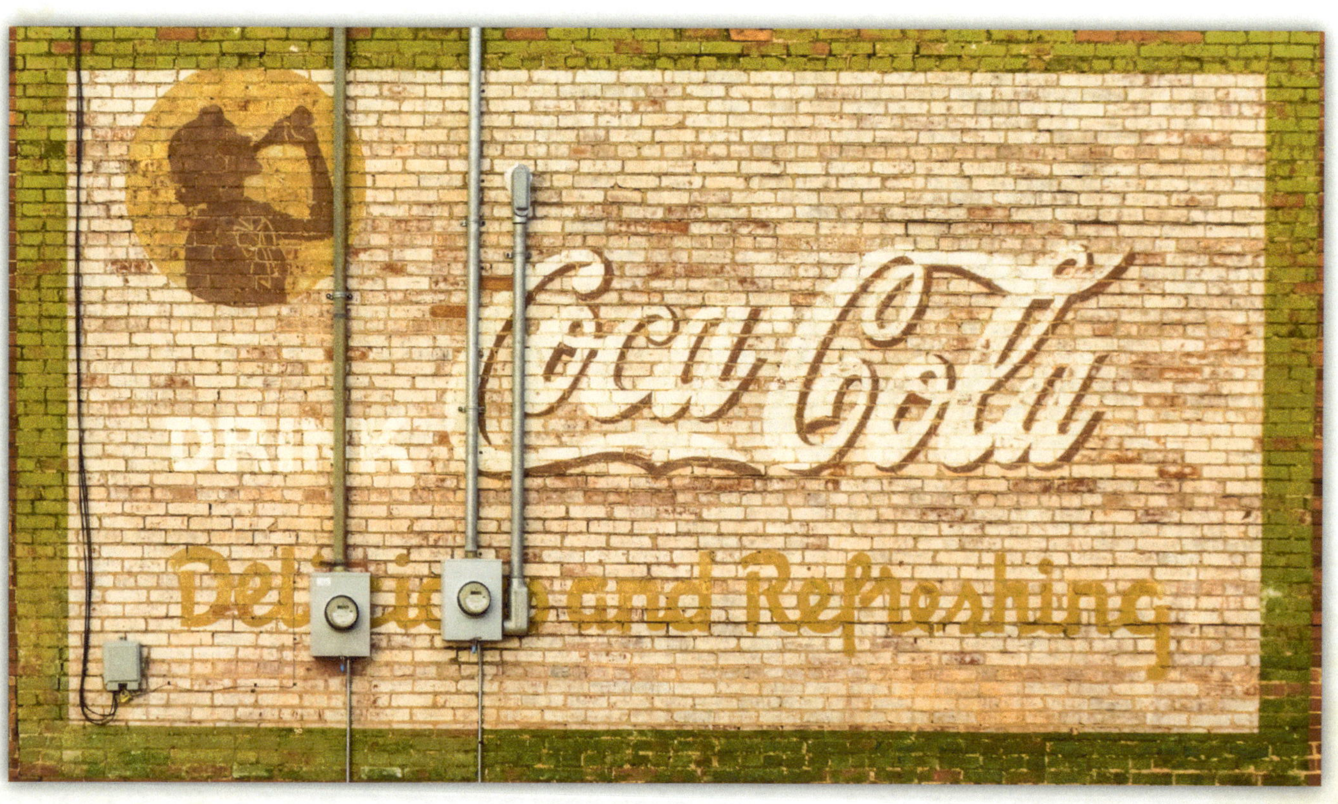

Delicious and Refreshing

Butler

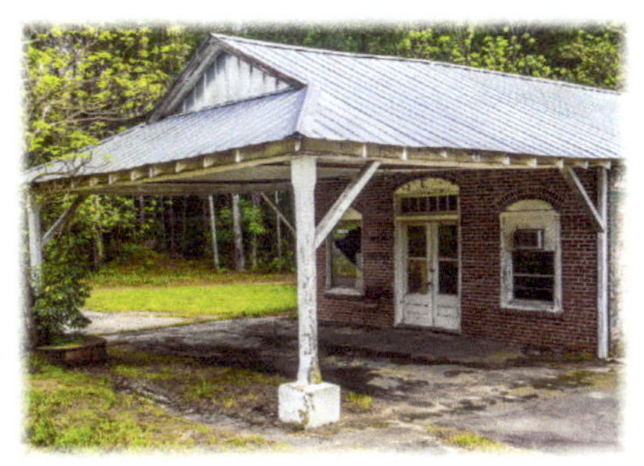

U.S. 19 near Garrett Road
GPS 32°37'0" N 84°14'41" W

According to Bill Amos, this sign is on the original location of McCants Mill Pond and Grist Mill, which became a country store. Bill grew up near the store and remembers the building being a home first, then a garage, and then a fish house and store.

It was very popular at one time, a place where people from all around the area would gather. When this sign was originally painted is unknown.

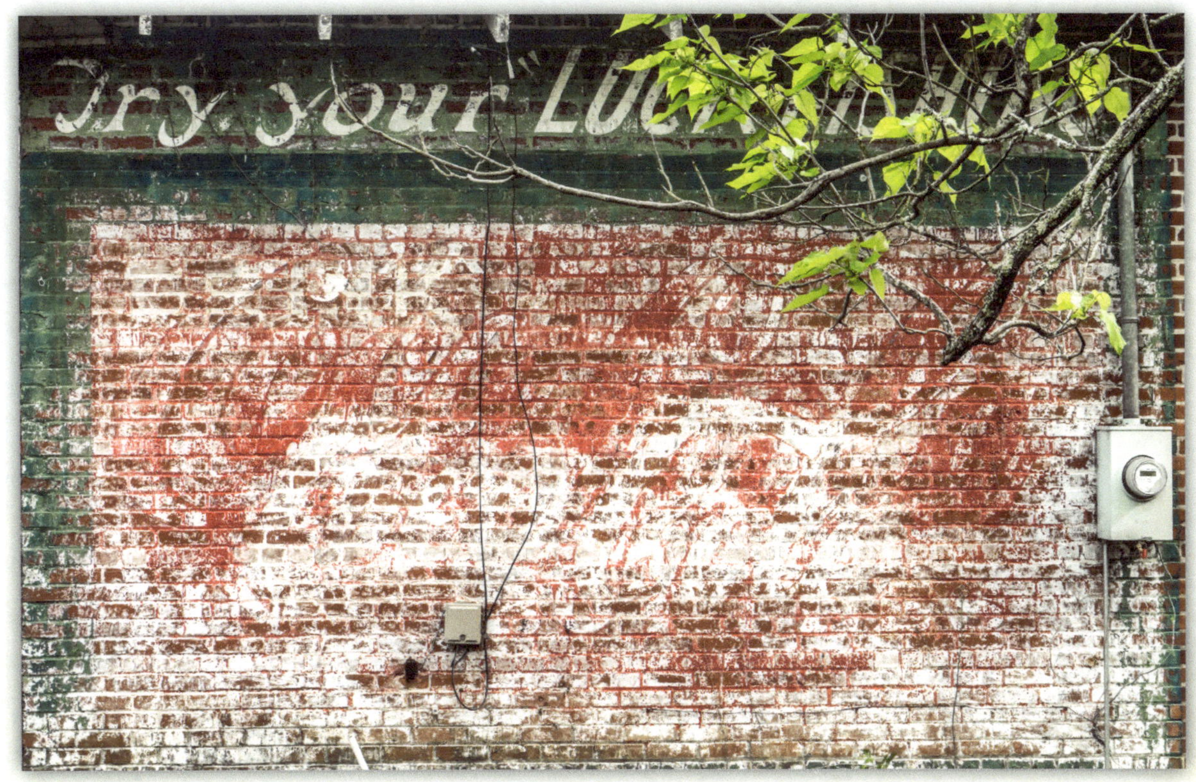

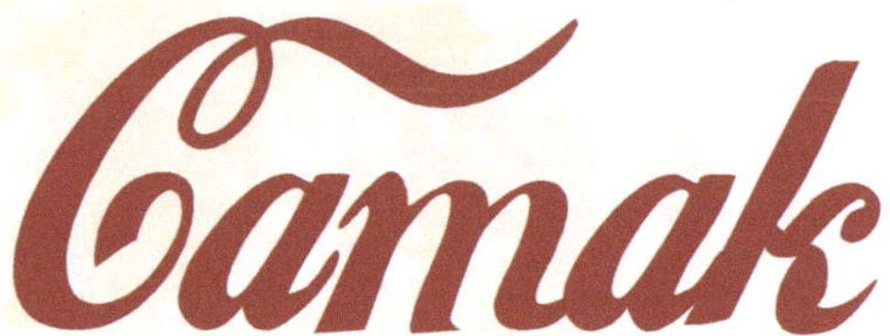

Camak

Between Baker Street and Johnson Street on Railroad Street

GPS 33°27'11" N 82°38'46" W

According to Margaret Pinion, this Coca-Cola wall sign was painted on the old William M. Moore store across from the railroad tracks. Nothing is known about when it was painted.

Since the building is located across from the railroad tracks and is obviously very old, my guess is this ghost wall sign was painted between 1894 and 1940.

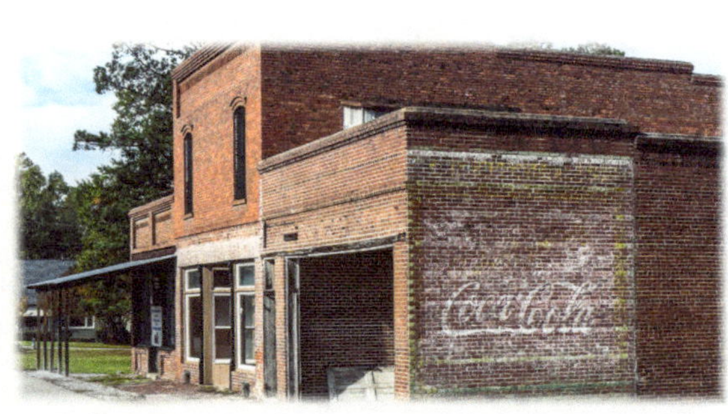

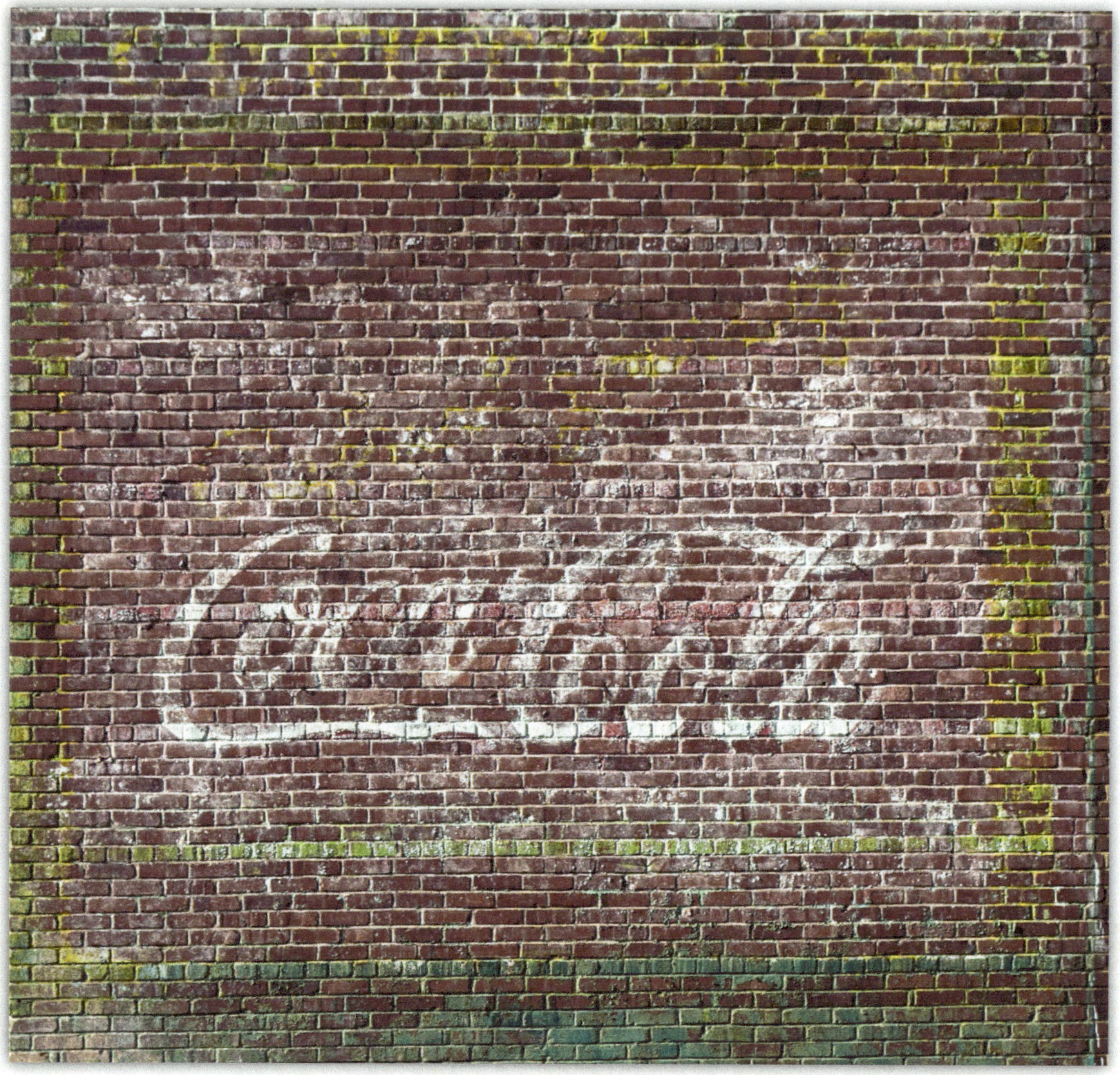

Carrollton

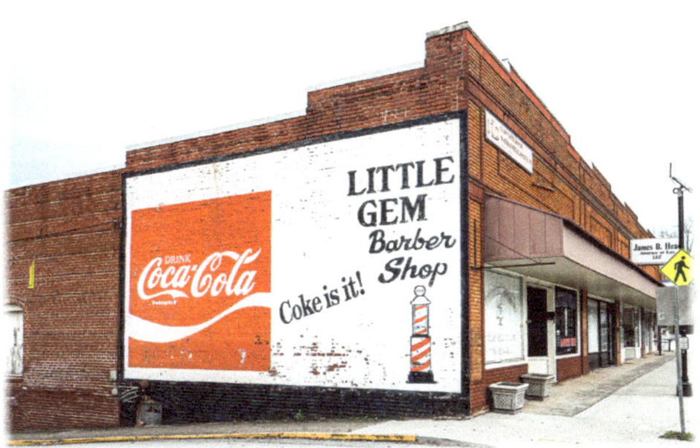

Little Gem Barber Shop - Corner of Tanner Street and State Route 166 Bus
GPS 33°34'48" N 85°4'24"

The Little Gem Barber Shop first opened in 1895 as The Parlor, and is the oldest barber shop in Georgia. In the 1900s, "Little" Jimmy Jackson began working there and eventually became the owner, changing the name to Little Gem after his town nickname, Little Jim.

Jess Crawford became the owner in 1939 and the shop has stayed in the Crawford family to this day. I spoke with Jess's grandson, John Crawford, who says this Coke wall sign was originally on the grocery store at this location in the 1930s.

When the barber shop was moved in 1982, the sign was repainted by the Coke distributor, which is how we see it today.

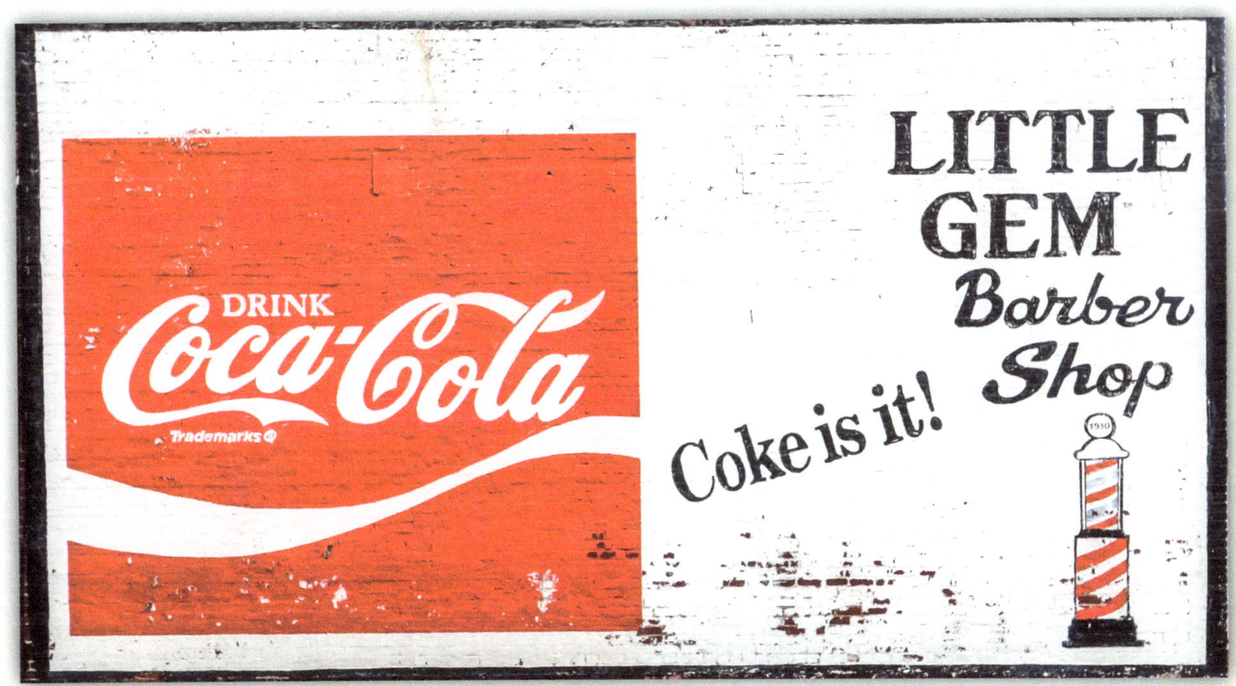

Carrollton

C.M. Tanner Grocery -
Maple Street where it crosses the Railroad Tracks
GPS 33°34'35" N 85°4'53" W

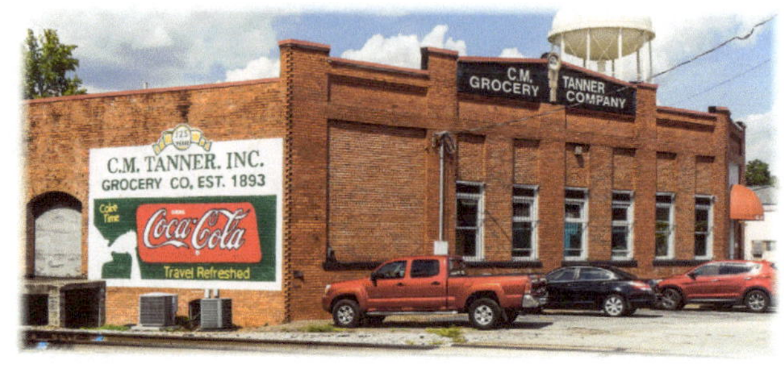

I had the opportunity to speak with Johnny Tanner, whose great-grandfather, Charles Mobry Tanner, started the wholesale mercantile store in 1893. When the original Coca-Cola sign was painted is not known.

Alan Kuykendall repainted the sign around 30 years ago. Kim Wolfe has repainted the sign two or three times since.

The sign has been updated over the original, but the presence of the silhouette girl suggests the original sign may have been painted after 1938.

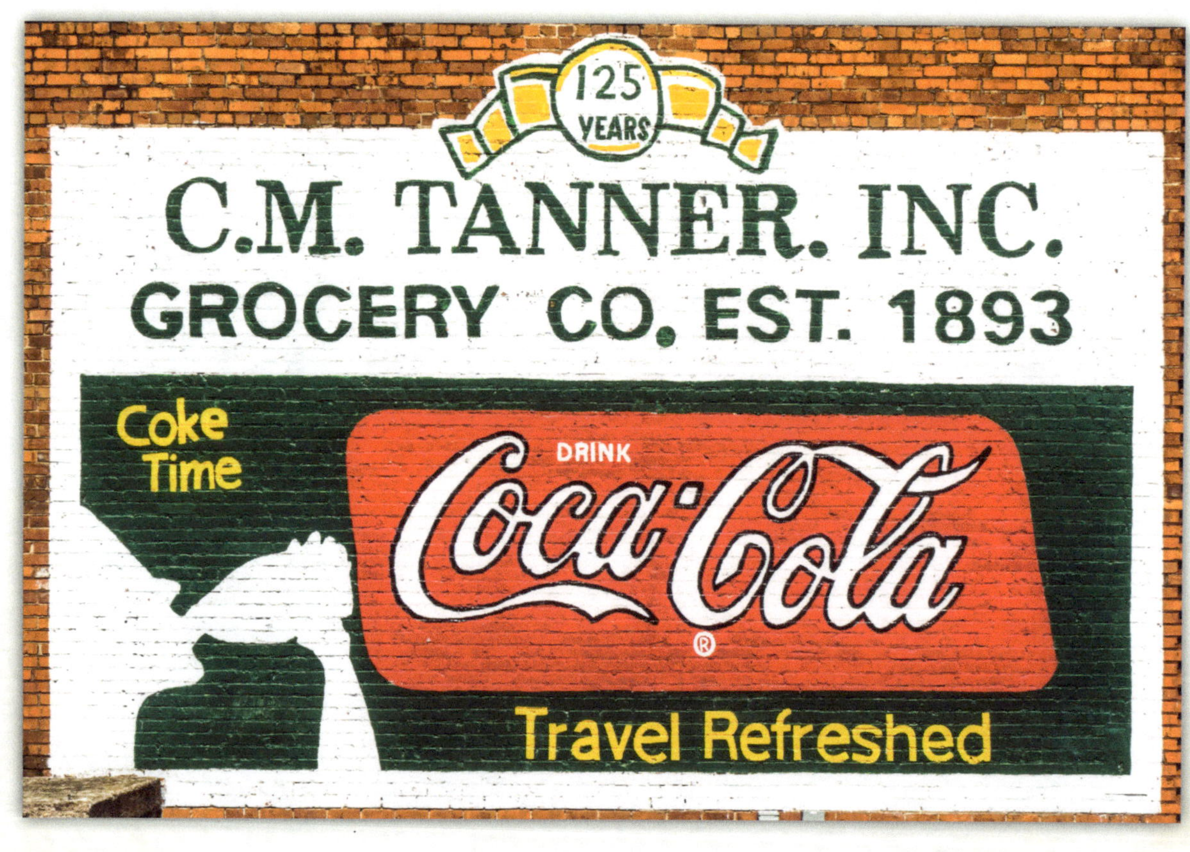

Delicious and Refreshing

Cartersville

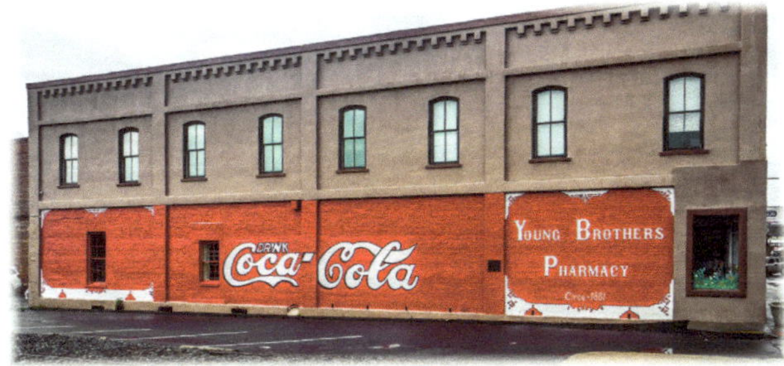

Corner of W Main Street and S Railroad Street
GPS 34°9'55" N 84°47'44" W

The Cartersville Coke sign has the distinction of being the earliest known painted wall sign. It was originally painted in 1894 on the side of Young Brothers Pharmacy by Coke syrup salesman James Couden.

This sign is located near the railroad tracks just down from the train depot. Alison Free and Aggie Ferguson restored the original sign, removing many layers of paint to reveal the wall sign underneath.

The current owner, William Tatum, shared that his brother-in-law, Dean Cox, worked at the pharmacy for 50 years, buying it in 1968. Later, it was passed on to William, who has owned it since.

Ronald Fowler repainted the sign in 2005 and remembers seeing the sign as it now looks over 60 years ago. Ronald points out that James misspelled DRINK as "DRNK," then went back and added in the "I."

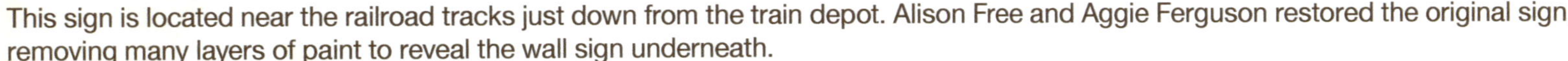

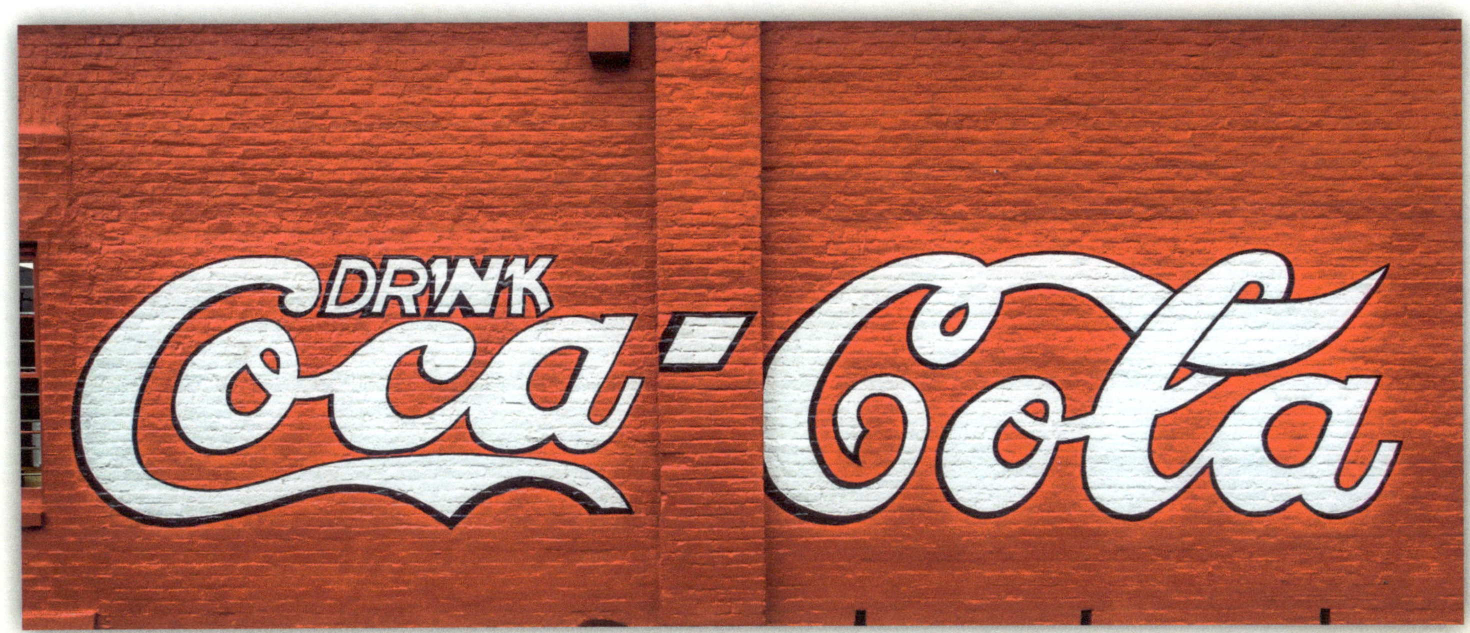

Cave Spring

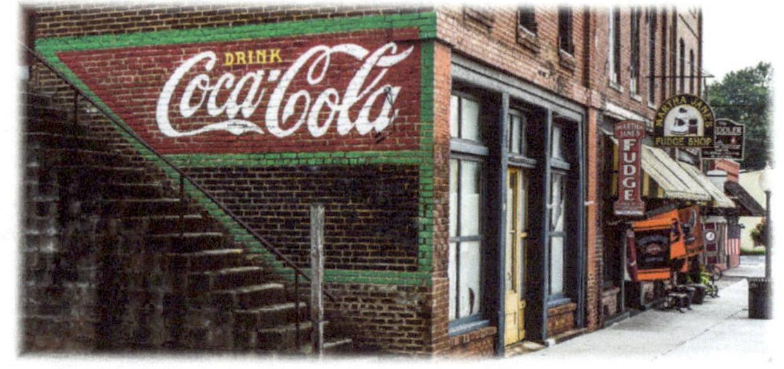

Between Church Street and Broad Street on Highway 53
GPS 34°6'28" N 85°20'14" W

The Cave Spring Coca-Cola sign was painted on the side of what Pete Mathis tells me was the Griffin drugstore. Pete shares that he remembers going to the drugstore as a child to read comic books. He thinks the building dates back to the 1880s.

John Johnson first restored the wall sign. If this wall sign was restored like the original, the trademark style and placement suggest the original painting was between 1894 and 1903.

John Christian recently restored the wall sign again.

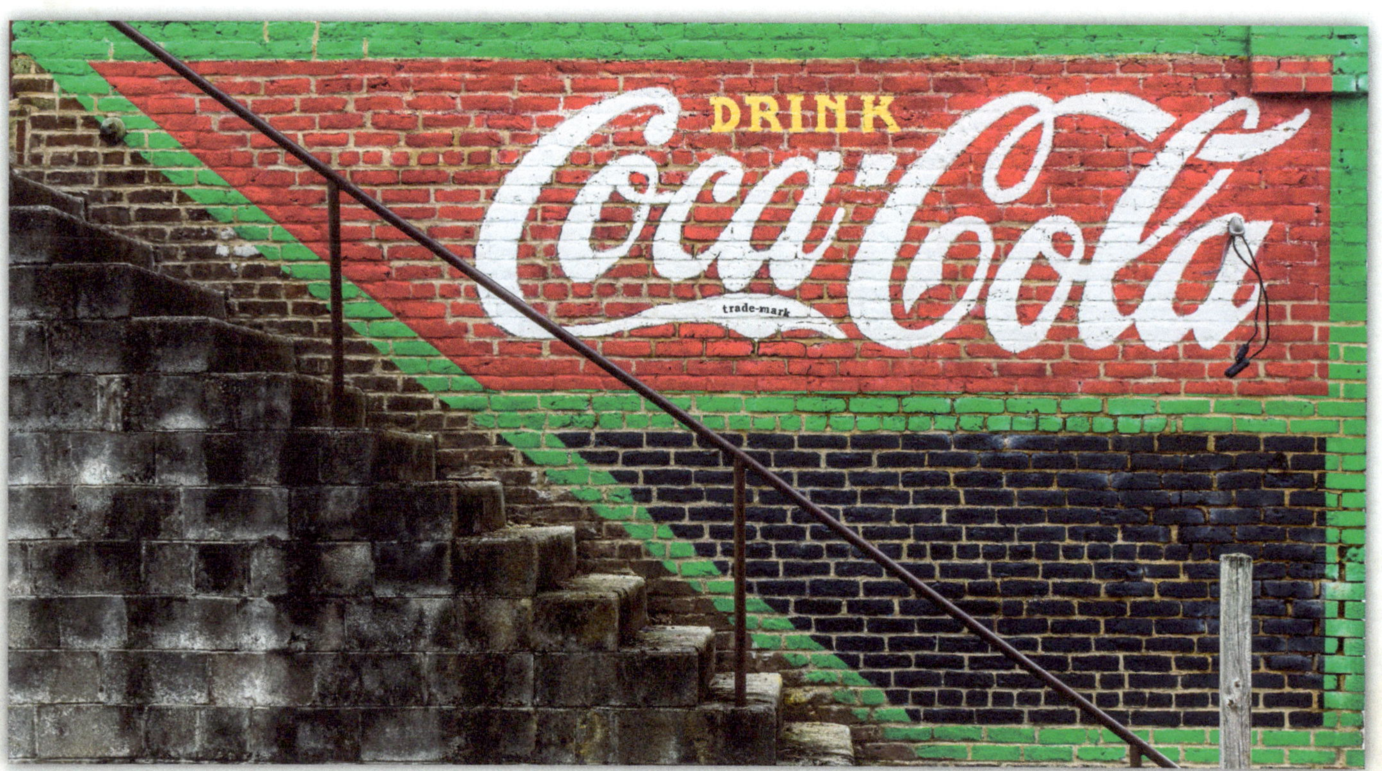

Delicious and Refreshing

Cedartown

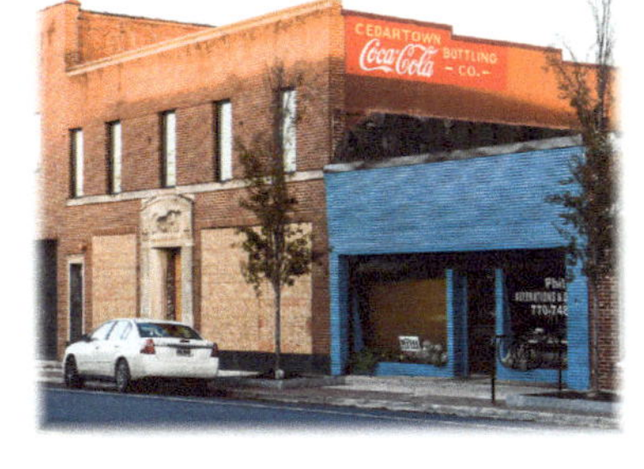

Corner of Sterling Holloway Place and S Main Street
GPS 34°0'44" N 85°15'18" W

This Coca-Cola sign was recently restored as part of the building's renovation by the Morris family.
The building is home to the Cedartown Museum of Coca-Cola Memorabilia.

The sign's trademark placement and style date the original wall sign to between 1903 and 1931.

Daniel Morrison, whose family founded the Cedartown Museum of Coca-Cola Memorabilia, said the building became a Coca-Cola bottling plant in 1920, with further renovations in 1939. The sign's trademark placement and style would indicate this time period.

In 2014, the sign was repainted exactly as it had appeared.

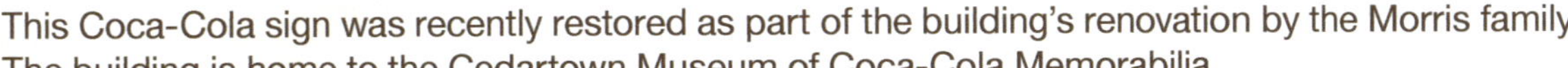

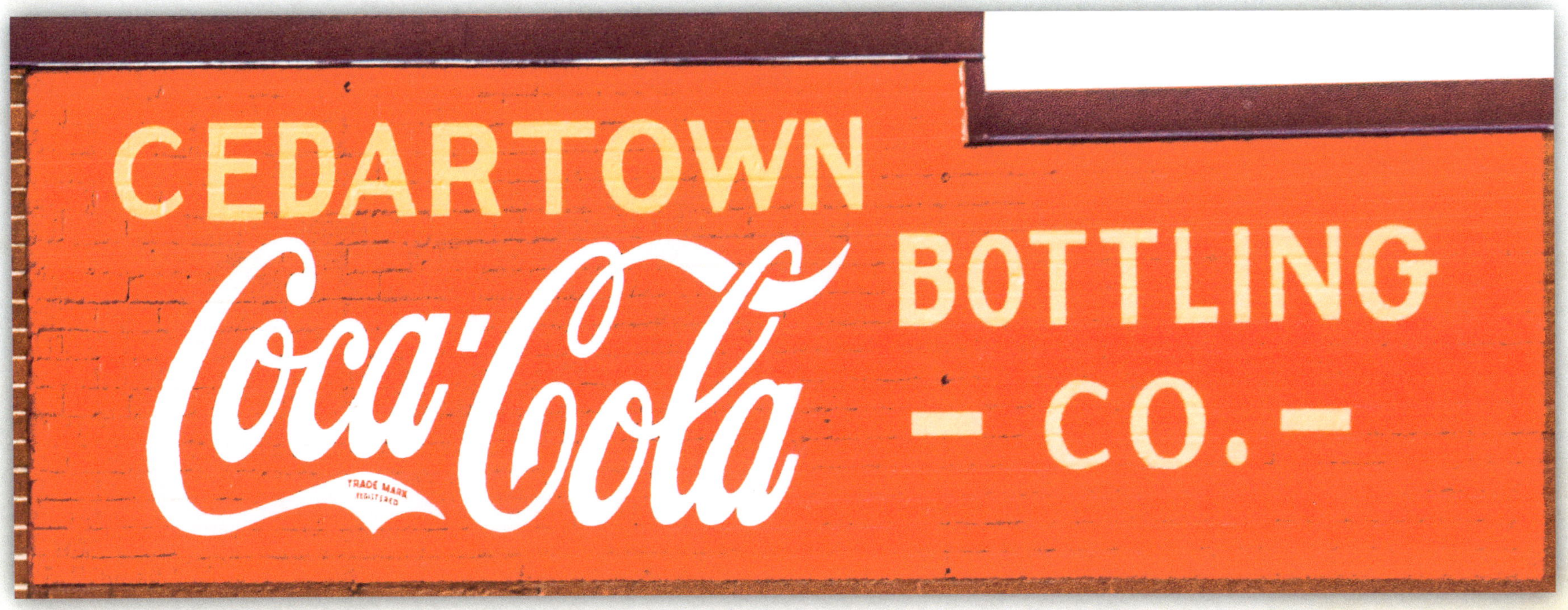

Colbert

Corner of 4th Avenue and S 4th Street
GPS 34°2'17" N 83°12'44" W

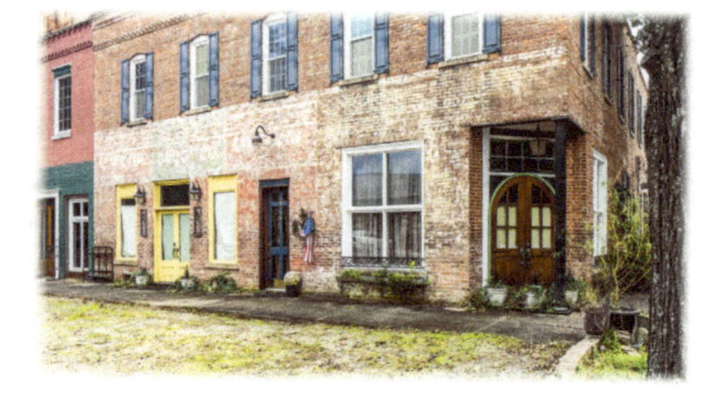

Building owners Ellyn and Carl Trinrud have been diligently restoring this landmark for the past 19 years.
Ellyn thinks the Coca-Cola sign was originally painted on the old Hardman Drug Co. between 1920 and 1947.

At the time, Hardman Drug Co. had the only soda fountain and "sit-up counter" located across from the Colbert train depot.

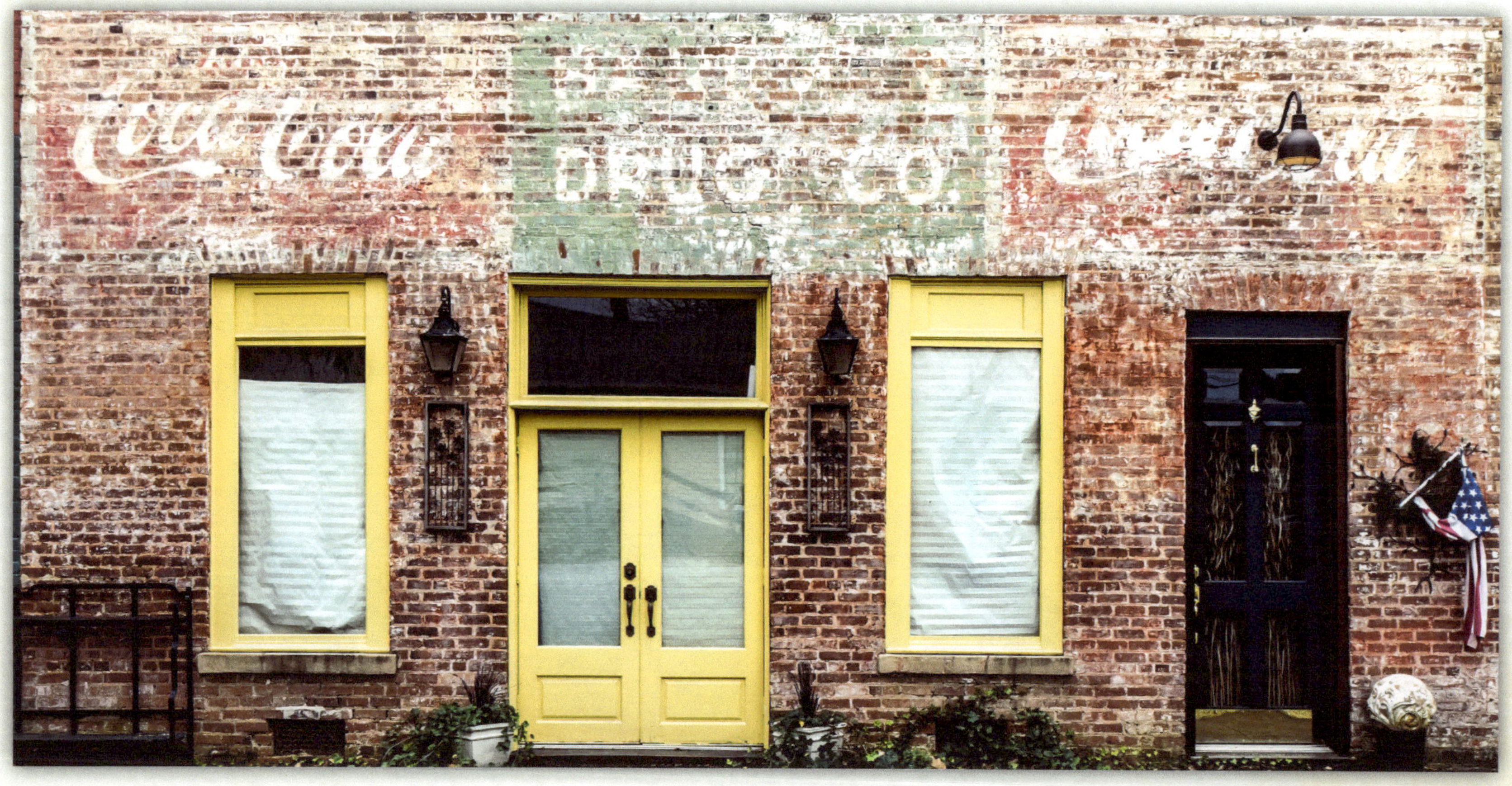

Delicious and Refreshing

Commerce

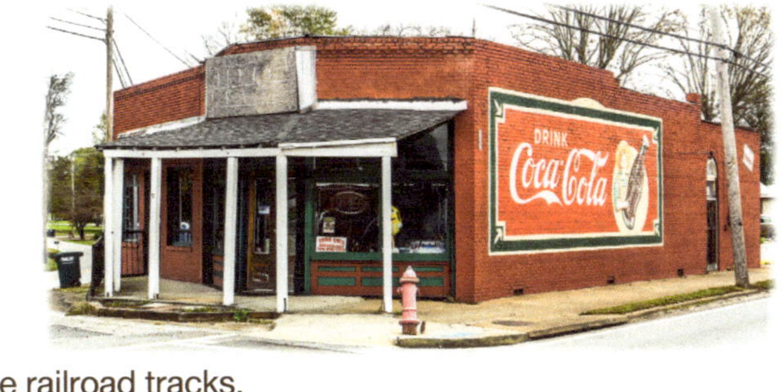

Corner of S Broad Street and Madison Street

GPS 34°11'32" N 83°26'49" W

This is the only sign of its type I found in Georgia. It is located on an old building across from some railroad tracks. Unfortunately, little could be found out about the sign or its history.

My best guess as to when the sign was originally painted is after the 1950s, because of the figure pointing at the Coke bottle. The newness of the wall sign indicates it might have been painted over a much older sign.

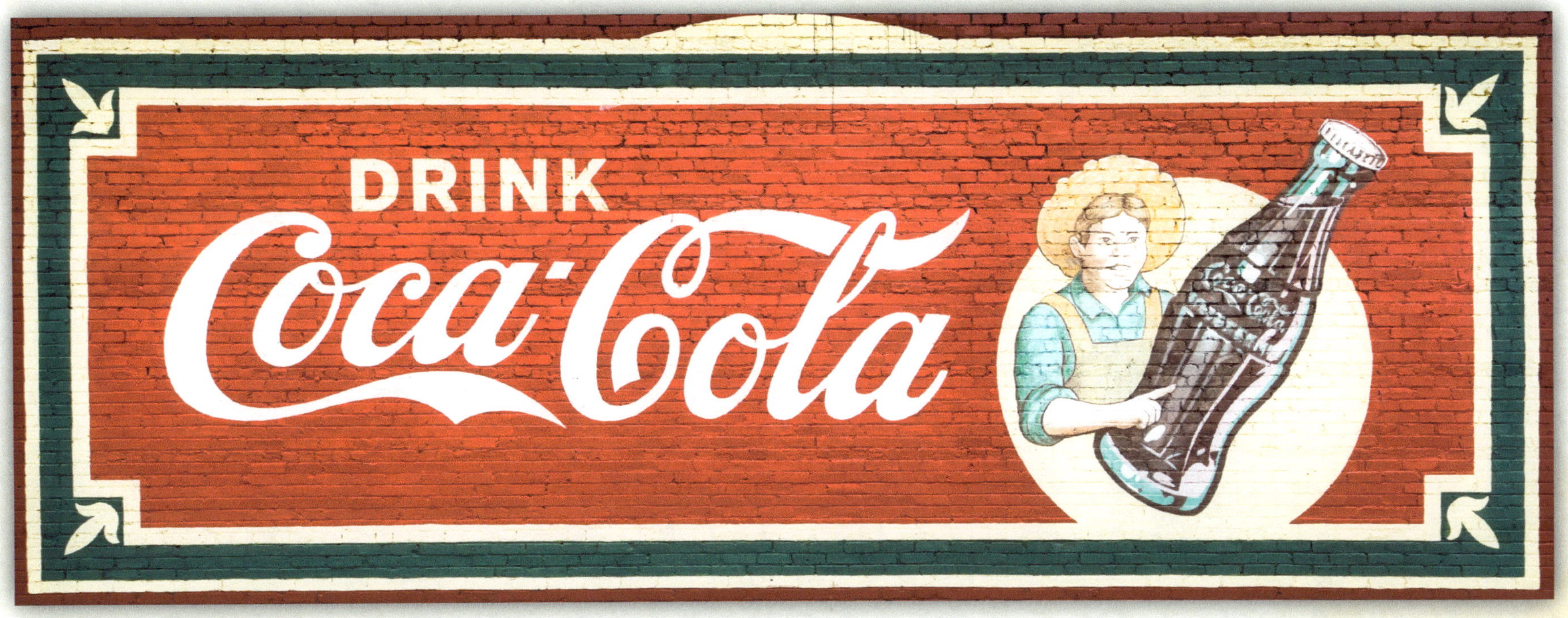

Conyers

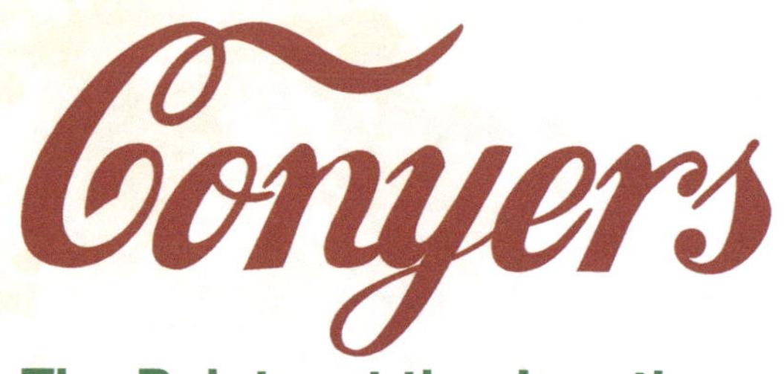

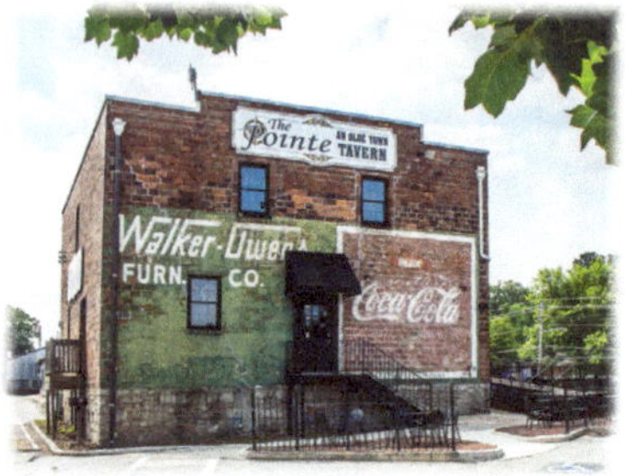

The Pointe, at the Junction of Railroad Street NW, Railroad Street, and Warehouse Street

GPS 33°39'57" N 84°1'2" W

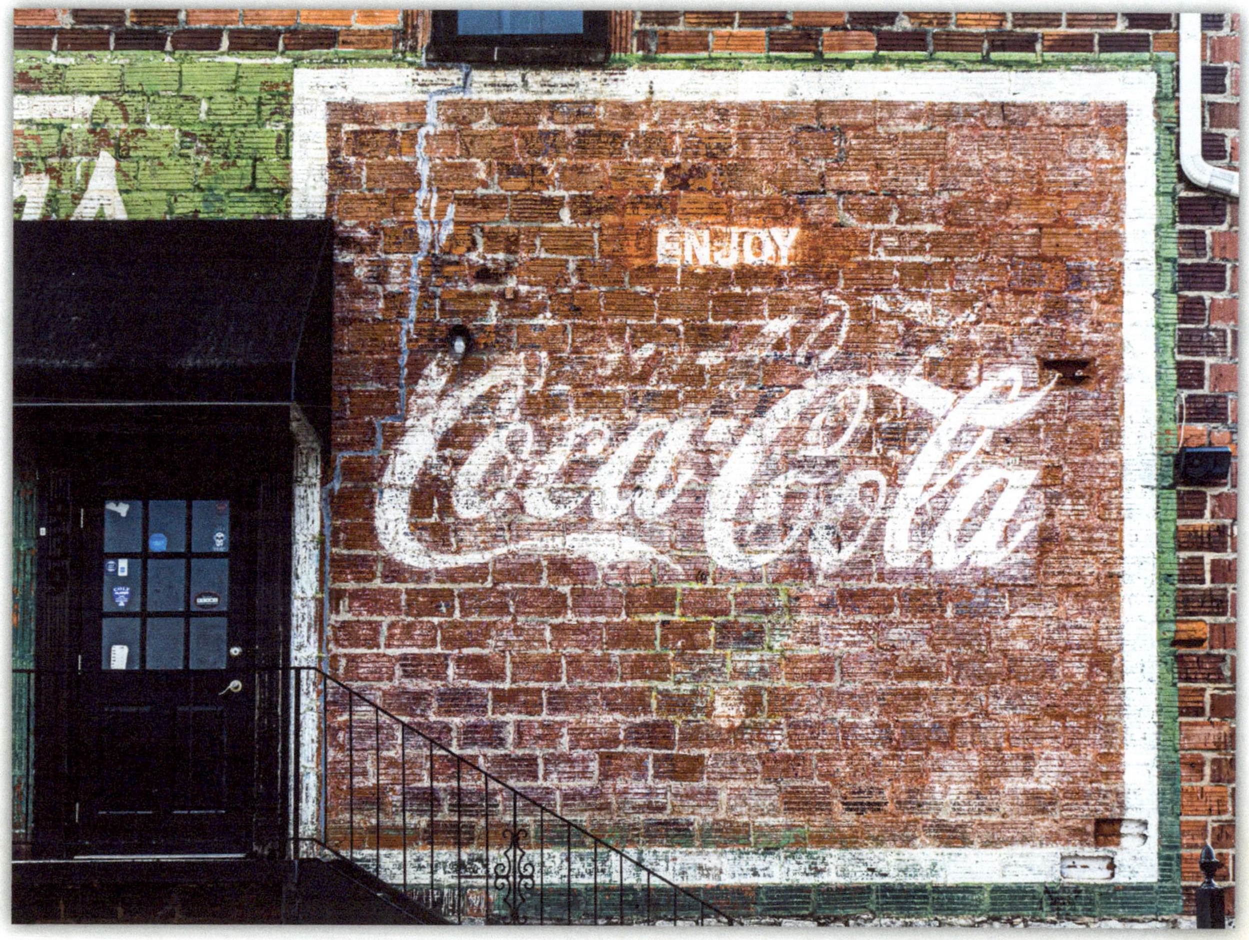

Delicious and Refreshing

Walker-Owens Furniture Co.,
Back of the Same Building in the Parking Lot Off Railroad Street NW
GPS 33°39'56" N 84°0'60" W

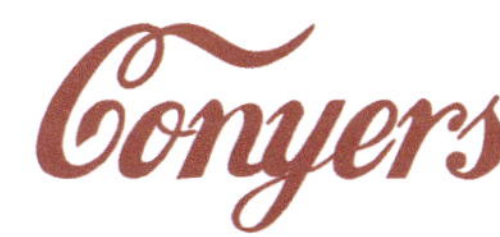

Conyers local Judy Bond remembers the two Coca-Cola signs on the building across from the railroad depot. These signs date back to the 1950s, when they stood in the center of the commercial district and community gathering place.

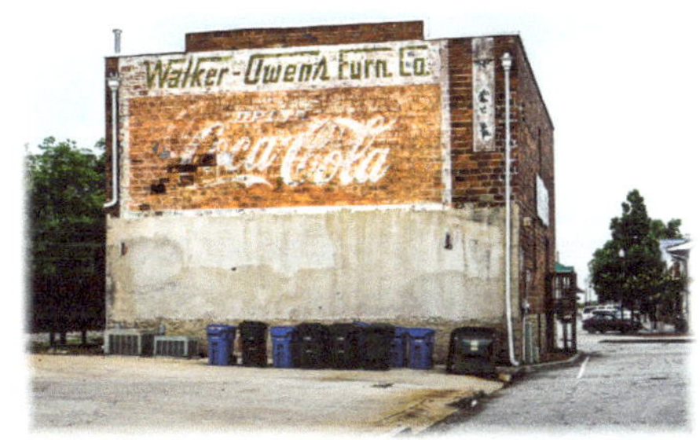

The wall signs were recently restored as a joint venture between the Conyers-Rockdale Council for the Arts, the City of Conyers, and the University of Georgia Lamar Dodd School of Art's "Color the World Bright" program.

Shelli Siebert, executive director of the Conyers-Rockdale Council for the Arts, shared that the restored wall signs are true to the appearance of the originals.

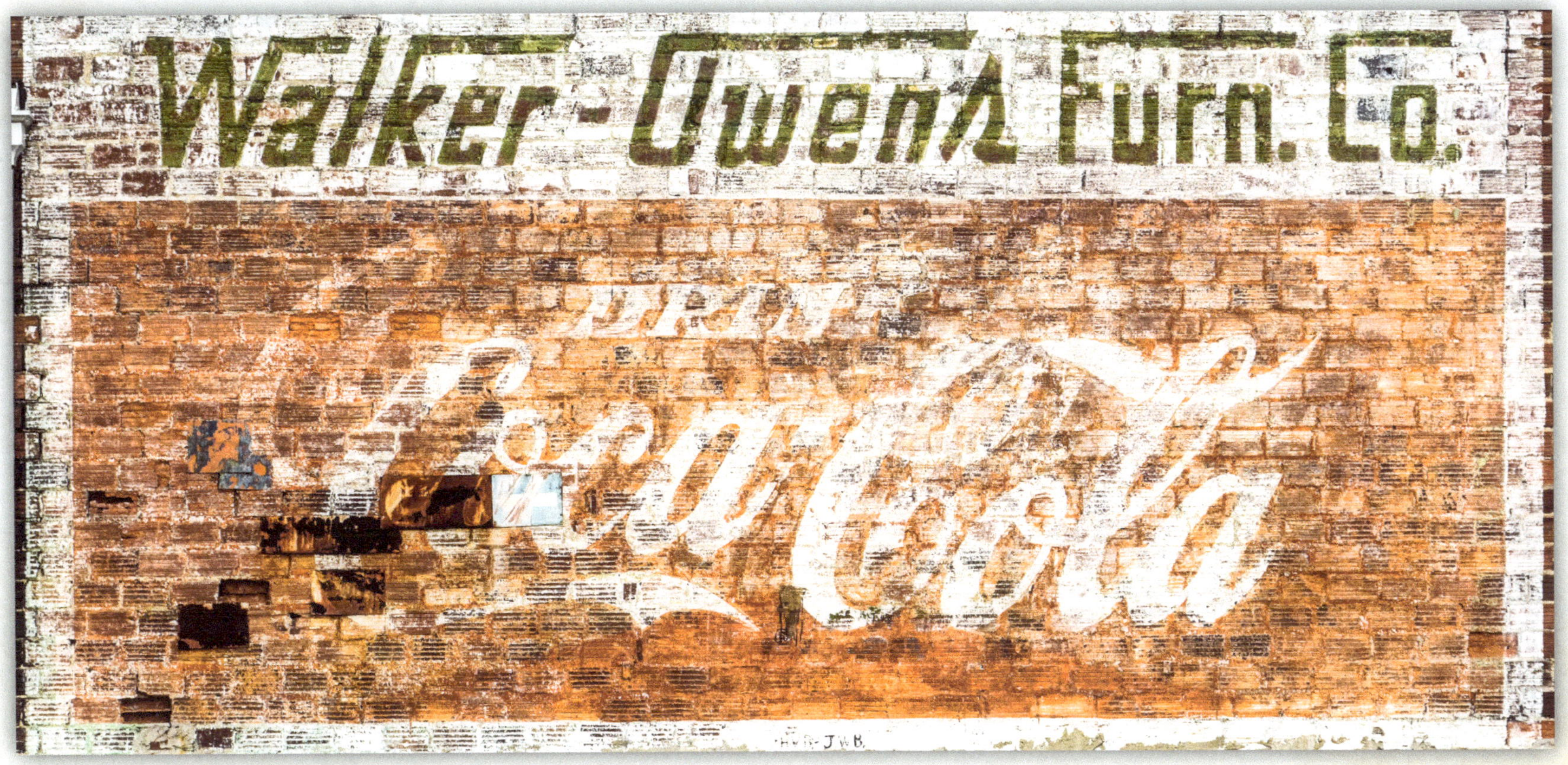

Douglas

Corner of E Bryan Street and Peterson Avenue S, Parking Lot
GPS 31°30'26" N 82°51'1" W

By chance I noticed this Douglas sign, but could find very little information about it.
The slogan "It's the Real Thing" and the added wave suggest it was painted around 1969.

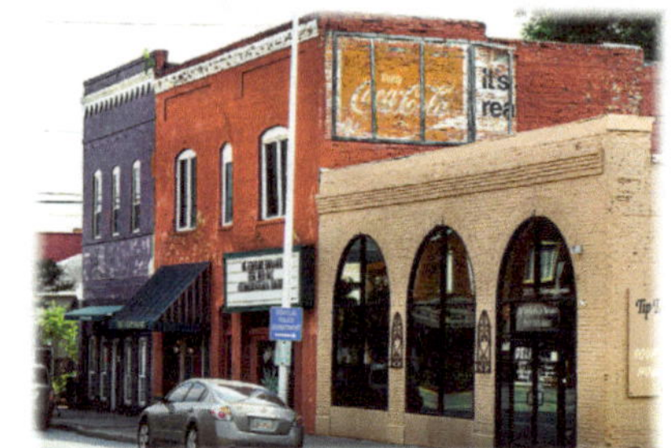

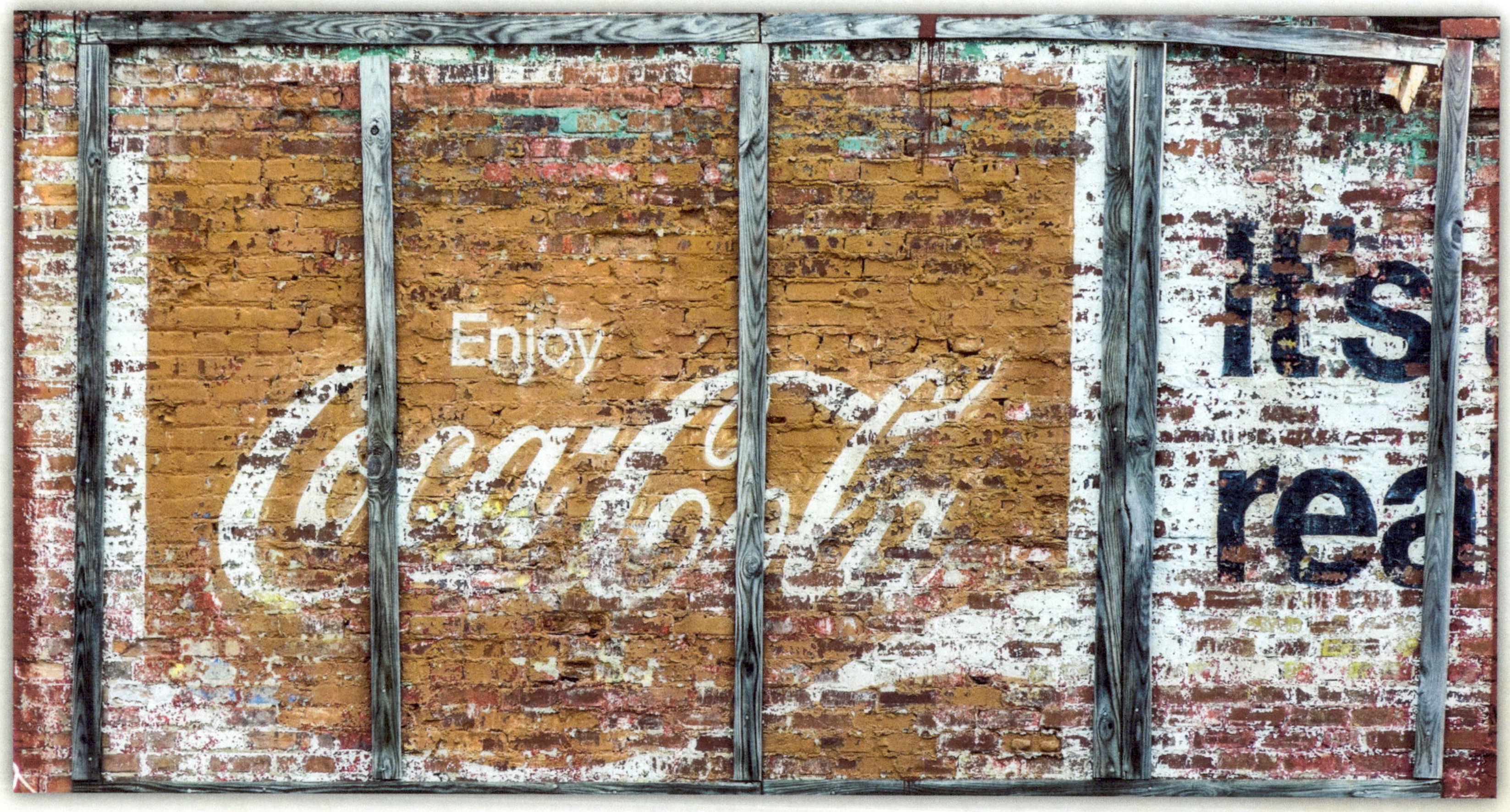

Delicious and Refreshing

Douglasville

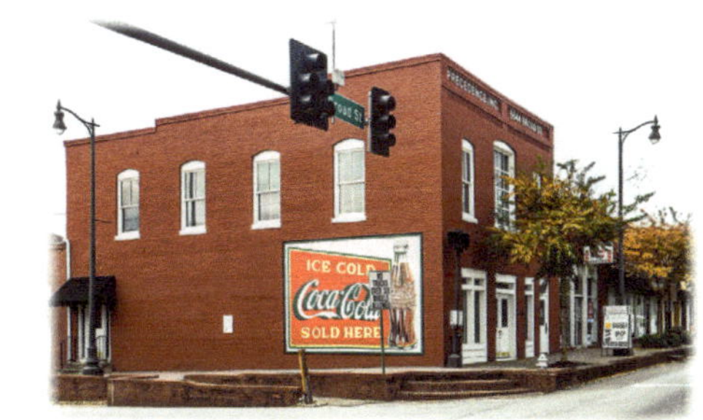

W.E. Johnson's
On Martha Berry Highway (GA 27) near Roopville Baptist Church
GPS 33°28'29" N 85°6'37" W

This sign was recently restored by Dianna Love Snell and Karl Snell of Art Productions, Inc.
It is located along the railroad track in the historic section of town.

The trademark location and sign location suggest that the original sign might have been painted between 1930 and 1941.

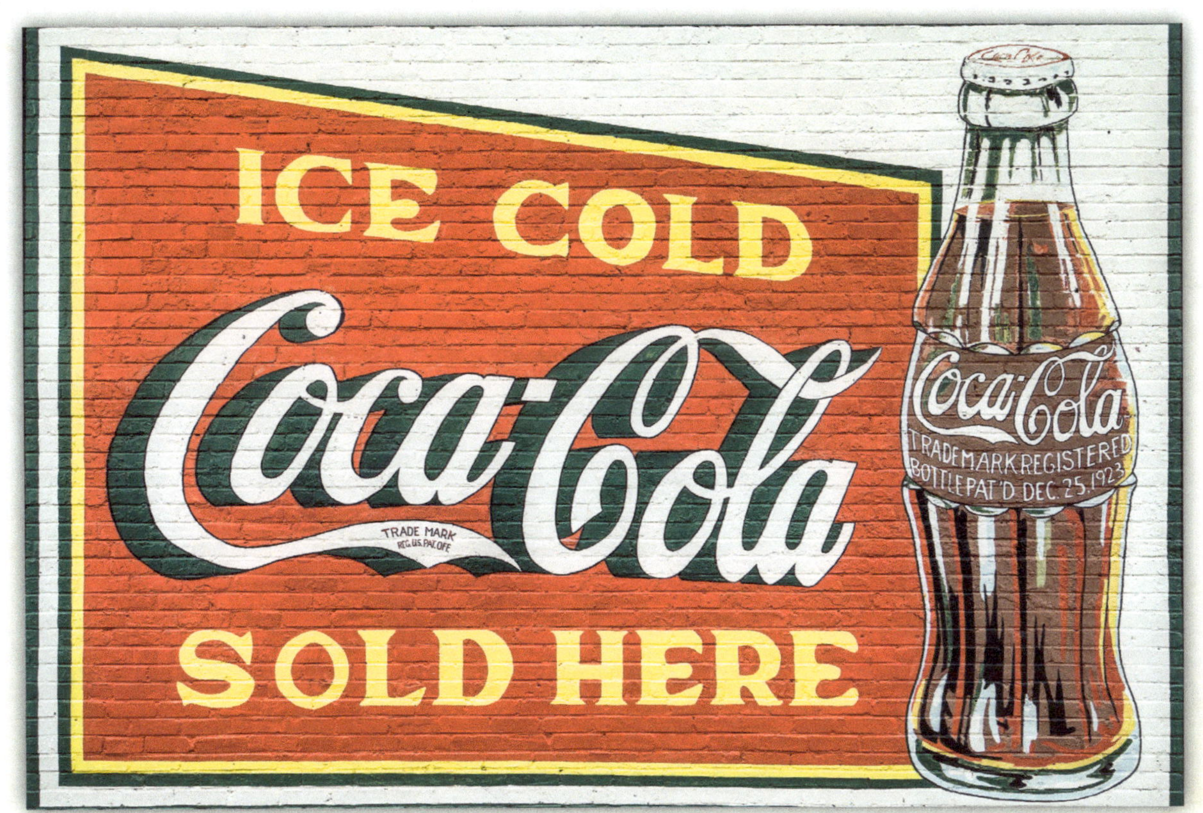

Ellijay

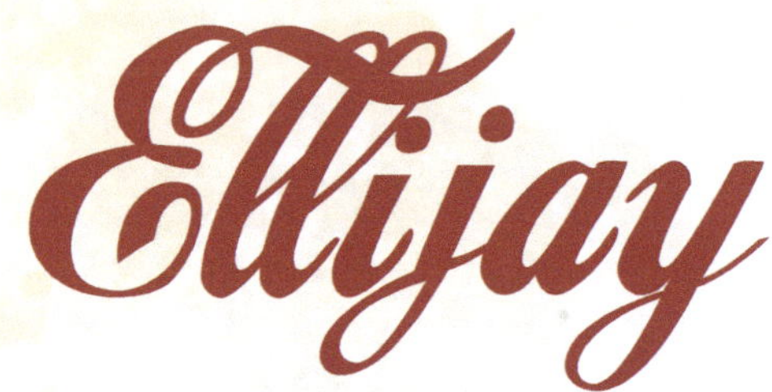

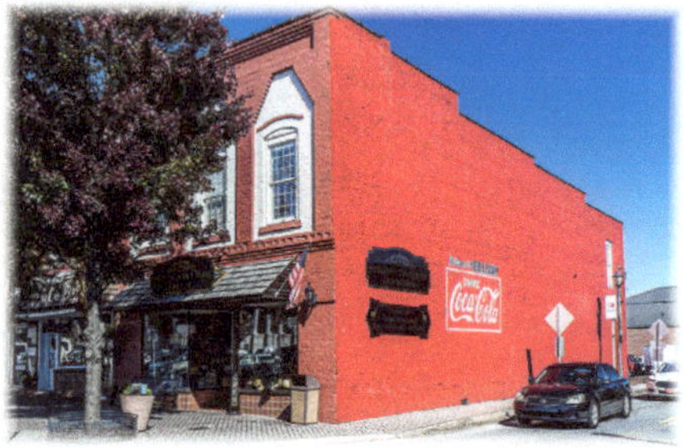

Old Highway 5 at the Town Square
GPS 34°41'42" N 84°28'56" W

The town decided to include a Coca-Cola sign as part of its historic renovation. The Ellijay sign is newly painted by Ken Lynch, who has been painting wall signs for 40 years. He completed the work in September of 2017.

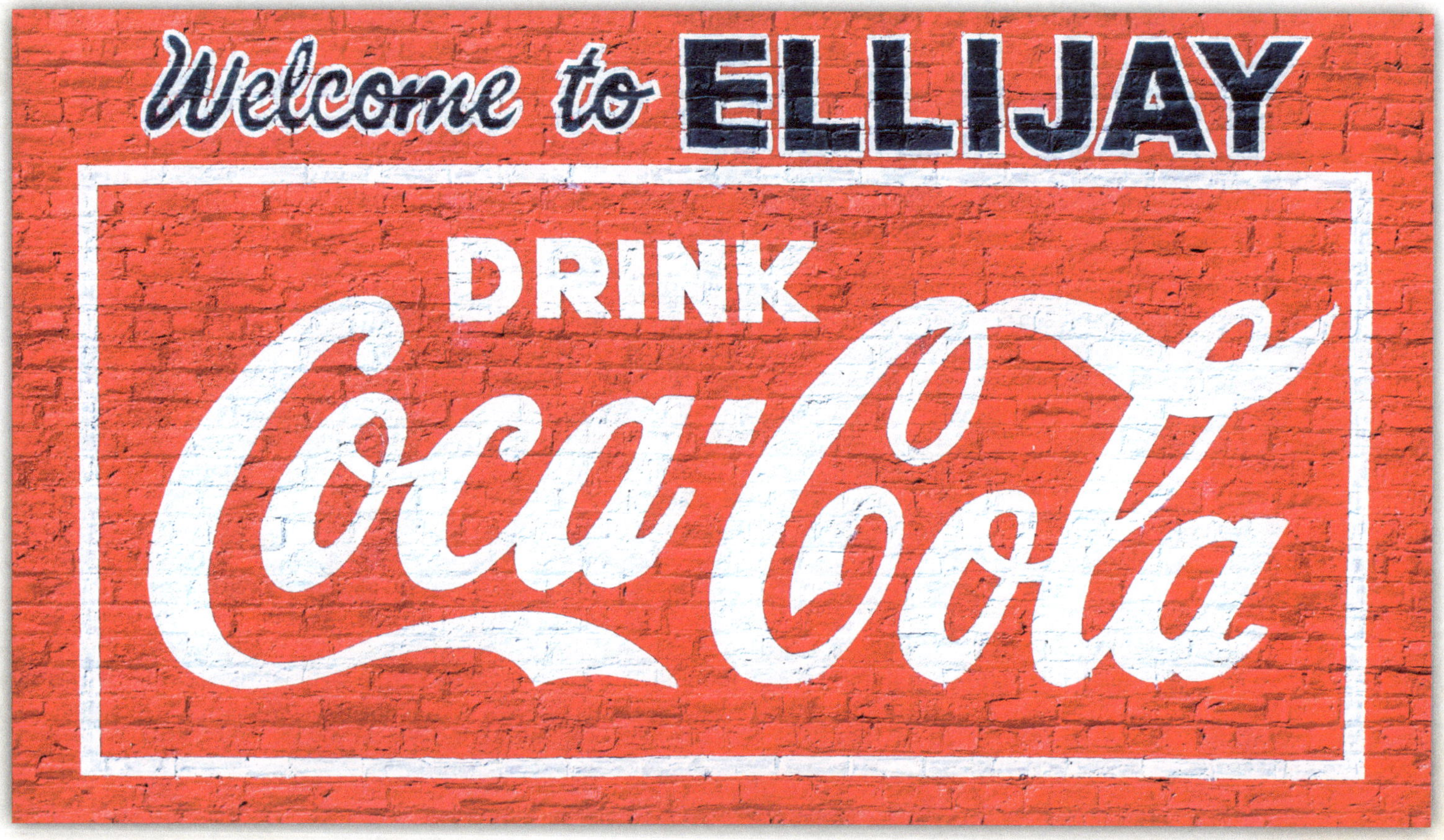

Delicious and Refreshing

Fairmont

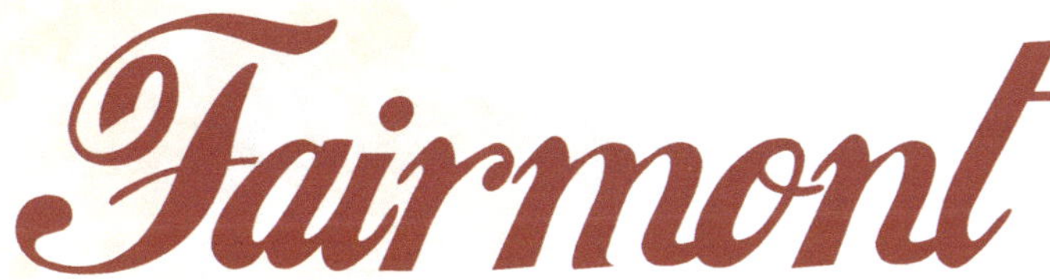

Corner of South Avenue and Highway 53
GPS 34°26'6" N 84°42'2" W

Mayor Calvin Watts shared that this building was built in 1918, and housed the local grocery store. Originally, it was near the railroad tracks.

If you look closely, you will see how this wall sign, repainted in the 1990s, is over the original sign.

In my opinion, the original wall sign might have been painted between 1918 and 1940 because of the age of the building, its use as a grocery store, and its closeness to the railroad tracks.

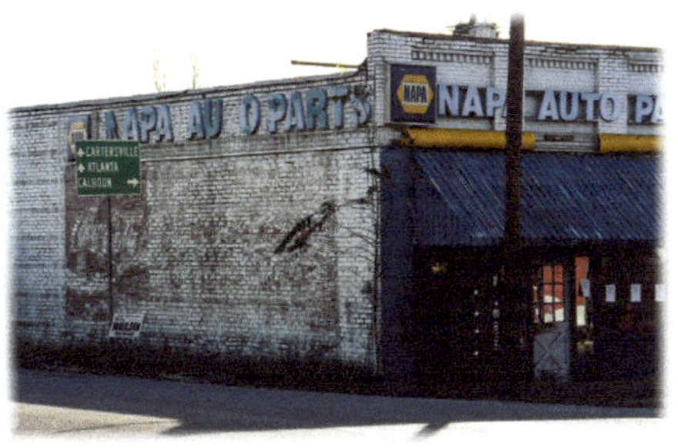

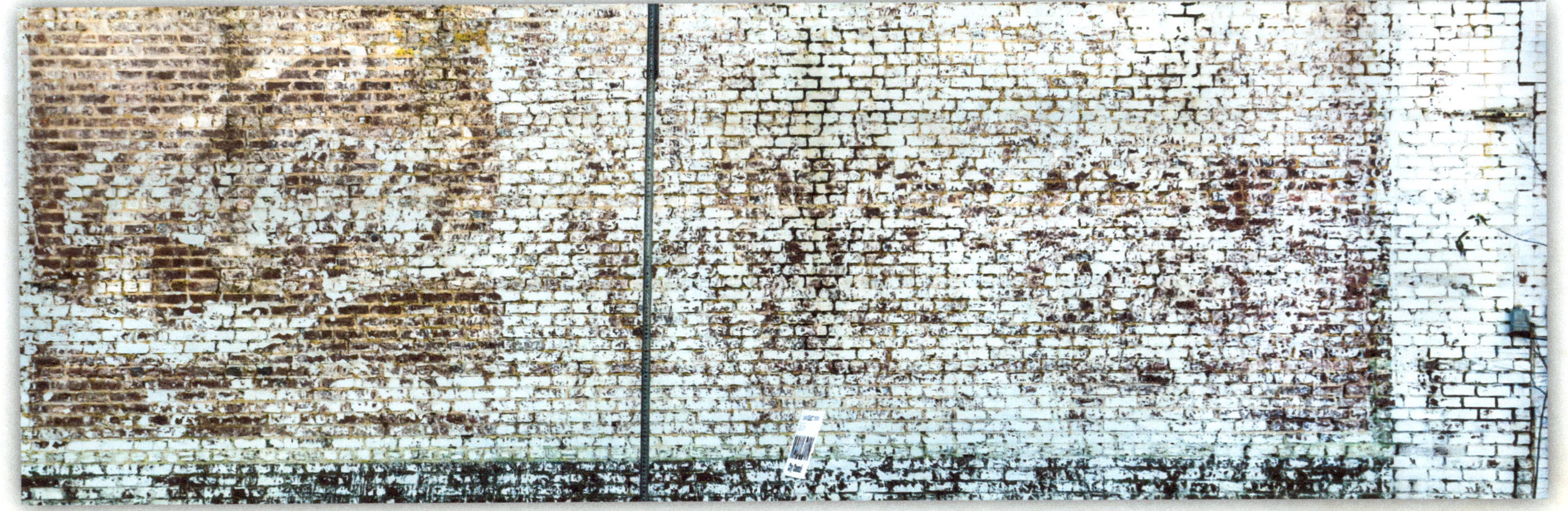

Fort Gaines

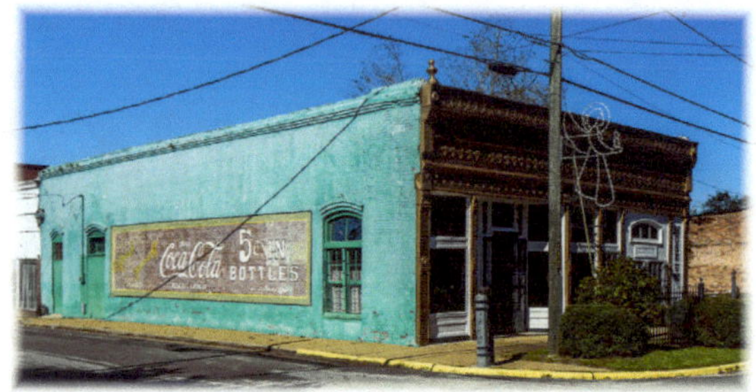

Corner of E Carroll Street and Washington Street
GPS 31°36'20" N 85°2'57" W

The Fort Gaines Coca-Cola wall sign's bright blue background makes it impossible to miss. Karen Klear was sorry to say that "no one seems to know when the original sign was painted, but it was repainted in the 1980s."

The slogan "Refresh Yourself" and trademark placement could place the original wall sign between 1924 and 1931.

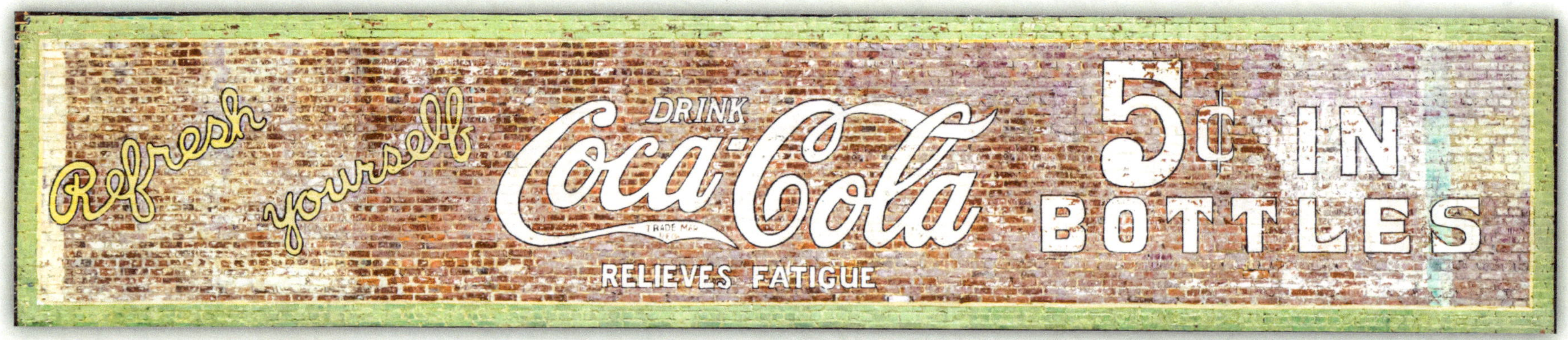

Delicious and Refreshing

Gainesville

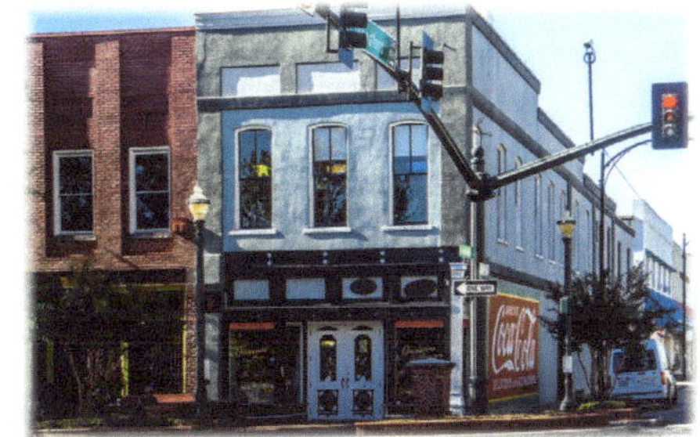

This Coca-Cola wall sign is located on the Imperial Building in the historic town square. Built in 1871, it at one time housed a drugstore.

The trademark location and wording would suggest the original sign might have been painted between 1930 and 1941.

Gainesville is the hometown of past Coca-Cola CEO Douglas Ivester. When Dianna Love Snell and Karl Snell of Art Productions, Inc., were repainting the wall sign, Doug said, "I would like to paint on the wall with her."

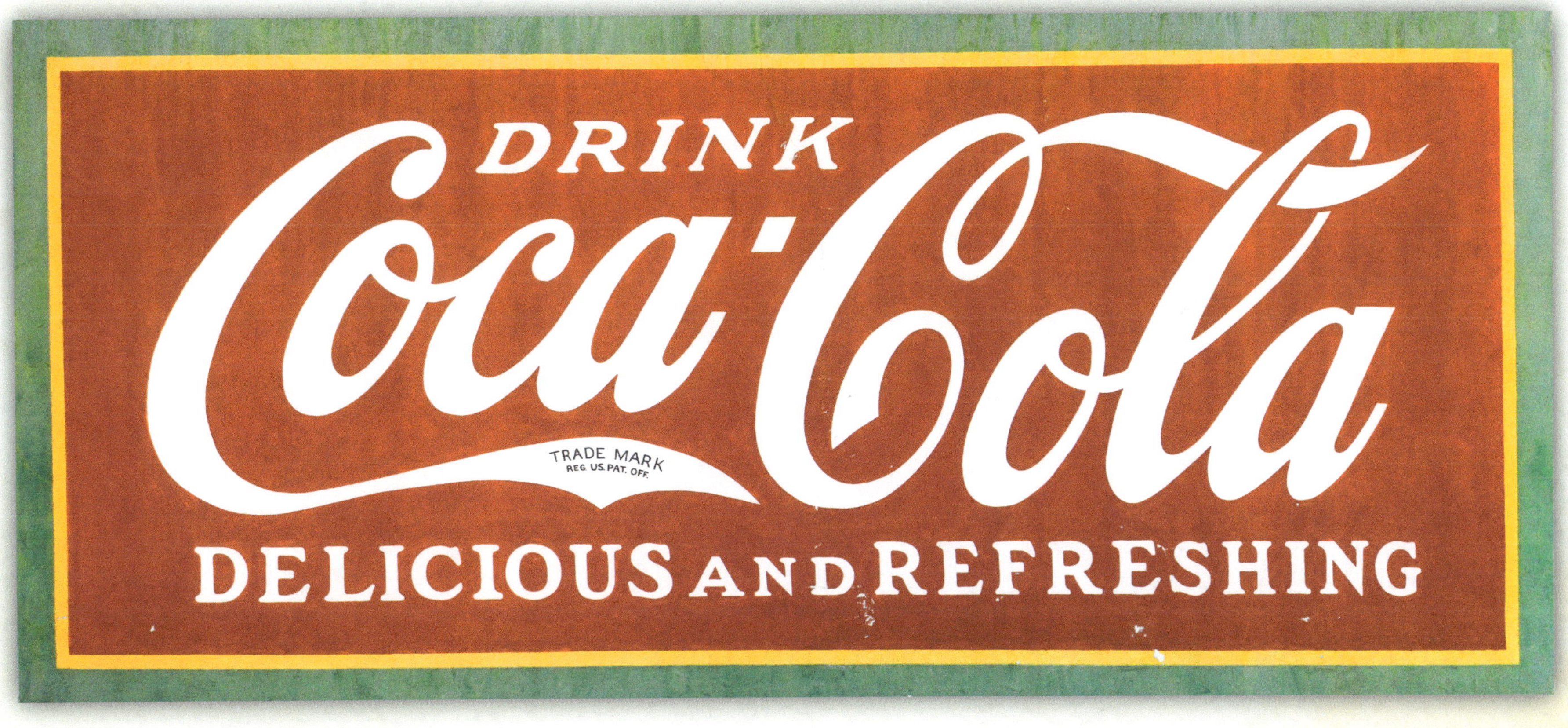

Grantville

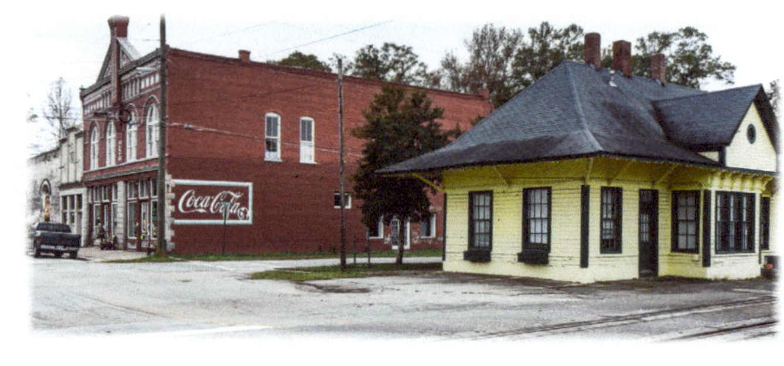

**Near the Train Depot -
Corner of W Broad Street and Church Street**

GPS 33°14'4" N 84°50'7" W

Originally placed where passengers disembarking from the train would see it, the Grantville Coca-Cola sign was likely painted after 1938, since the silhouette girl is included in the design.

According to Jeff Bishop, the director of the local historical society, the building was built in 1893 and has been used as the farmer and merchant building, a general merchandise store, and a bank. The sign was originally painted when the building was used as a general merchandise store.

Delicious and Refreshing

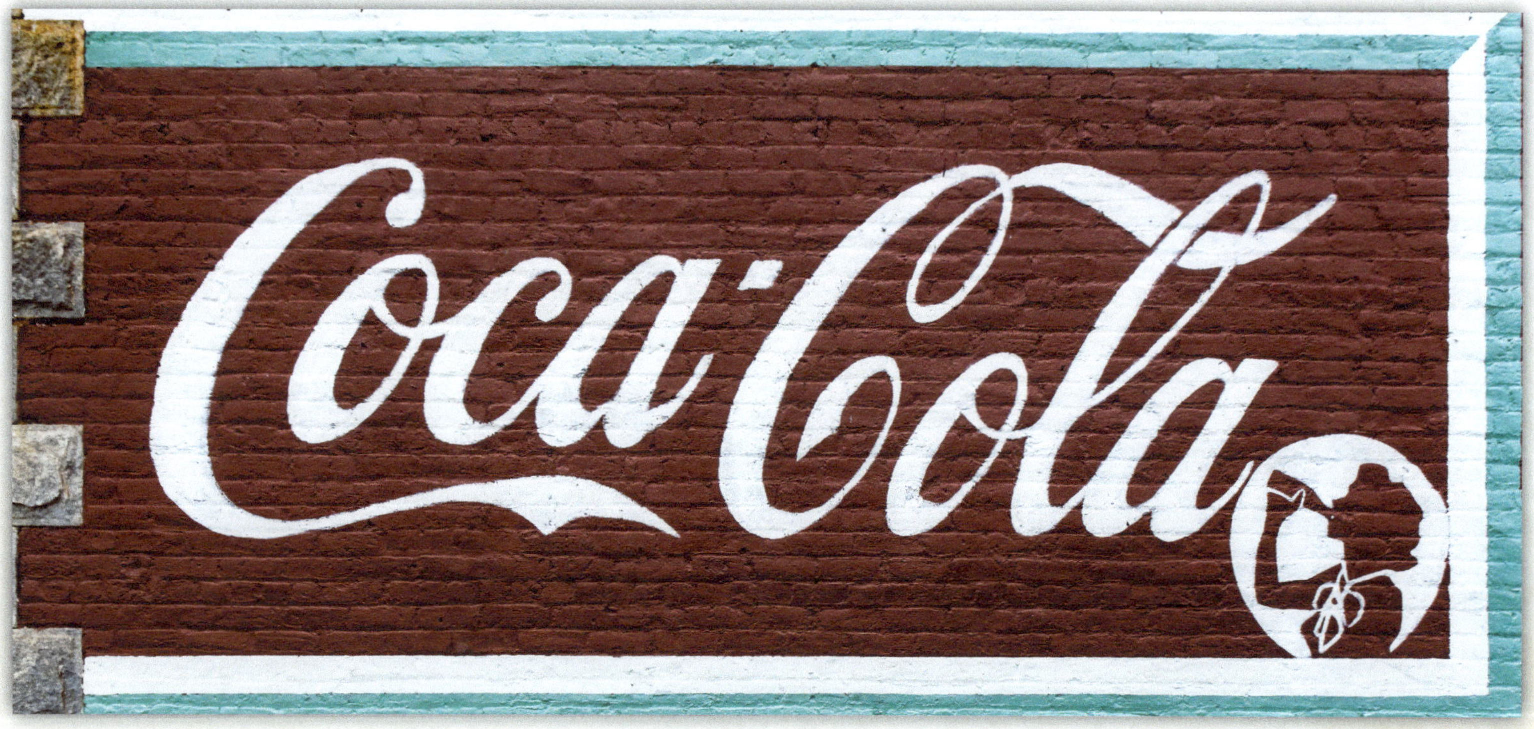

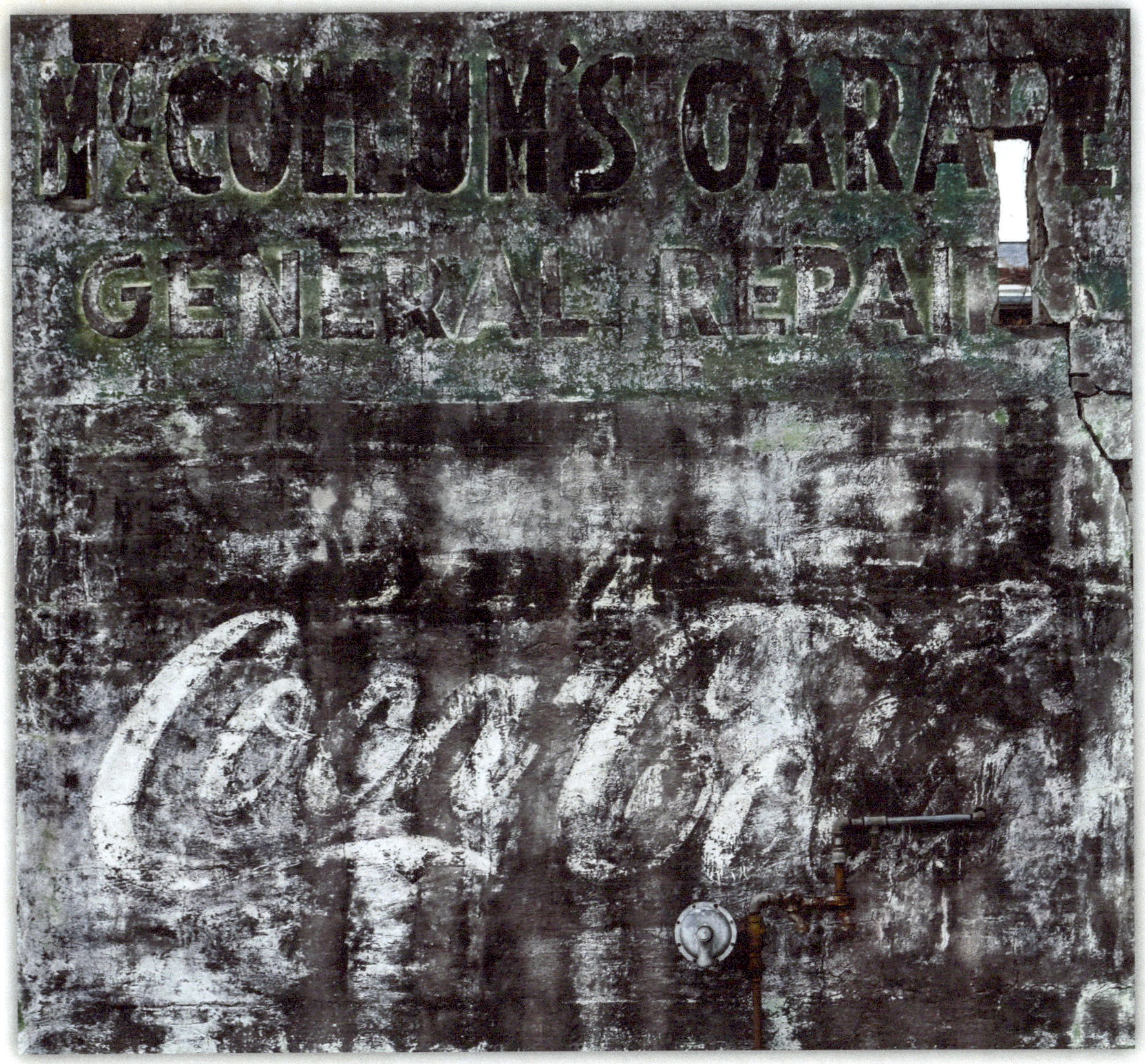

Grantville

Old Shop at the Junction of Church Street and Lone Oak Street

GPS 33°14'1" N 84°50'4" W

It was just by chance I discovered this ghost wall sign. My guess is it was painted on the side of the garage so drivers traveling into town would see it.

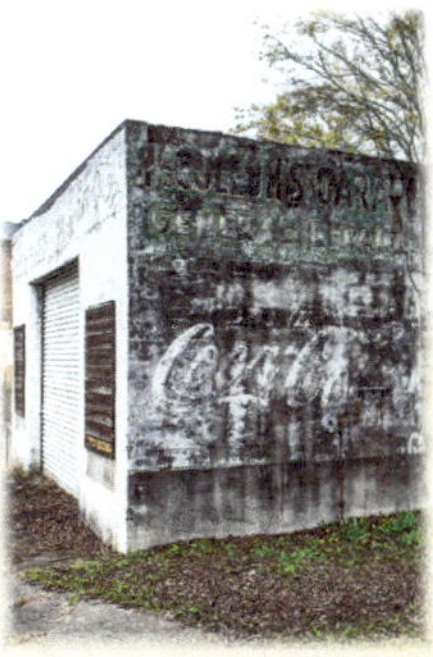

Hampton

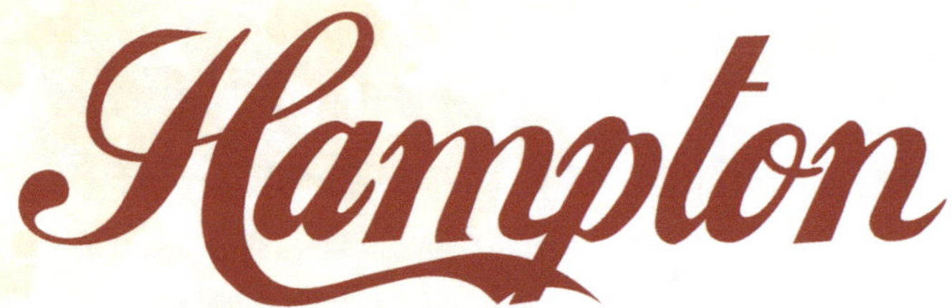

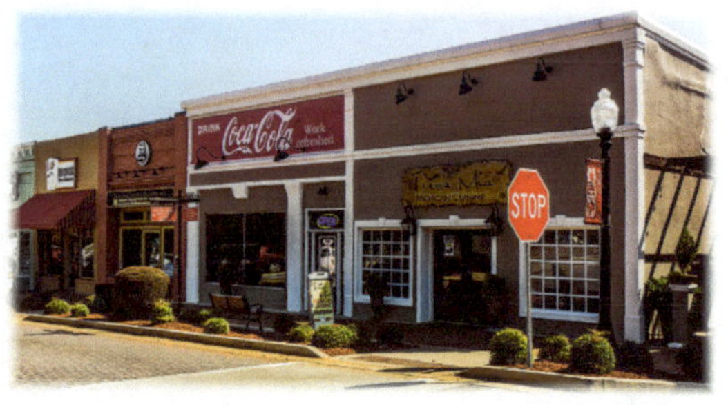

End of Oak Street and E Main Street S
GPS 33°23'12" N 84°16'58" W

Betty English's daughter, Mary Ellen English Kiszka, remembers the sign on Marvin Daniel's Meats and Grocery store. Betty found the "Work Refreshed" slogan in an old photograph. This slogan is associated with the early Sprite Boy wall signs, which means this sign was probably painted in the early 1950s.

As a child, Mary remembers walking to the supermarket with her mother to buy groceries and have a Coke. The owner's son would deliver the groceries later that day.

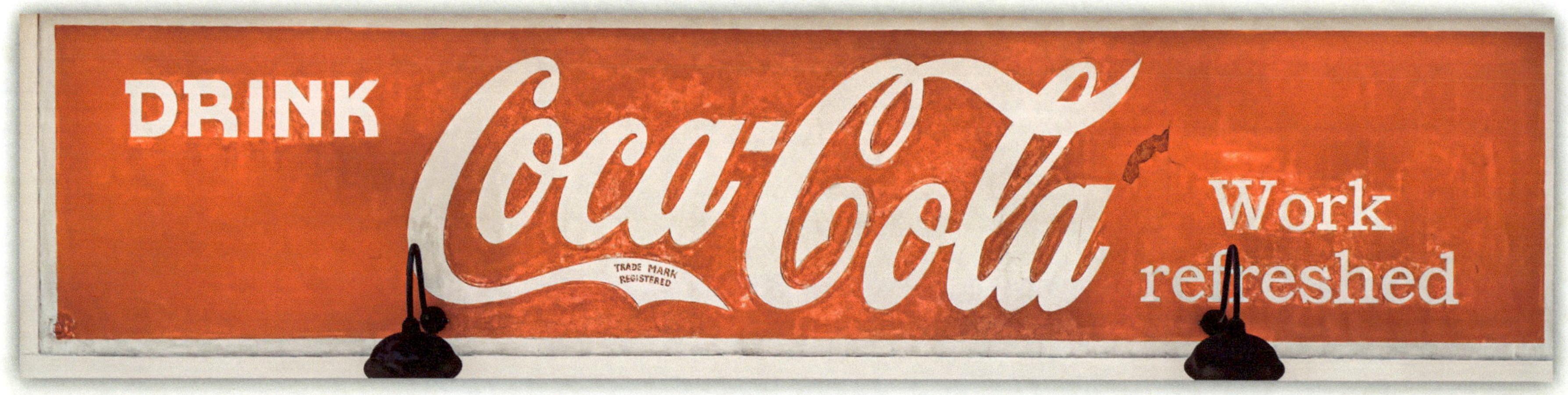

Delicious and Refreshing

Hapeville

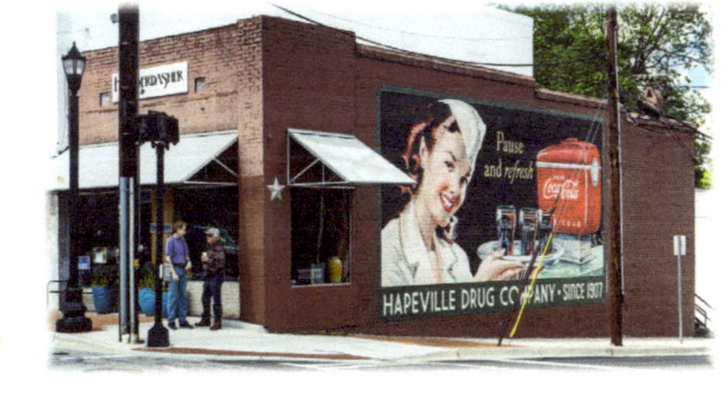

Corner of N Central Avenue and N Fulton Avenue

GPS 33°39'32" N 84°24'32" W

This Coca-Cola wall sign in Hapeville is located on a building that was a bank in 1911, and became a drugstore in 1921. The drugstore had a metal Coke sign with a bottle cap that was removed.

This beautiful wall sign was painted by Shannon Lake in 2001 as a historic reproduction for the town.

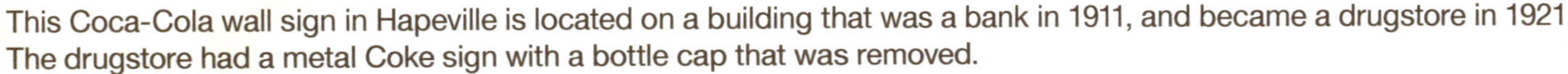

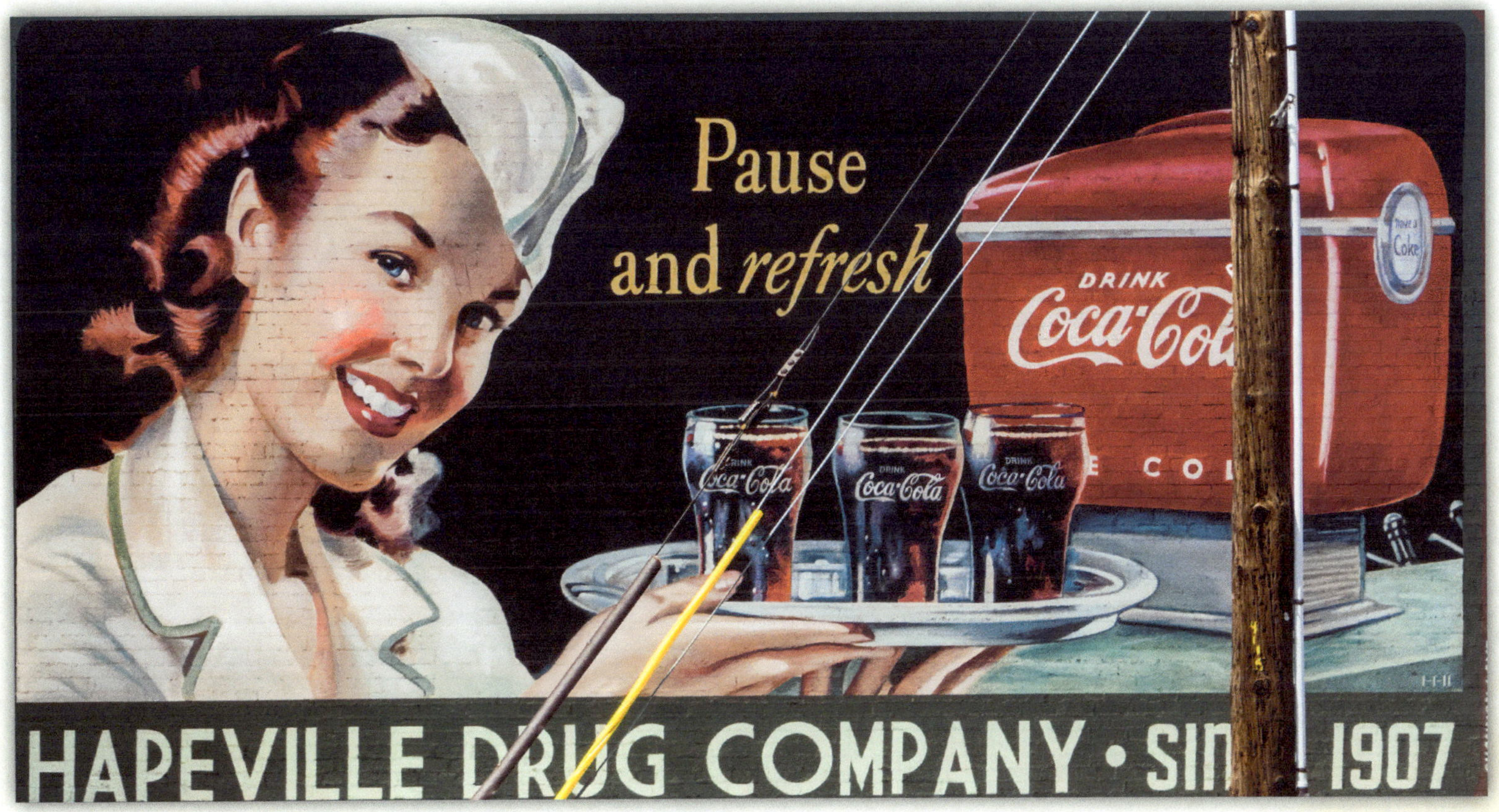

Hiram

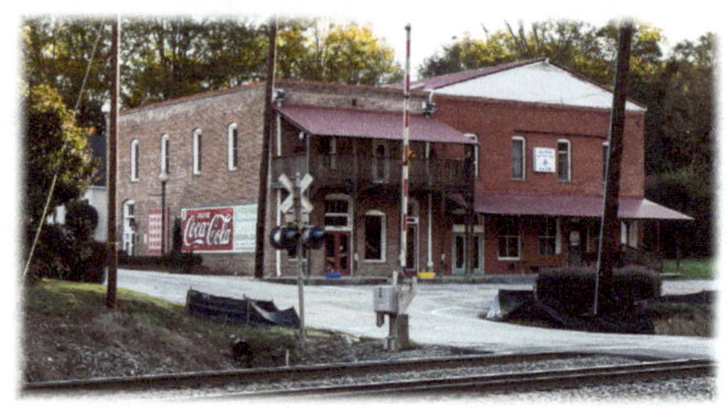

On Main Street across the Railroad Tracks and Beatty Street
GPS 33°52'30" N 84°45'41" W

Local Kathy Bookout believes the building was likely built around 1889. In 1956, when the original Coca-Cola sign might have been painted, it served as a restaurant.

The sign was repainted in 2004 by Matt Porter and Rick McClung. Interestingly, it was featured in the opening scenes of the 1984 movie *Footloose*, starring Kevin Bacon and Lori Singer.

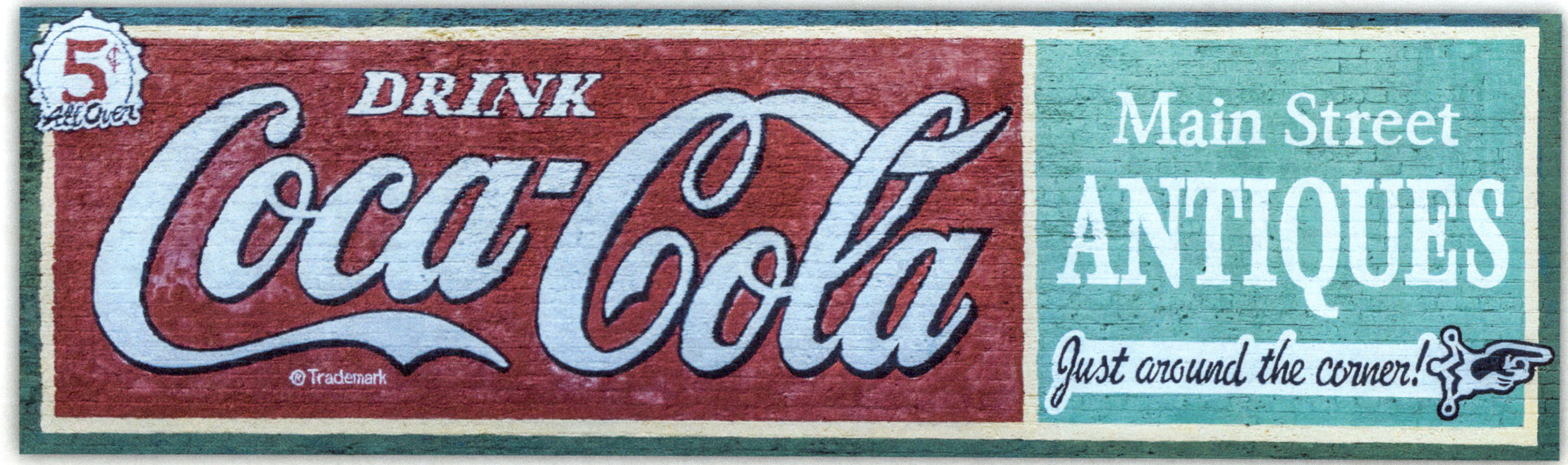

Delicious and Refreshing

Hoboken

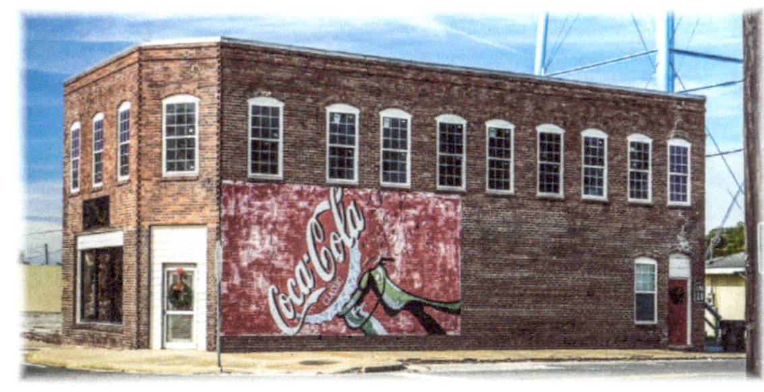

Corner of W Main Street and Palm Street
GPS 31°10'52" N 82°7'56" W

According to Hoboken resident Linda Henderson, the town's Coca-Cola sign was originally painted in the 1900s on what was then the Davis grocery building, in the center of town near the railroad tracks. Since then, the sign has been repainted and changed several times.

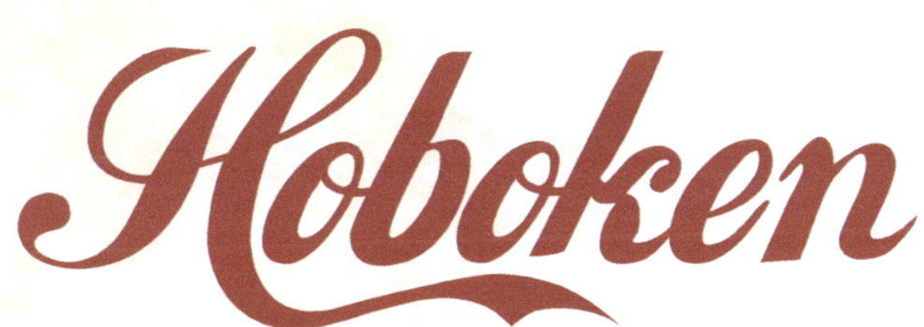

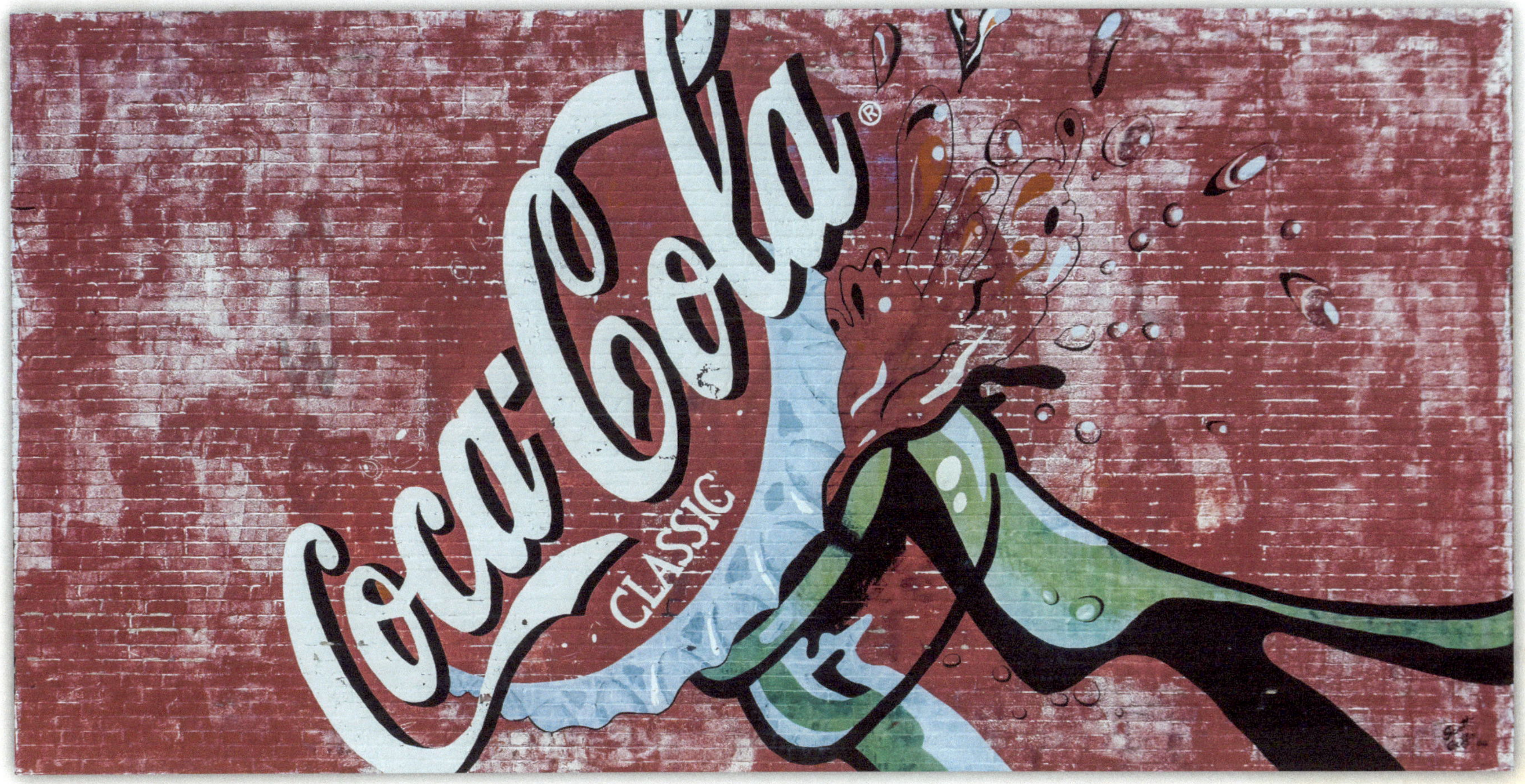

Jasper

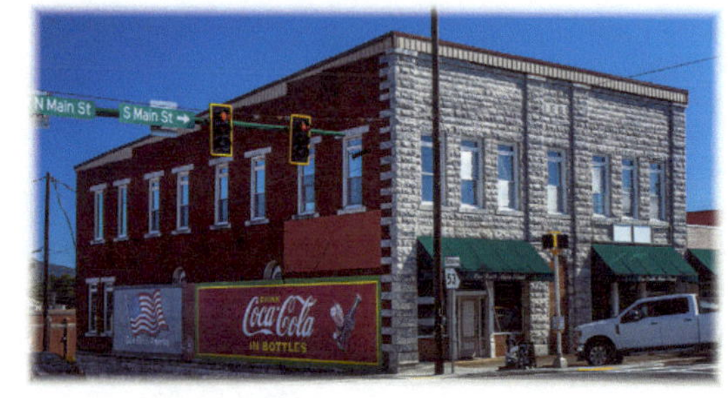

On Main Street across railroad tracks and Beatty Street
GPS 33°52'30" N 84°45'41" W

This Jasper sign is the most beautiful Sprite Boy sign I found in Georgia.
It was repainted in 2020 by John Christian, who first had to remove the old paint.

John believes the original sign was likely painted in the 1940s. That makes sense,
because the building is not far from the renovated train depot.

John is a muralist, creating wall art representing a lasting historic and cultural theme for cities along the Georgia Mural Trail.

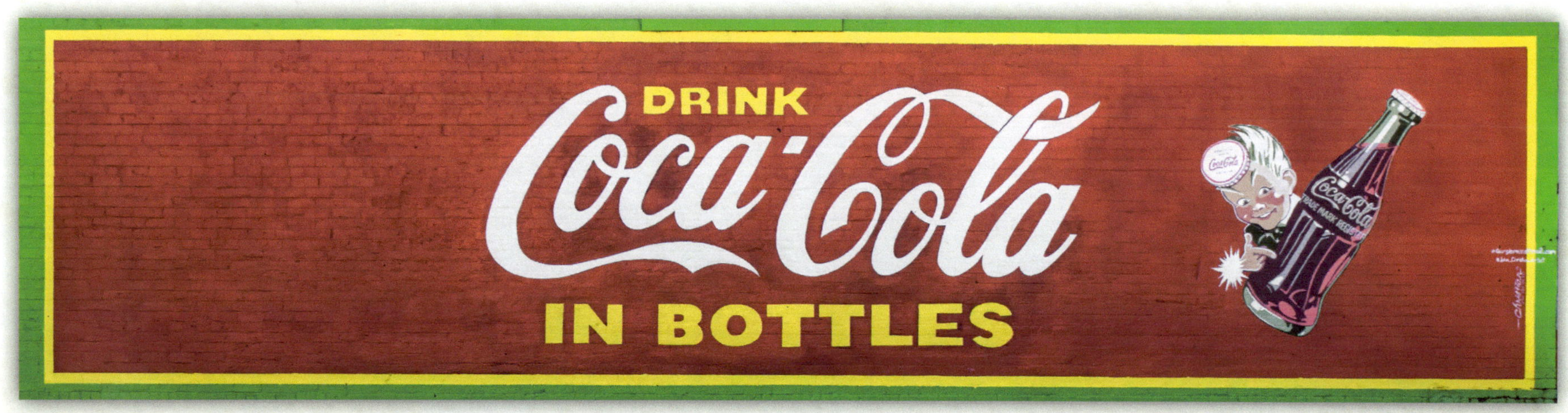

Jefferson

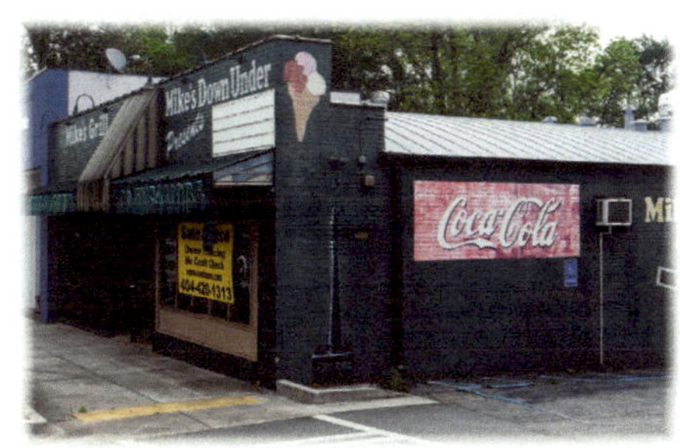

On GA 82 N/Sycamore Street across from College Street
GPS 34°7'4" N 83°34'21" W

This portion of the original wall sign on the side of Mike's Down Under was preserved when the building was repainted. However, little could be found out about the building or the original sign. Because of the trademark location, my guess is it was painted after the 1950s.

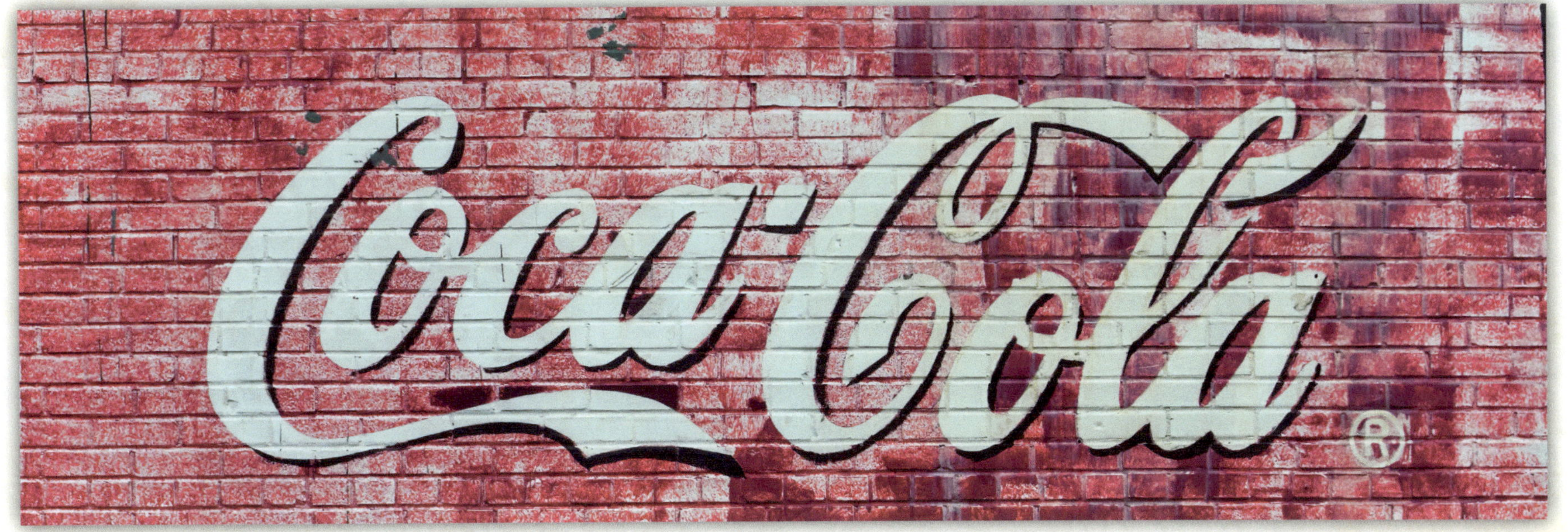

Lakemont

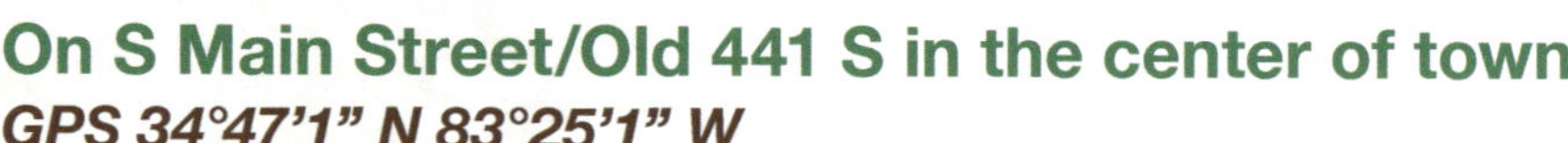

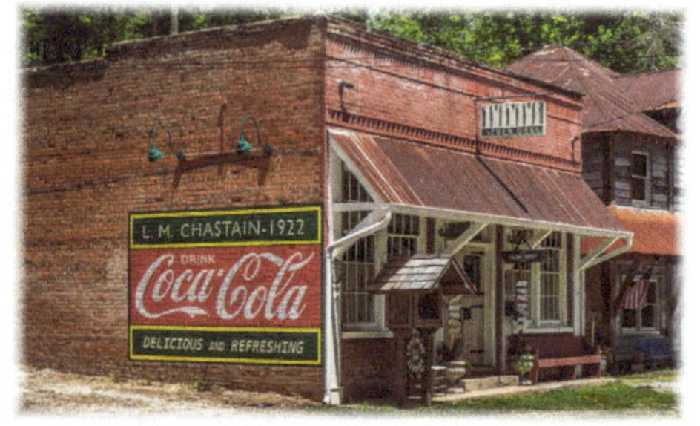

On S Main Street/Old 441 S in the center of town
GPS 34°47'1" N 83°25'1" W

Local Jim Loudermilk shared that the Lakemont Coca-Cola sign was painted in 1922, when the building was Chastain's Grocery. The grocery store was located across the tracks from the train depot, which no longer exists.

The Tallulah Falls railroad stopped in Lakemont at 11 a.m., and disembarking passengers would see the Coca-Cola sign. The "Delicious and Refreshing" slogan provides credibility to the original 1922 date.

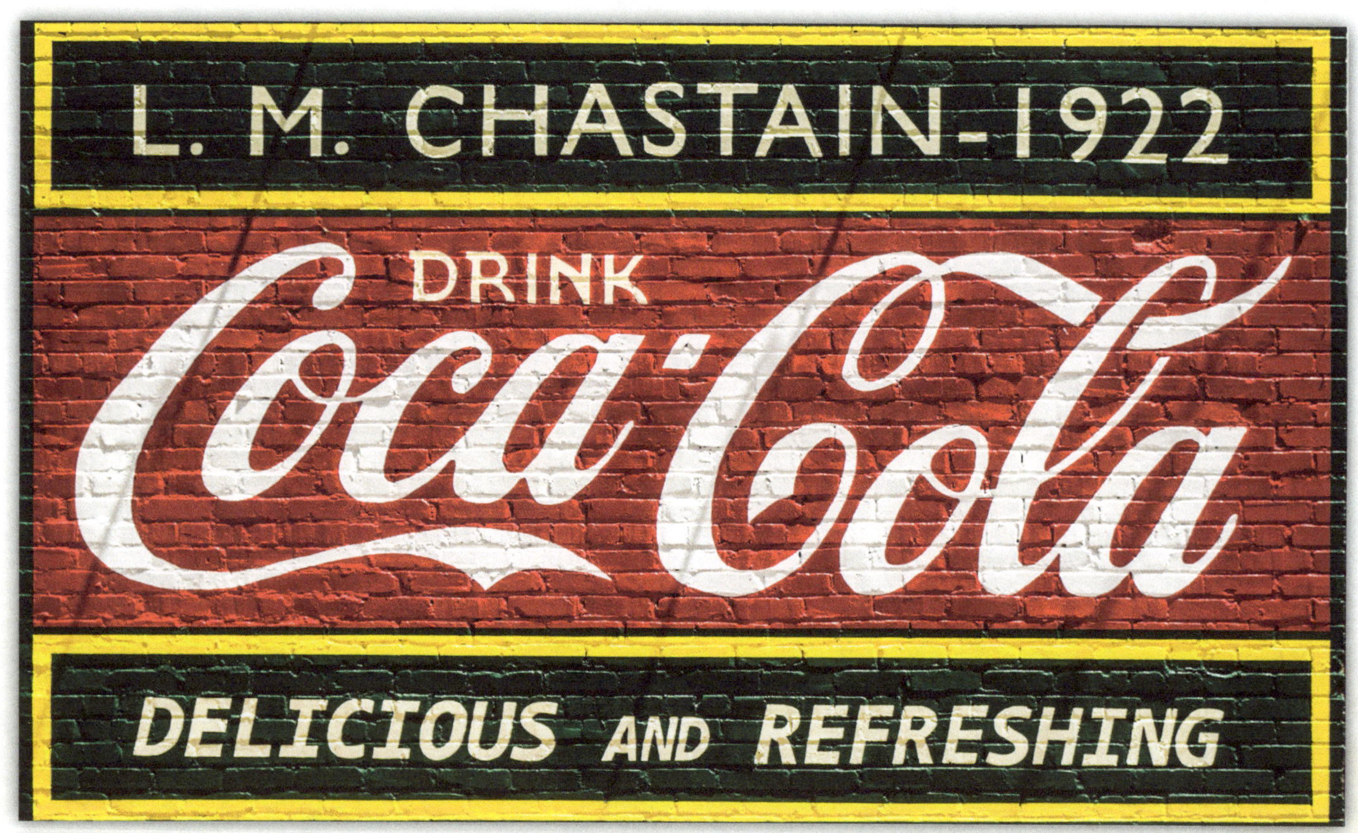

Delicious and Refreshing

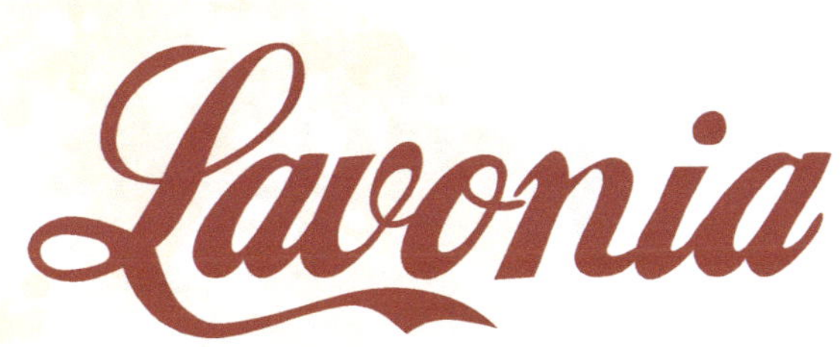

Lavonia

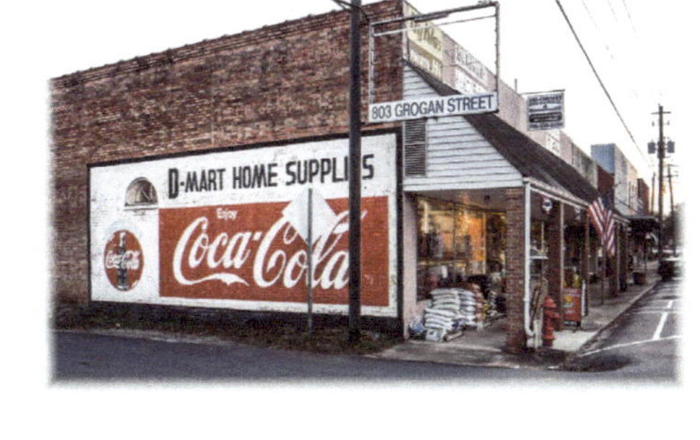

Corner of W Main Street and Grogan Street
GPS 34°26'7" N 83°6'22" W

Barbara Busby at Lavonia City Hall could find little about this wall sign. It was recently repainted over other signs.

Even after talking with the historical society and Barbara Busby at Lavonia City Hall, little could be found out about this wall sign, except that it was recently repainted over other signs that dated back to the 1960s.

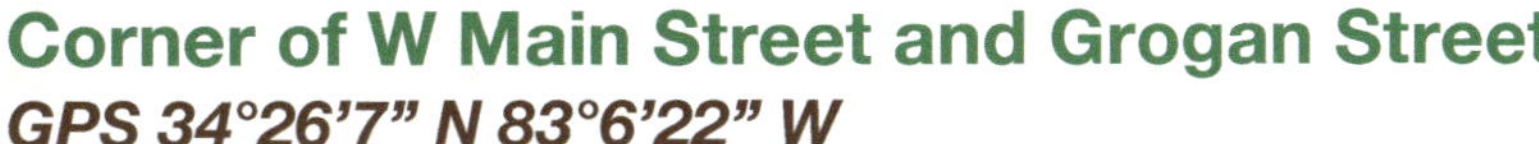

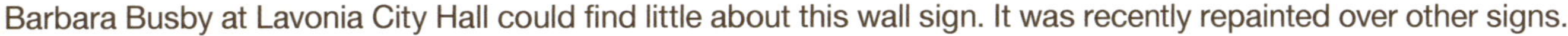

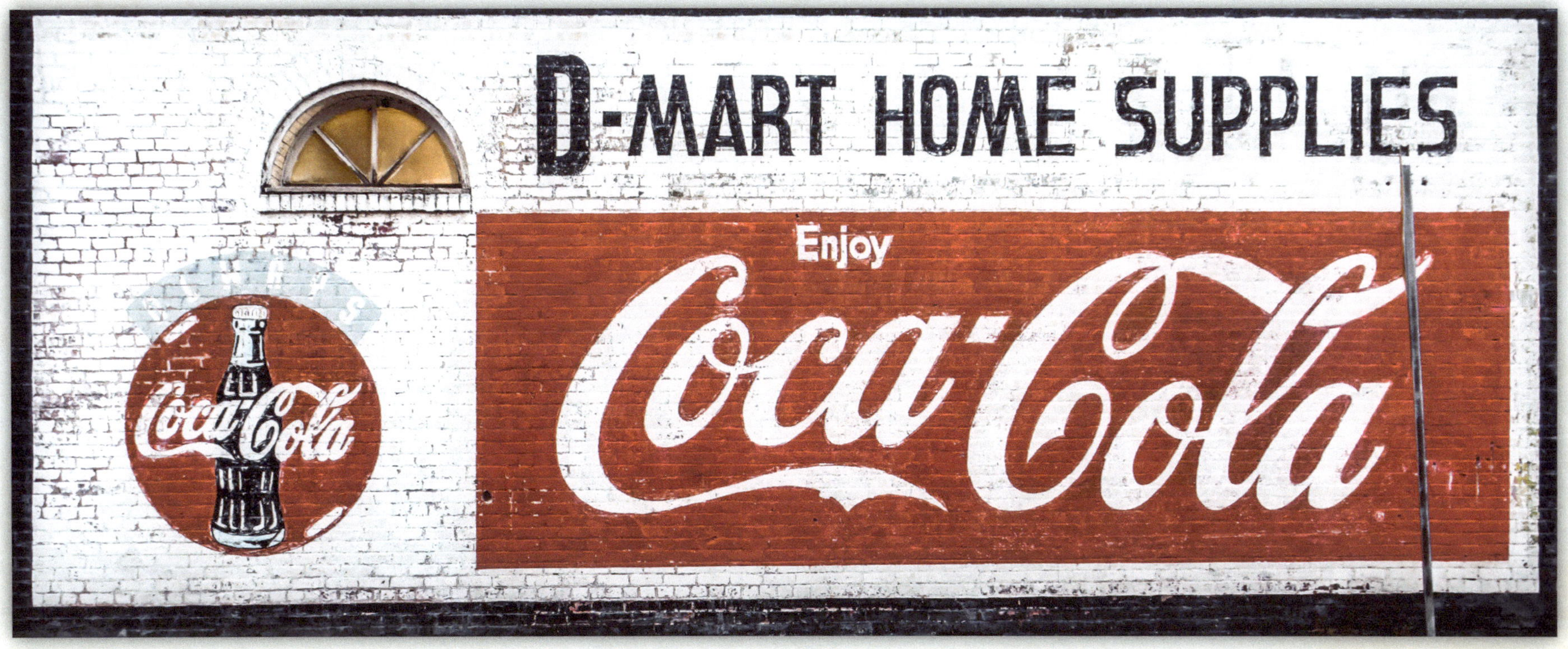

Corner of E Main Street and Grogan Street
GPS 34°26'9" N 83°6'20" W

Barbara Busby was able to confirm the Coke bottle cap wall sign was painted over several other signs that were on the building in the past. Because of the trademark used, the current sign was probably painted after 1969.

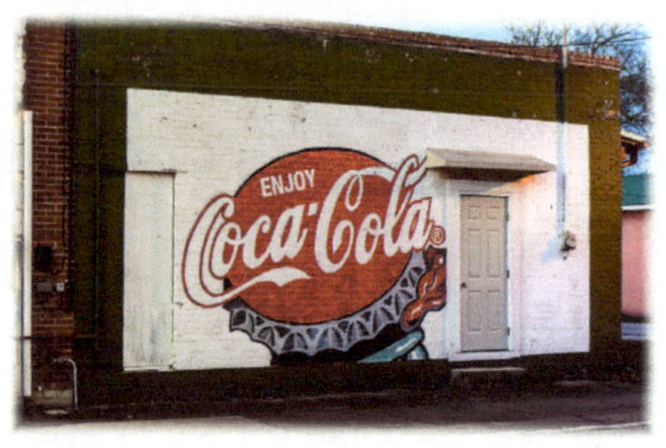

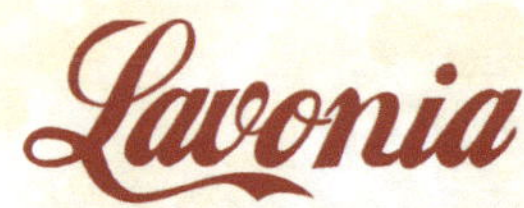

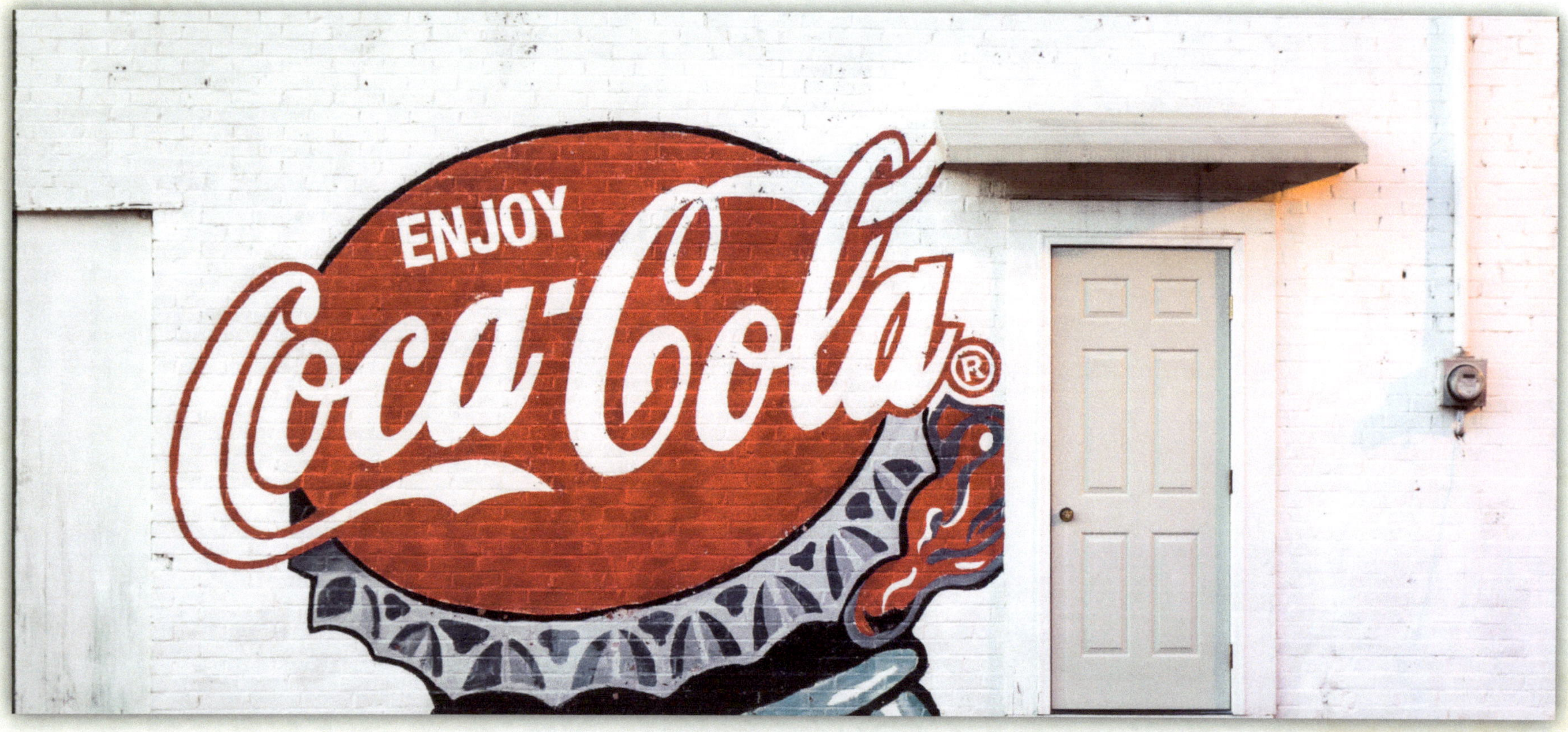

Lincolnton

Corner of N Peachtree Street and School Street

GPS 33°47'38" N 82°28'39" W

I spoke with Kevin Beggs, a history buff who has collected vintage Coke bottles since his youth, and who has a wealth of knowledge about Coca-Cola in the Lincolnton area.

This building, known as the L.H. Ward Building, was built in the early 1910s, and is one of the oldest buildings in town. Around 1939, it housed Mr. Dallas's grocery store.

The still-visible "R" is for Rees Oil Company. After the oil company, the building became home to a bowling alley in the 1950s.

I spoke to John Gumby, Hobby Corner owner, and learned he allowed the sign to be repainted in 2009 by Lincolnton High School's art class, if "Hobby Corner" was placed at the top.

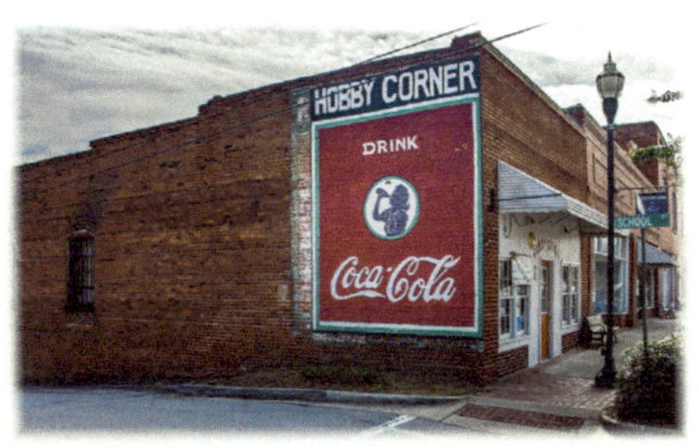

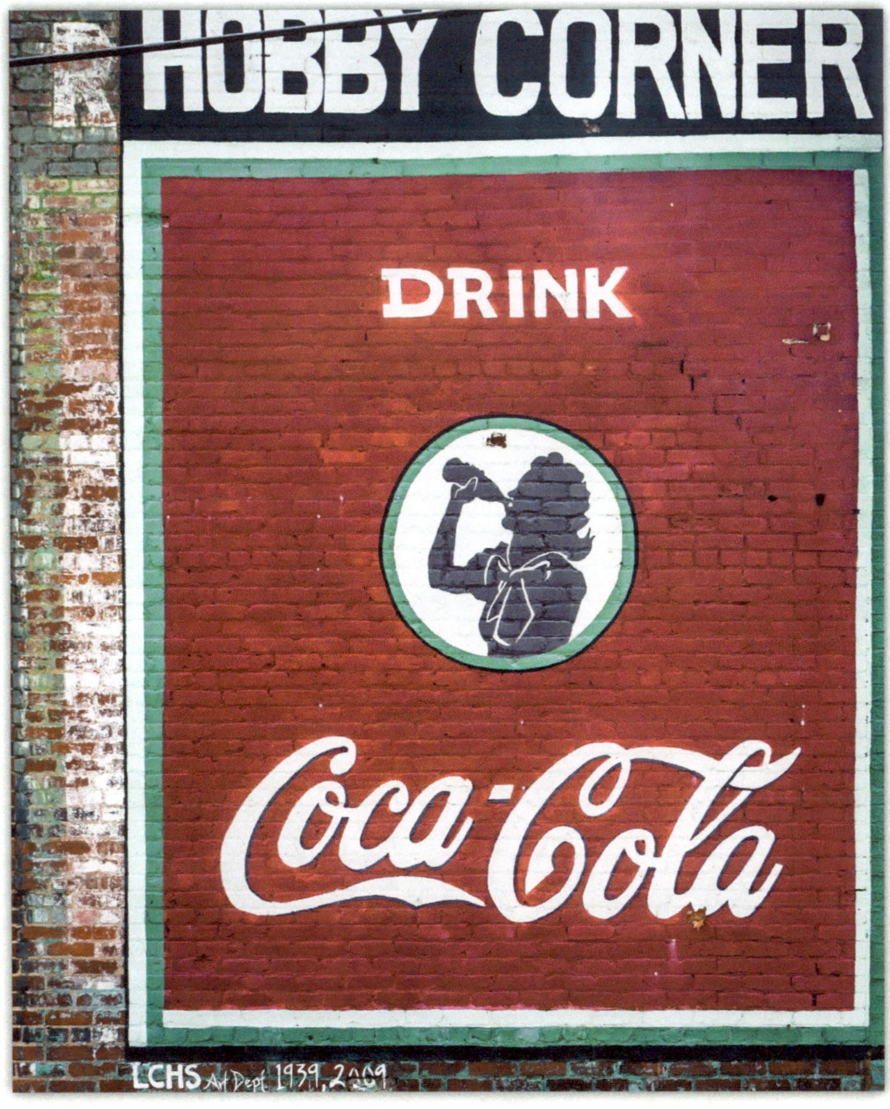

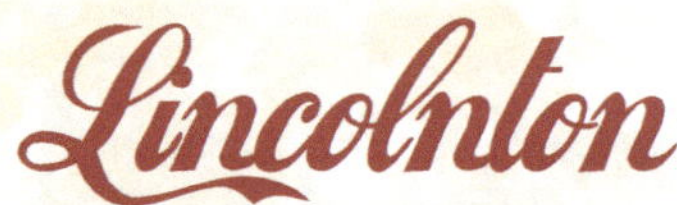

Lincolnton

N Peachtree Street and Ward Avenue
GPS 33°47'35" N 82°28'38" W

Kevin Beggs confirmed this was originally a Sprite Boy Coca-Cola wall sign painted on the side of M.L. Wright grocery store in 1951. The sign was repainted again in 1960, when a barber shop was located there.

This ghost sign is on the side opposite the Hobby Corner sign.

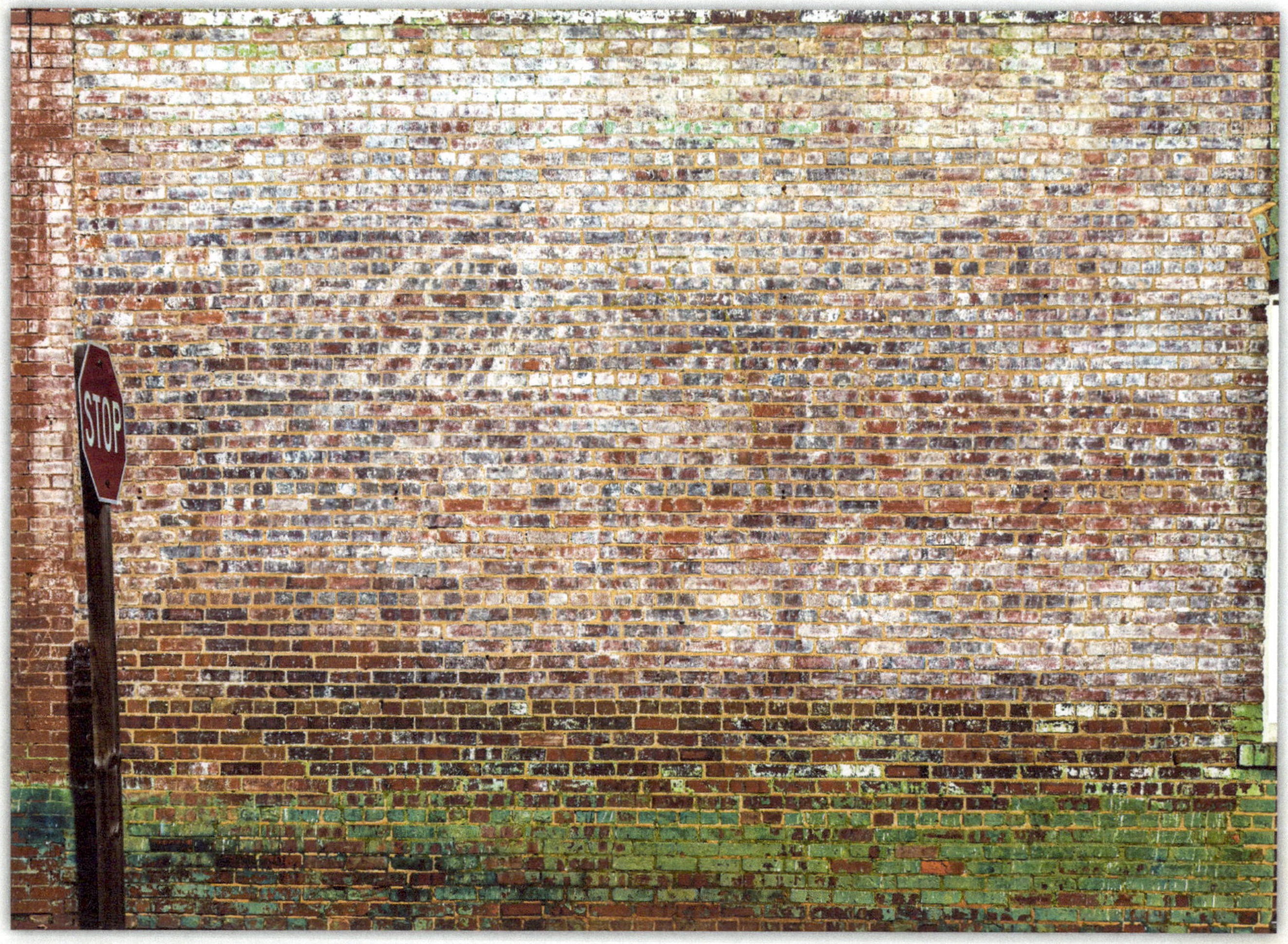

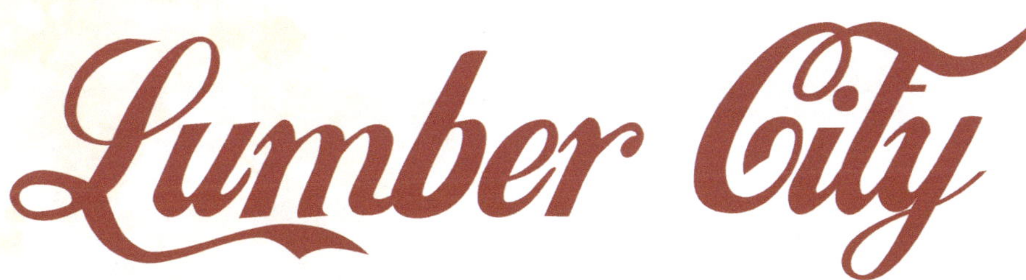

Lumber City

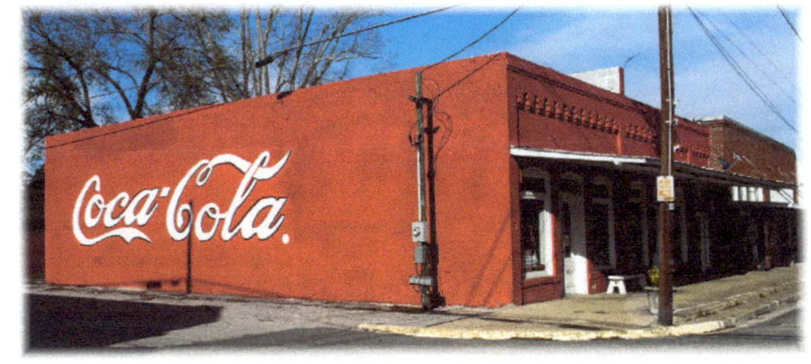

Corner of Main Street and Central Avenue
GPS 31°55'54" N 82°40'58" W

Building owner Craig Stinson confirmed this Coca-Cola sign was repainted by Charlie Shepherd, who "did the best he could, but couldn't paint the entire sign as it originally looked."

The building was built in the 1880s. In the 1930s it was the Phillips Five and Dime, which is when the original Coca-Cola sign might have been painted.

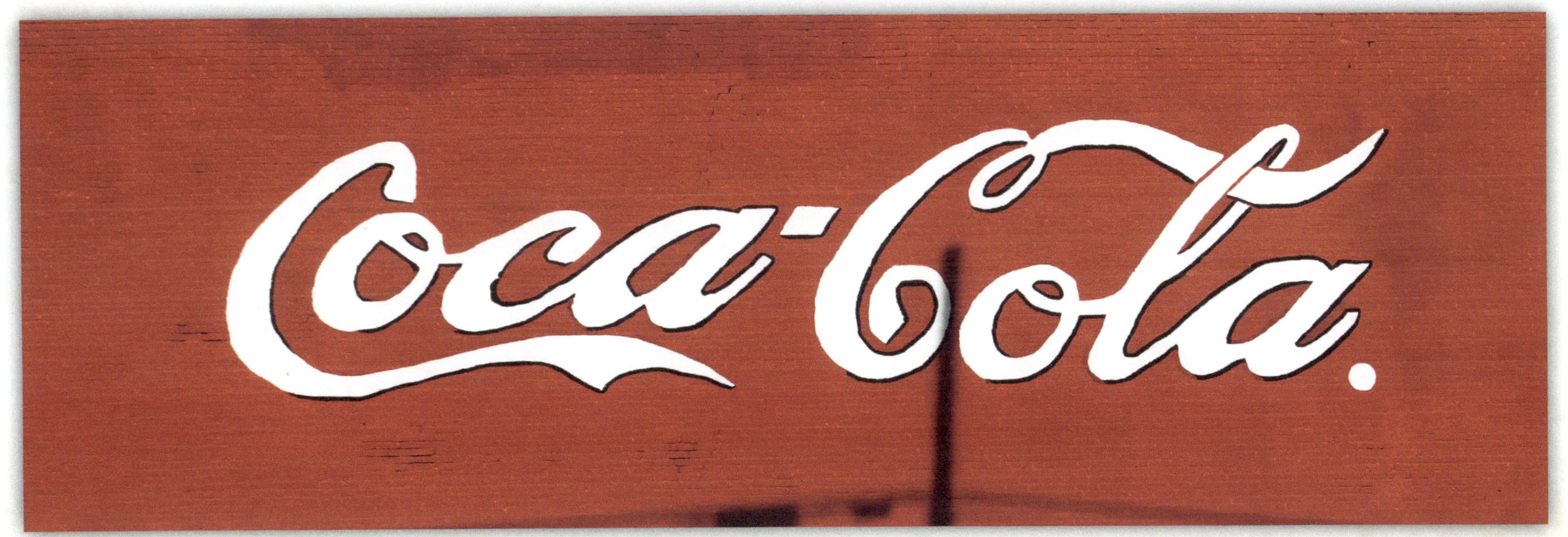

Macon

This Coca-Cola ghost wall sign is in the Black historic district of Macon. I called and spoke with many people in the town and area, but found very little history about when the wall sign might have been painted, or the building.

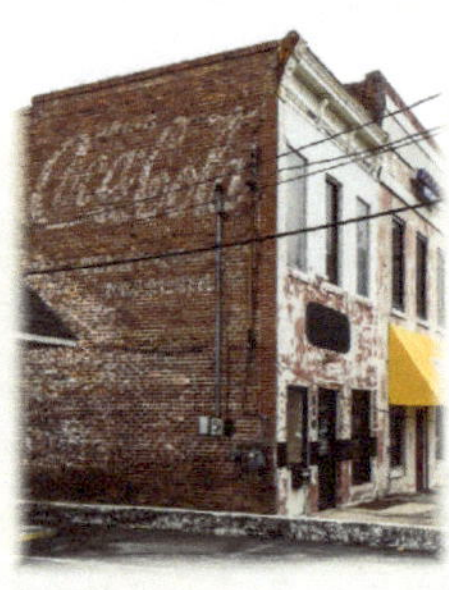

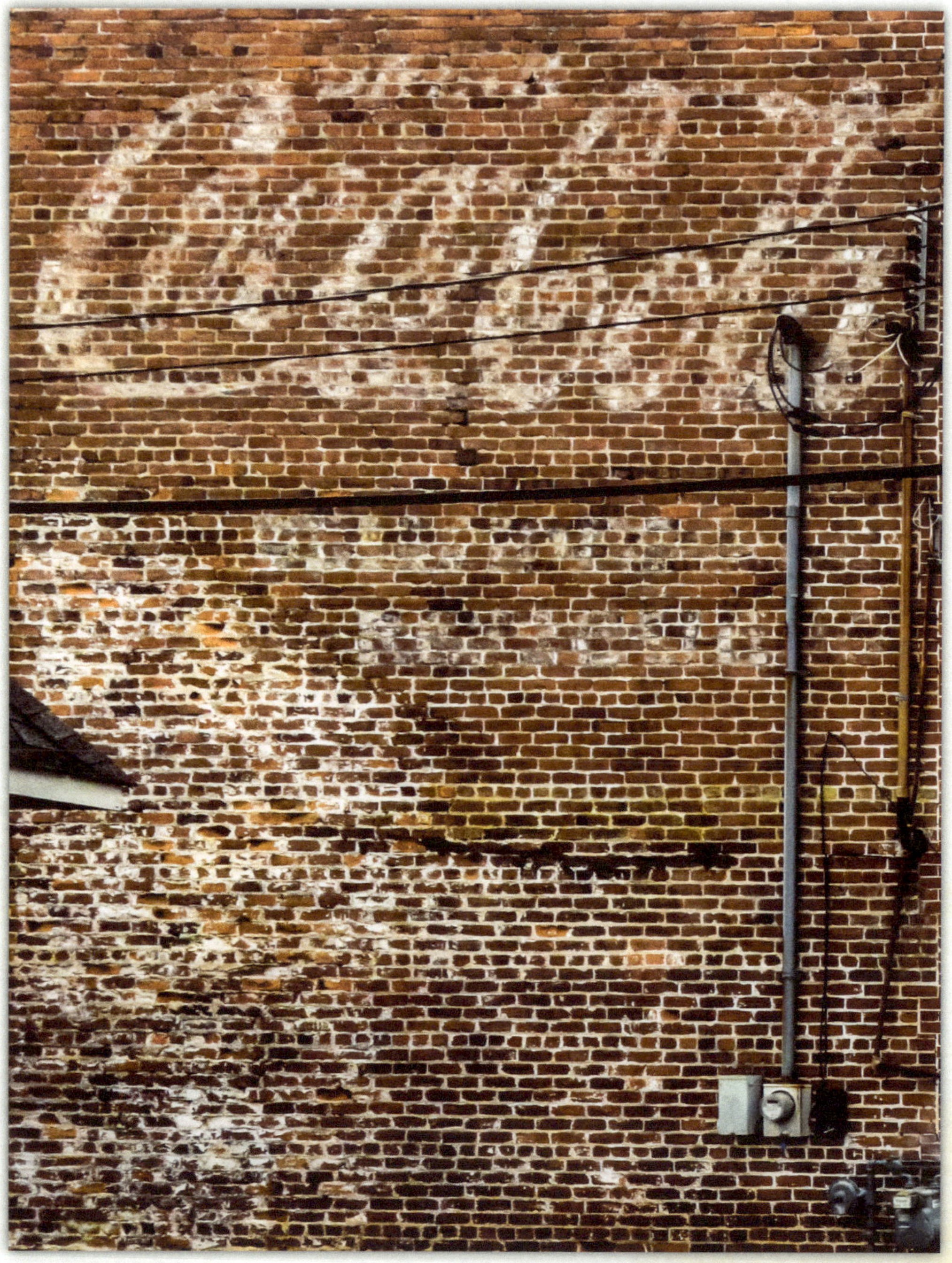

Delicious and Refreshing

Madison

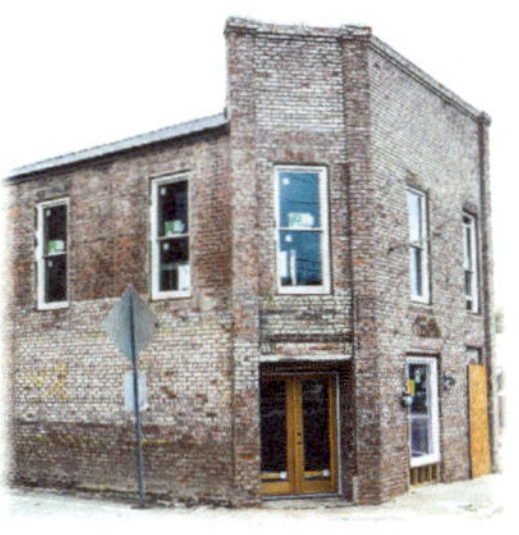

Corner of N 1st Street and W Jefferson Street
GPS 33°35'47" N 83°28'5" W

Thanks to Ken Kocher, Madison Information Specialist & Planner, the history of this sign can be pieced together.
This Coca-Cola wall sign was recently uncovered during renovation, when the old stucco was removed.

The building dates back to the early 1900s, and was the place where Black residents conducted business. Around 1918, two members of the Madison Black community, Dr. J.F. Smith and his wife, Eva, opened a medical practice upstairs and Star Drug Store downstairs.

This Coca-Cola sign clearly had the yellow "Refresh Yourself" slogan when discovered under a painted-over Red Rock Cola sign. The "Refresh Yourself" indicates the original wall sign was painted between 1924 and 1938, when Red Rock began distributing its cola.

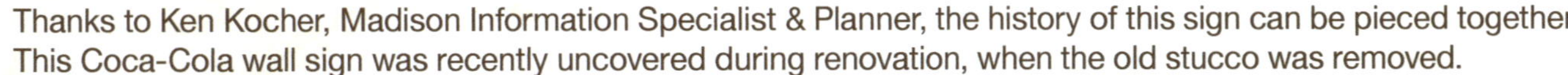

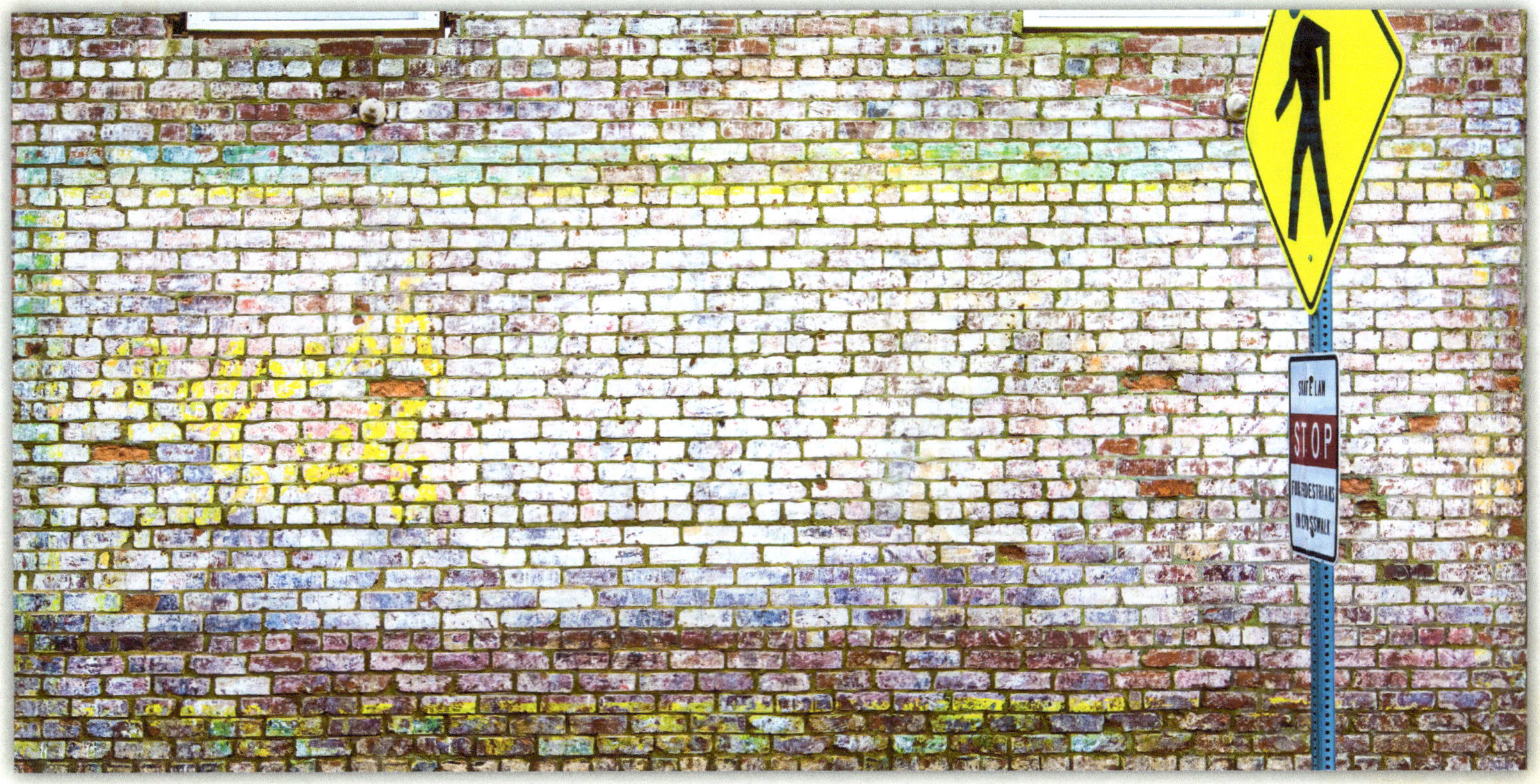

Maysville

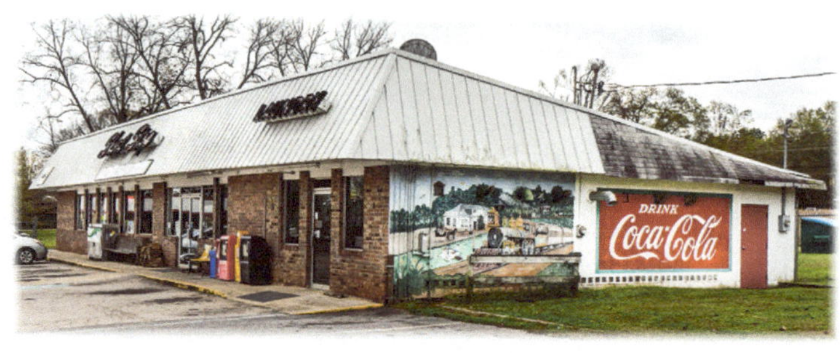

Corner of Maysville Road and Grace Street
GPS 34°14'53" N 83°33'30" W

According to Mayor Richard Presley, Mrs. Catherine Daniel had this sign painted around 2001. I had a wonderful conversation with Catherine and discovered she loves Coca-Cola, and had the historic sign painted to preserve the Coca-Cola wall sign history.

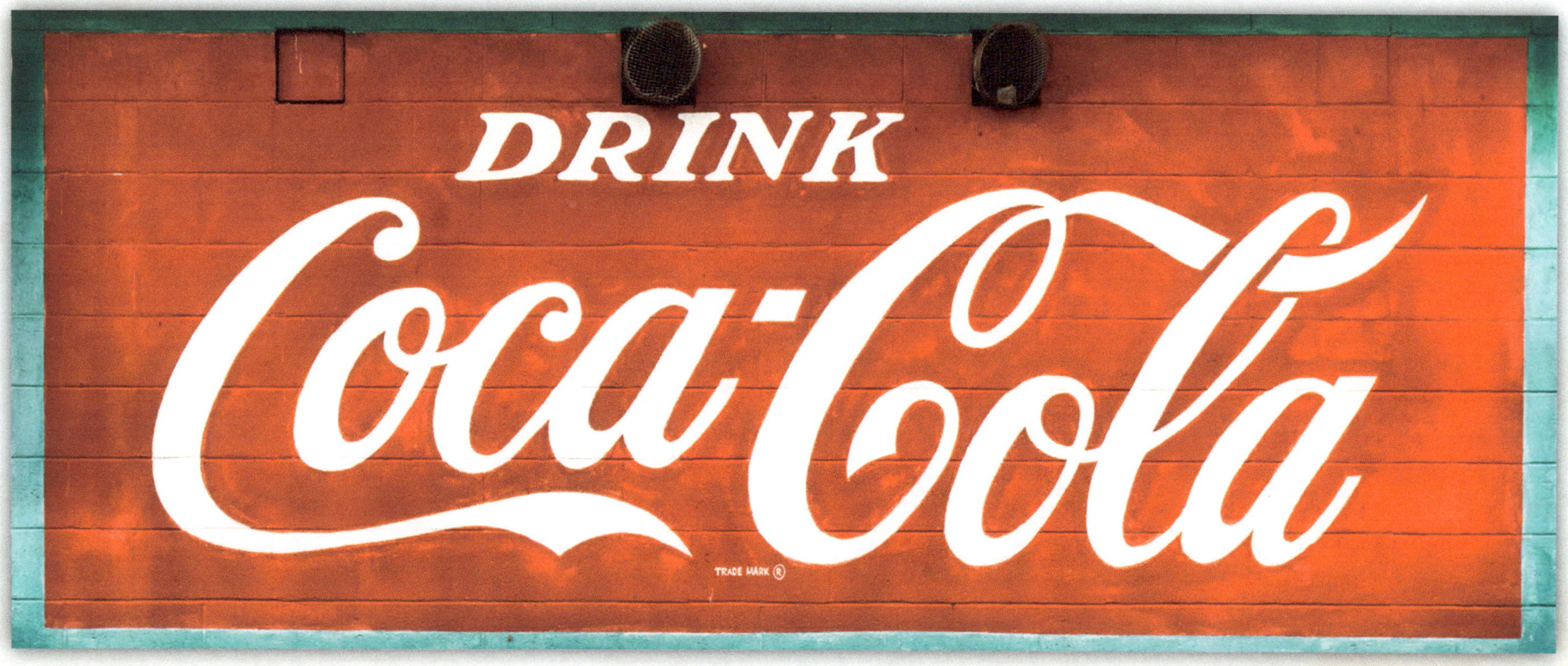

Delicious and Refreshing

McDonough

Corner of Macon Street and Sloan Street

GPS 33°26'47" N 84°8'47" W

I had the pleasure of speaking with McDonough Mayor Billy Copeland about the town's historic wall sign of the Sprite Boy pointing to a Coke. This sign was originally placed decades ago on Red Huffman and Analora Blankstown's popular hot dog restaurant.

The wall sign may have originally been painted between 1942 and 1950. In recent years, Shannon Lake repainted the sign.

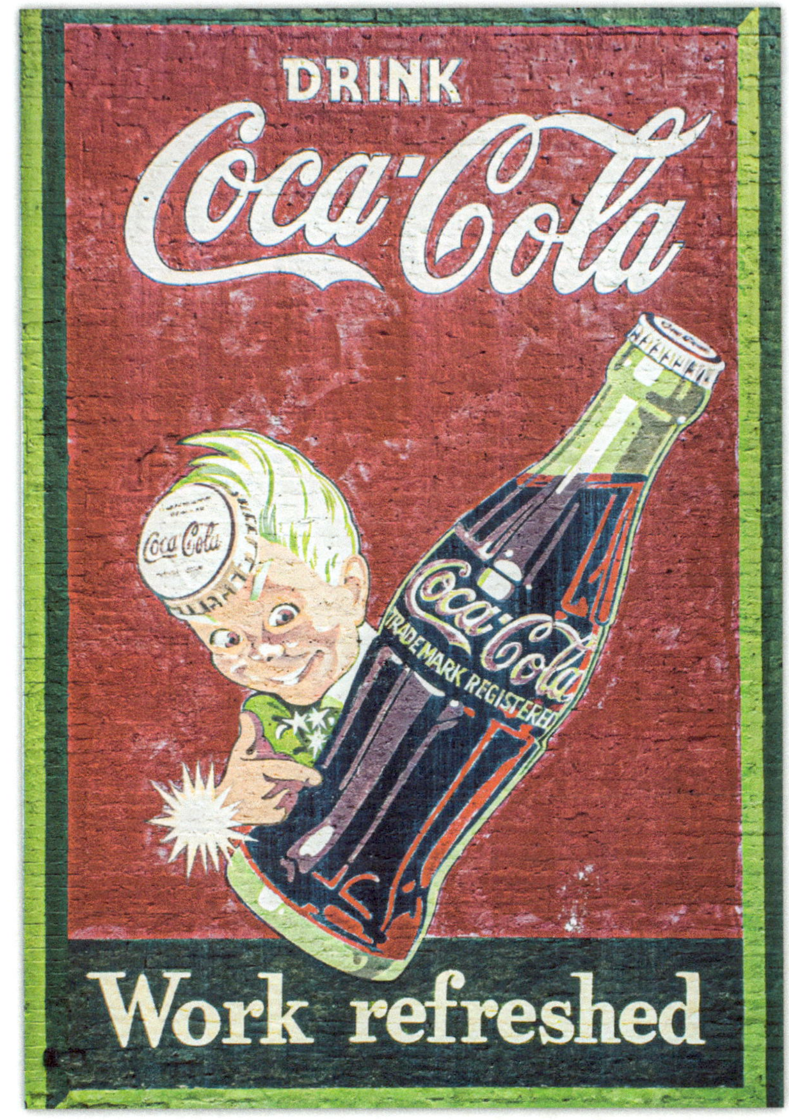

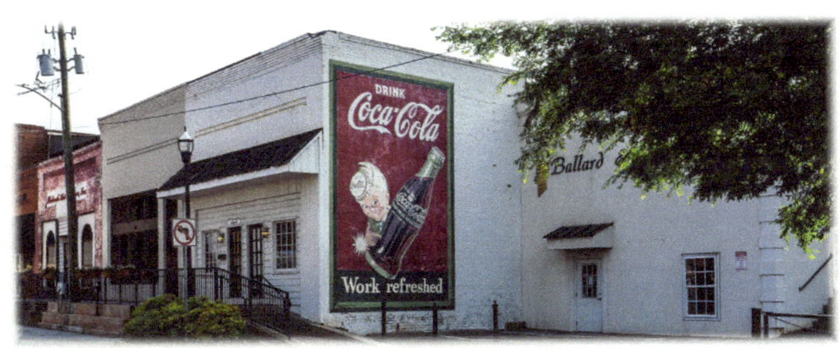

Meansville

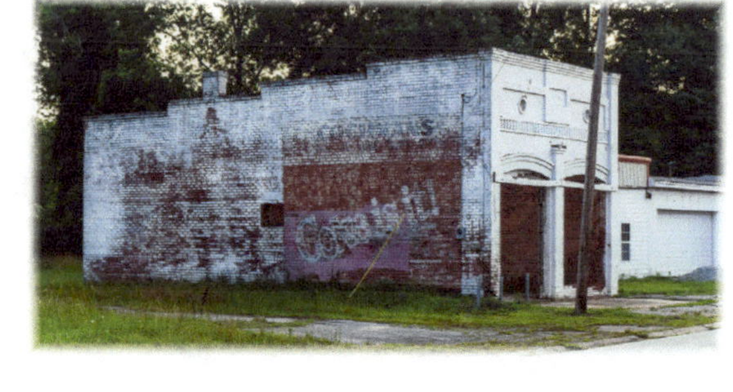

On Main Street across from Means Street
GPS 33°2'57" N 84°18'25" W

Thanks to city historian Lee Milby, the historical details of both the building and sign are known. First built in 1911 as a bank, the building shifted purposes in the 1950s or 1960s when it became the town post office.

Then, around 1970, Milton Cochran acquired the building and opened his store there, Cochran's, which is when the Coca-Cola wall sign was painted on the building. The "Coke is it!" slogan dates the sign to 1982 or later.

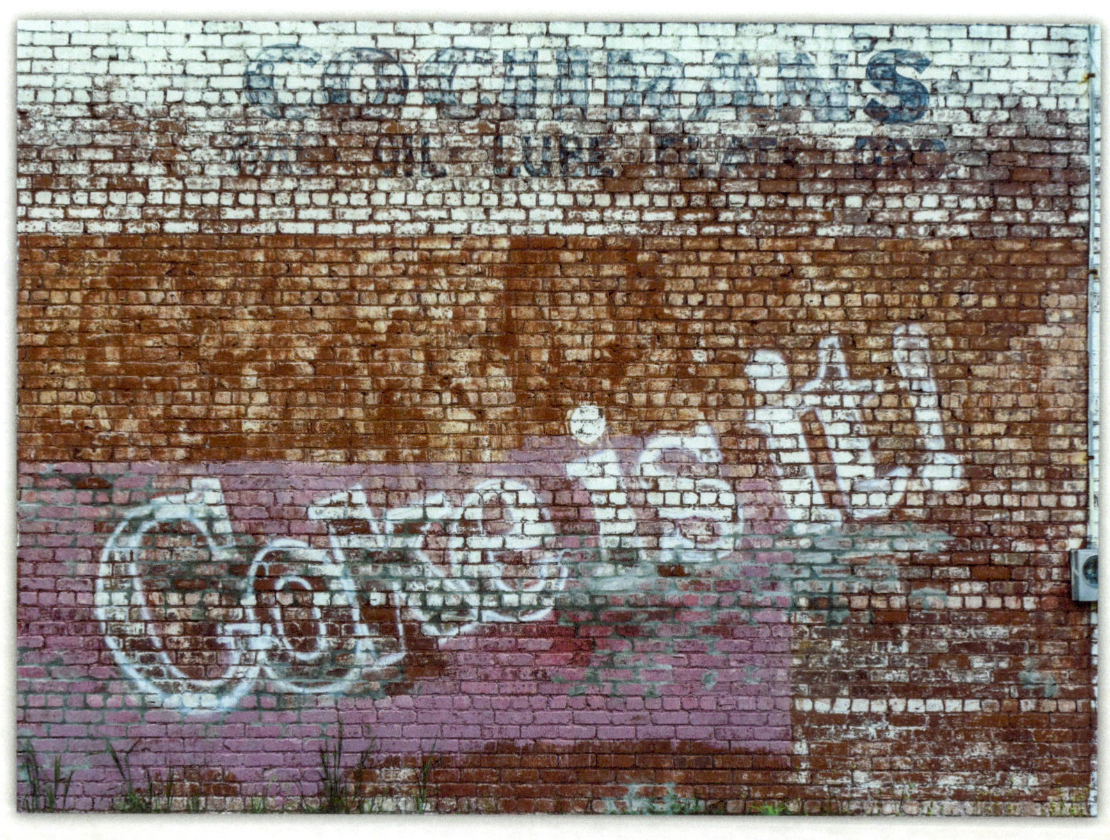

Milledgeville

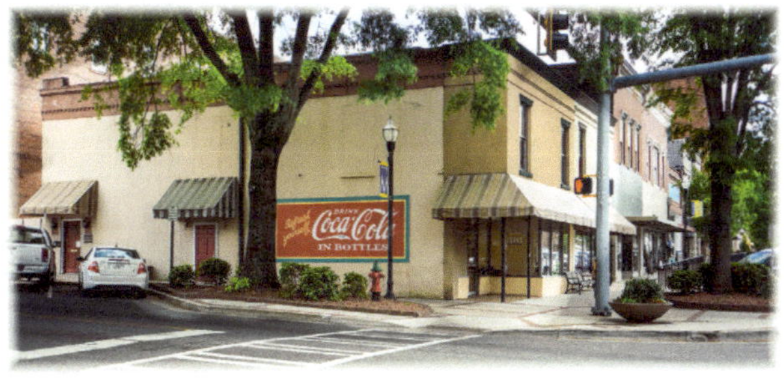

Corner of E Hancock Street and N Wayne Street
GPS 33°4'53" N 83°13'37" W

Former member of the Georgia House of Representatives E. Culver "Rusty" Kidd, whose great-grandfather owned the corner drugstore, shared the store's history. It was once the main meeting place in town, and home of a wholesale and retail druggist.

Rusty worked for his father at the soda fountain serving up Coca-Cola. He remembers the train passing right in front of the store, and sometimes stopping for the stoplight. The Milledgeville light was the only stoplight in Georgia trains had to obey.

The sign was repainted in 2005 by Dianna Love Snell and Karl Snell of Art Productions, Inc.

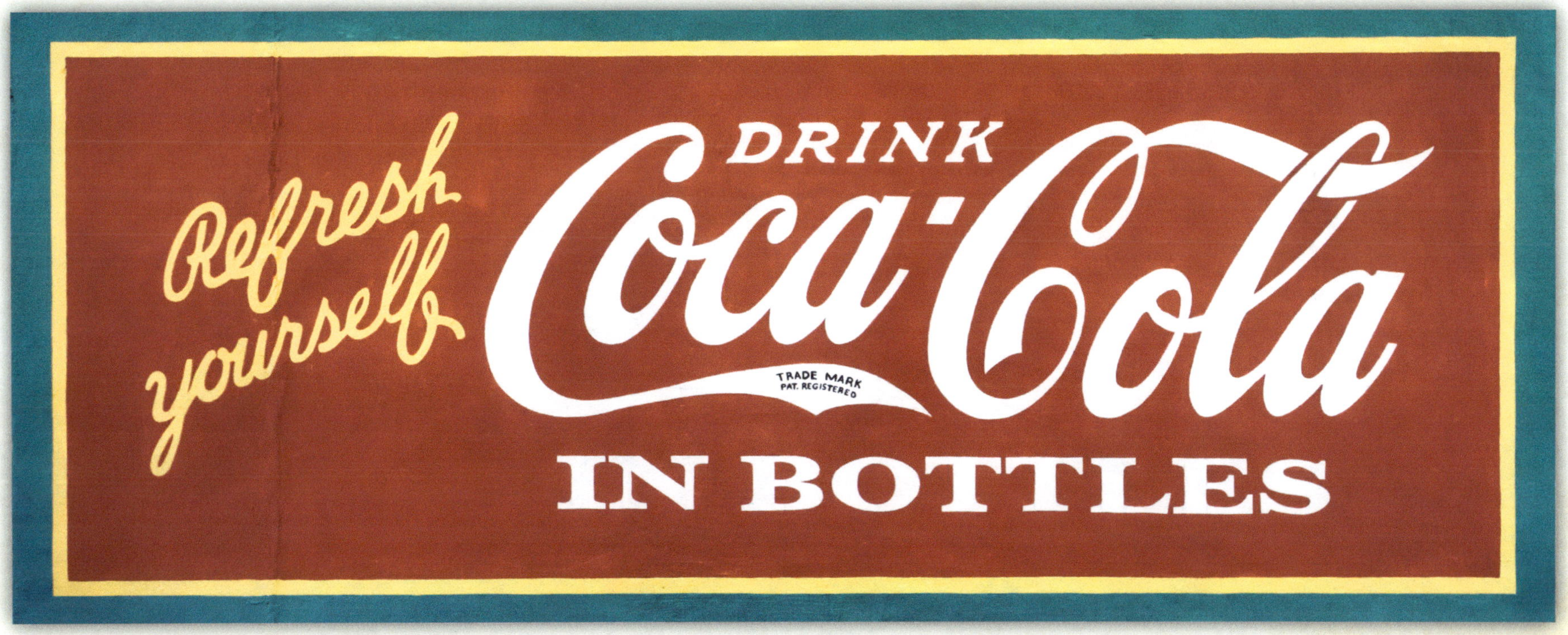

Mount Vernon

Corner of S Railroad Avenue and Broad Street
GPS 32°10'30" N 82°35'43" W

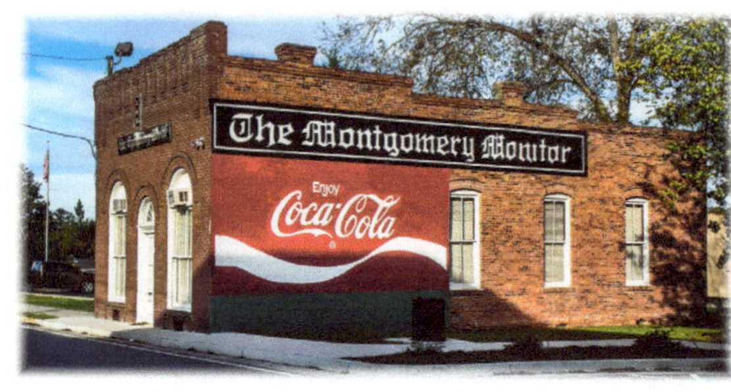

83-year-old Hugh Peterson explained that his father acquired
the *Montgomery Monitor* newspaper, which has been housed in this building since the early 1900s.

The sign has been on the building as long as he can remember. Hugh had it repainted about fifteen years ago.

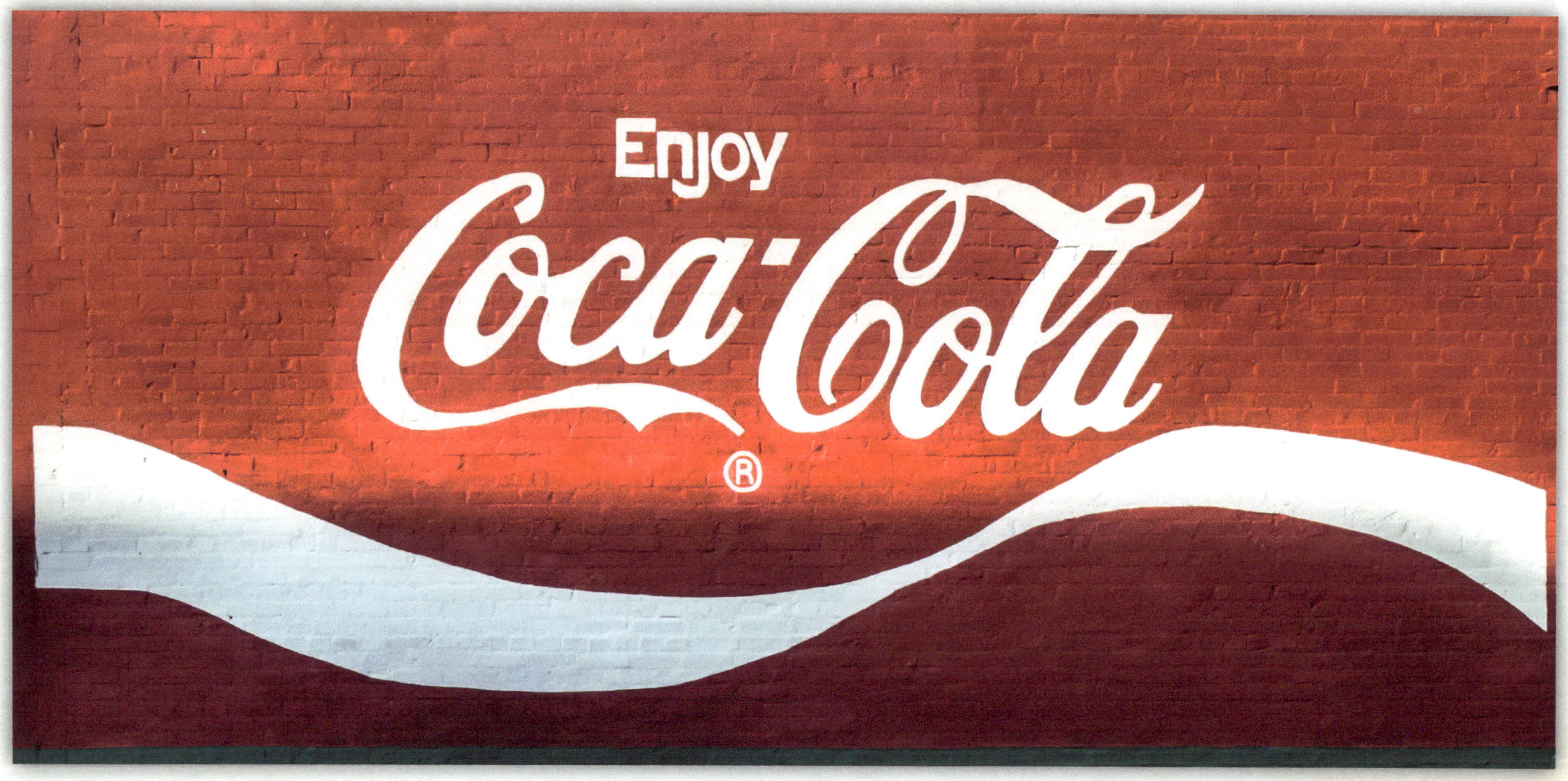

Delicious and Refreshing

Musella

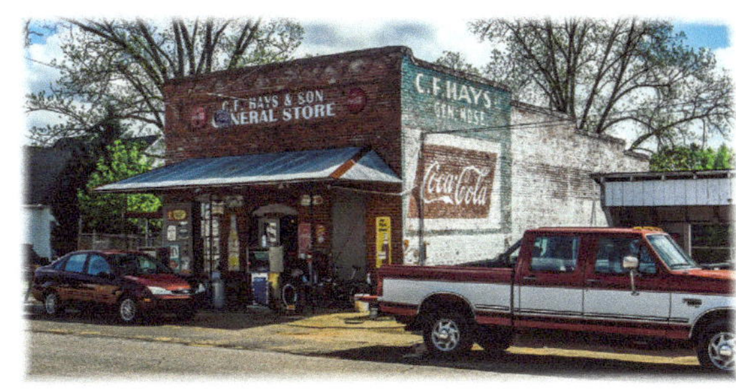

On Musella Road across from Post Office Road
GPS 32°47'51" N 84°1'46" W

The C.F. Hays & Son General Store was established in the early 1900s by Robert Lee Dickey. The store has been in continuous operation for more than 110 years, possibly making it the oldest store of its kind in Georgia, and maybe the nation.

I was unable to find out when the sign was originally painted.

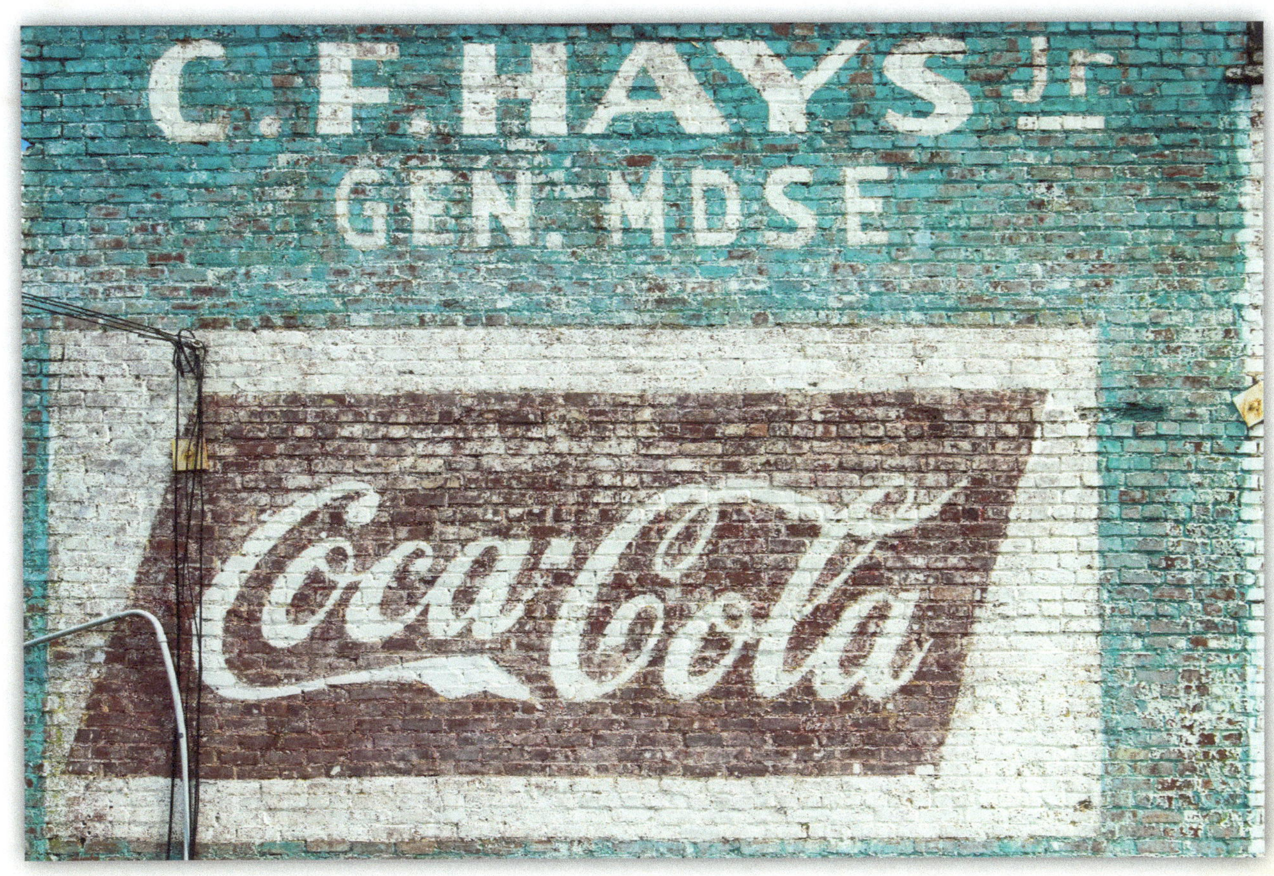

Newnan

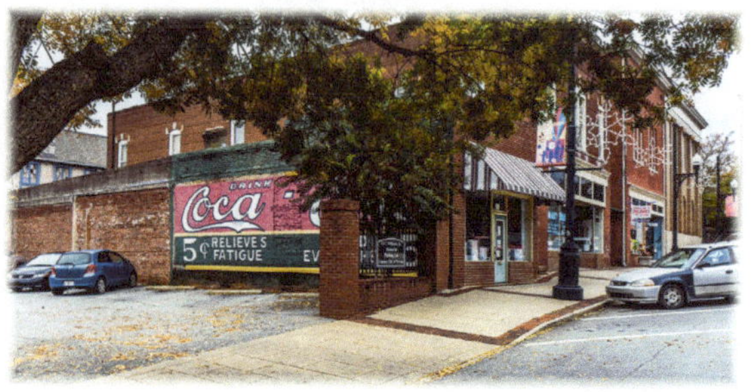

Corner of Spring Street and Lagrange Street
GPS 33°22'26" N 84°48'3" W

The Newnan Coca-Cola sign was rediscovered in the 1960s, when the adjacent building was demolished. Elizabeth Beers remembers that there might have been a grocery store in the building. The trademark dates the original wall sign to between 1930 and 1941.

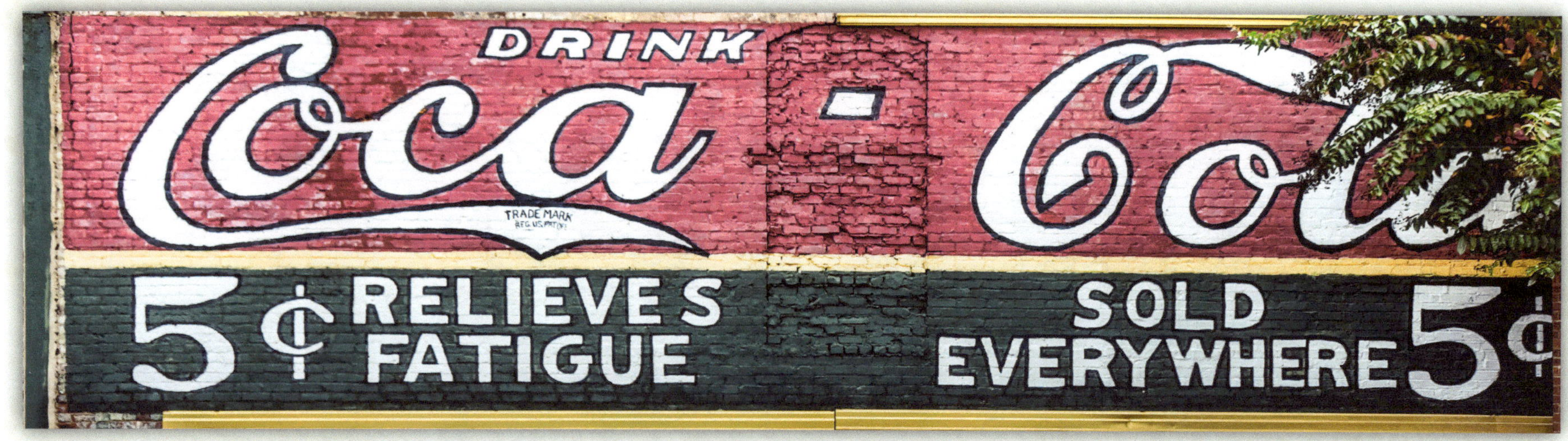

Delicious and Refreshing

Norristown

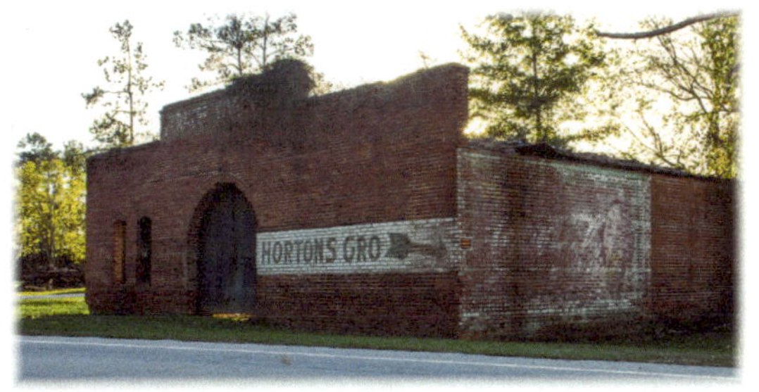

Corner of Norristown Covena Road and U.S. 221 N Highway
GPS 32°30'26" N 82°29'40" W

While passing through Norristown on U.S. 221 N Hwy., I ran across the old Horton's Grocery Coca-Cola wall sign.
The visible ghost image of the woman holding a Coke bottle appears to have been painted over the older yellow silhouette girl.

This is the only wall sign I have found with the painted woman holding a Coke. It is a rare Coca-Cola ghost wall sign!

The silhouette girl dates back to 1938. The rare over-painting dates back to the 1950s.

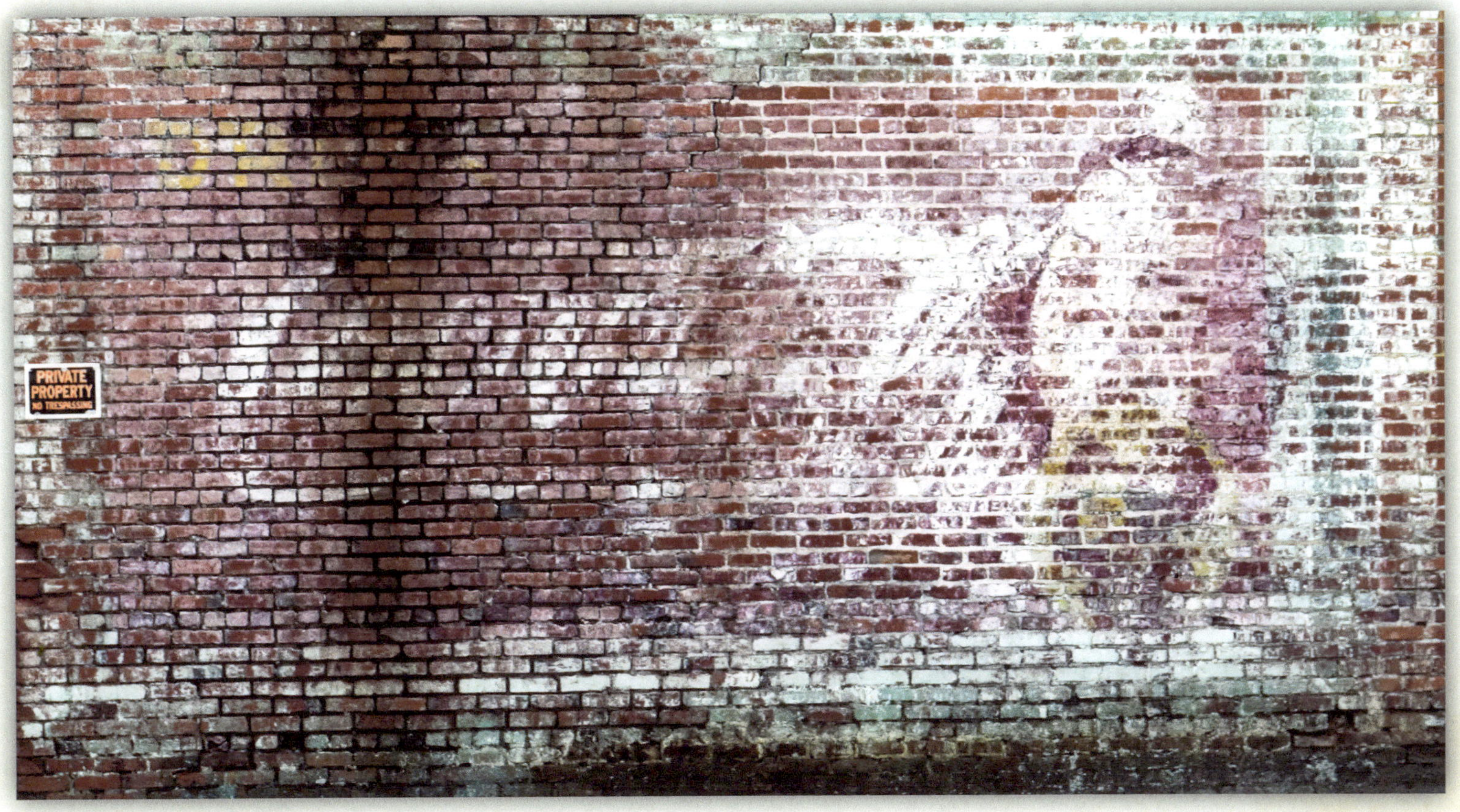

Pitts

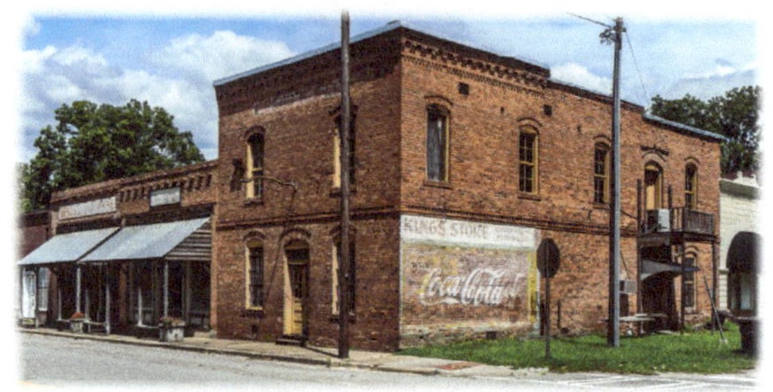

Corner of McDonald Avenue and 8th Street N
GPS 31°56'47" N 83°32'26 W

City clerk Wilton King remembers this Coca-Cola wall sign on King's Store when he was a young boy.
King is sure the wall sign dates back 75 years, and has been repainted many times.

The 1938 silhouette girl visible in the lower right-hand corner suggests the original sign could be 75 years old or older.
As a young boy, Wilton remembers J.A. King, the owner of the general store, as an older gentleman.

The postmaster general wanted a shorter name for King's Crossing, so J.A. King suggested Pitts after his son-in-law, Ashley J. Pitts.

In response, on November 1, 1888, King's Crossing became Pitts, with Ashley Pitts as postmaster.
Both the north-south railroad and the east-west railroad ran through town near the Coca-Cola sign.

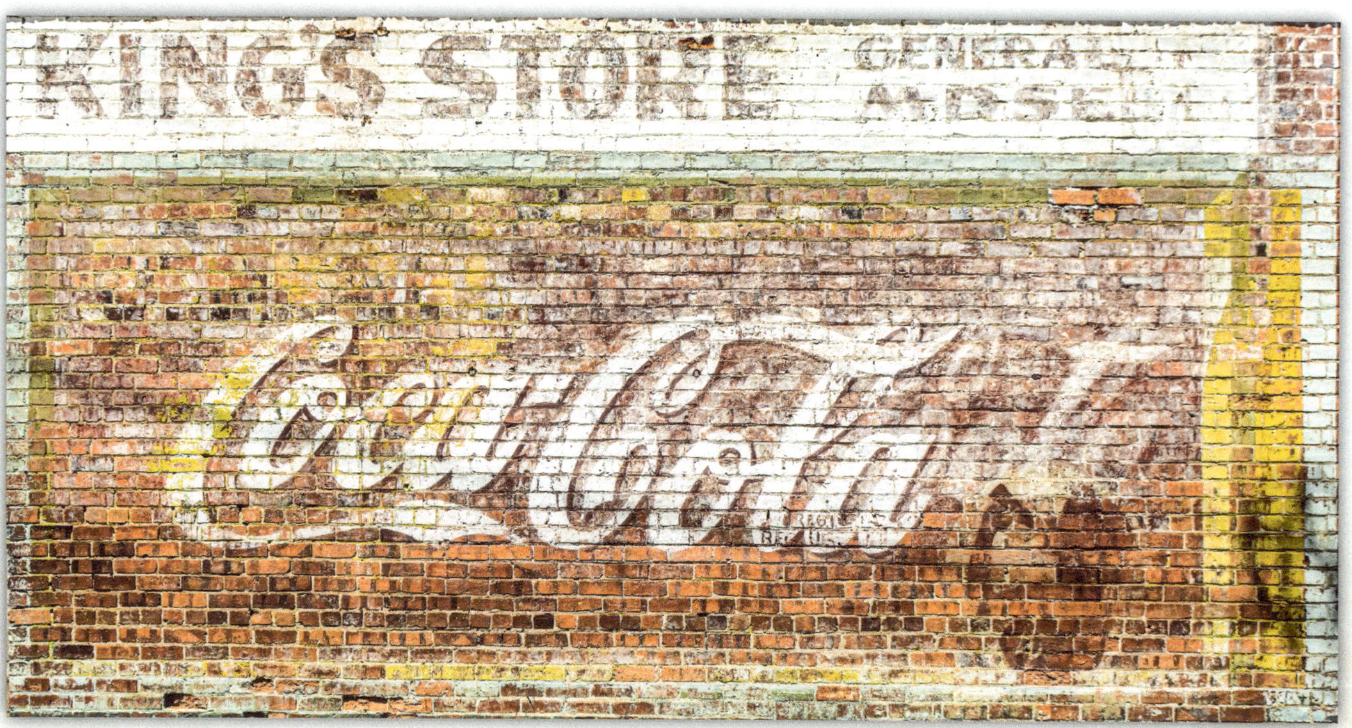

Delicious and Refreshing

Plains

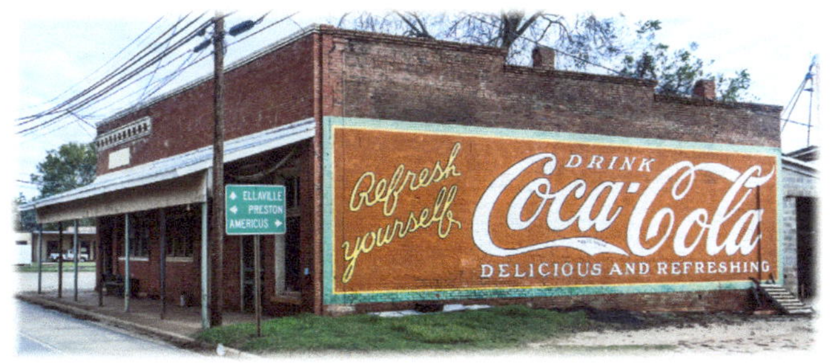

On S Bond Street between Main Street and Clark Street
GPS 32°1'60" N 84°23'33" W

The Plains sign was originally painted in 1924 on the side of a peanut warehouse located near the railroad tracks. The wall sign was restored in 1999 by Dianna Love Snell and Karl Snell, Art Productions, Inc.

Dianna shared that "when the sign was almost finished, President and First Lady Jimmy and Rosalynn Carter came by to put on the finishing touch of red paint."

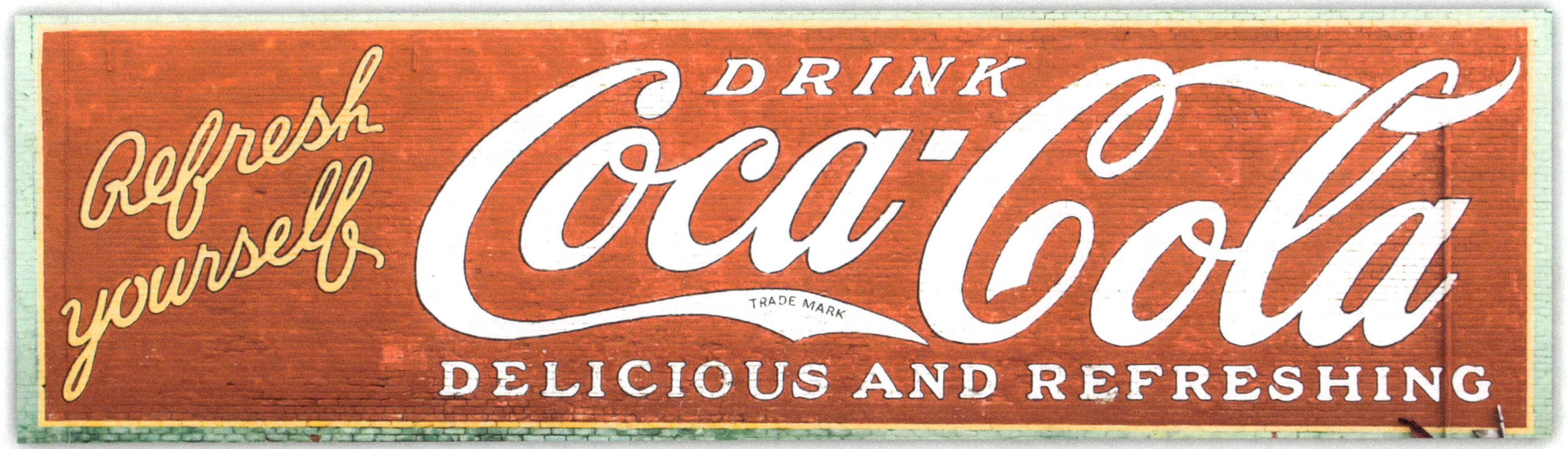

Powder Springs

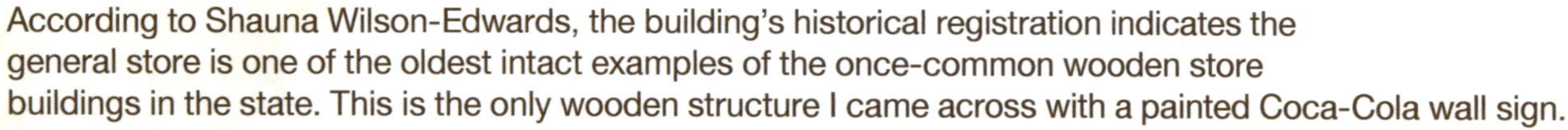

Corner of Marietta Street and Broad Street
GPS 33°51'34" N 84°41'3" W

According to Shauna Wilson-Edwards, the building's historical registration indicates the general store is one of the oldest intact examples of the once-common wooden store buildings in the state. This is the only wooden structure I came across with a painted Coca-Cola wall sign.

The trademark location indicates the original sign might have been painted between 1931 and 1941 when Butner-McTyre owned the store. The original sign was restored by Dianna Love Snell and Karl Snell of Art Productions, Inc.

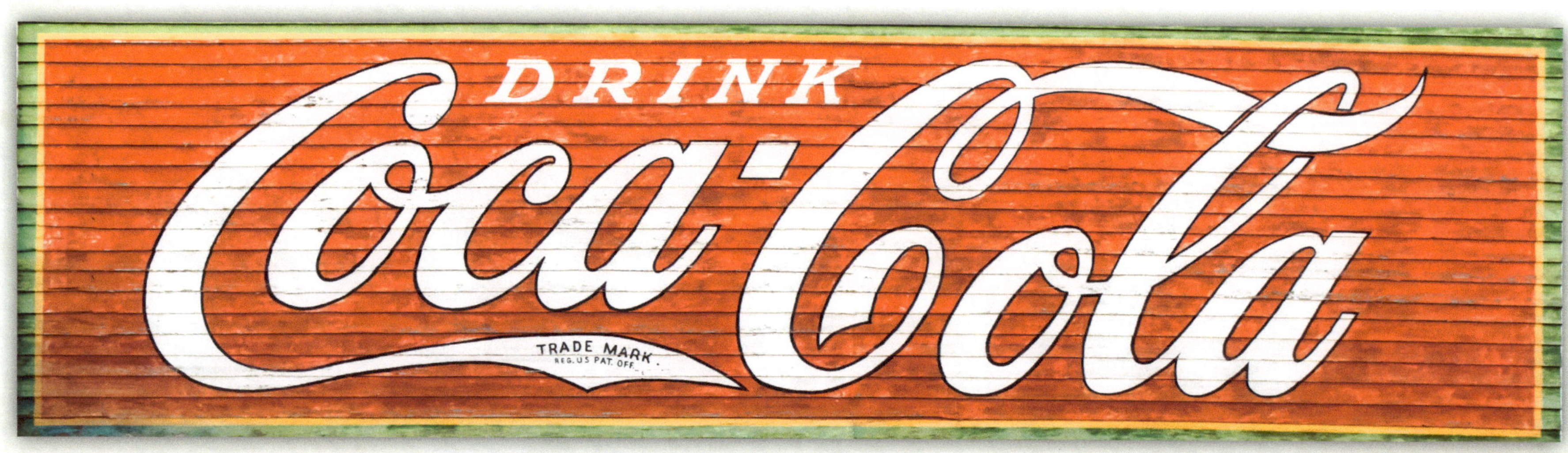

Delicious and Refreshing

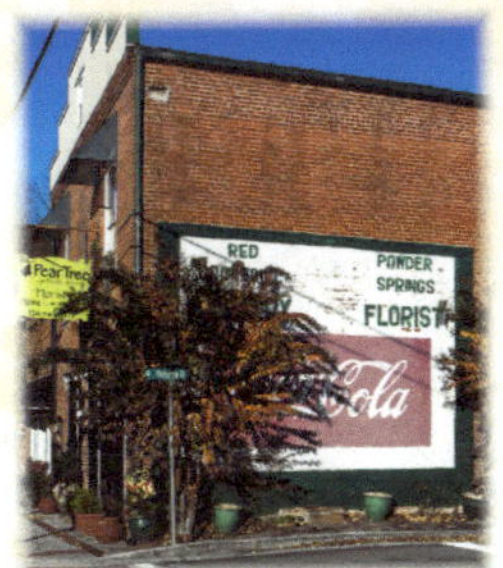

Corner of Oakview Drive and Marietta Street
GPS 33°51'34" N 84°41'0" W

This Coca-Cola wall sign was repainted by Kim Wolfe in 2007 over the original sign painted for Cooper Drugs. Mr. Wolfe used a pattern he had, so the trademark location does not indicate the year. He remembers little about the original sign.

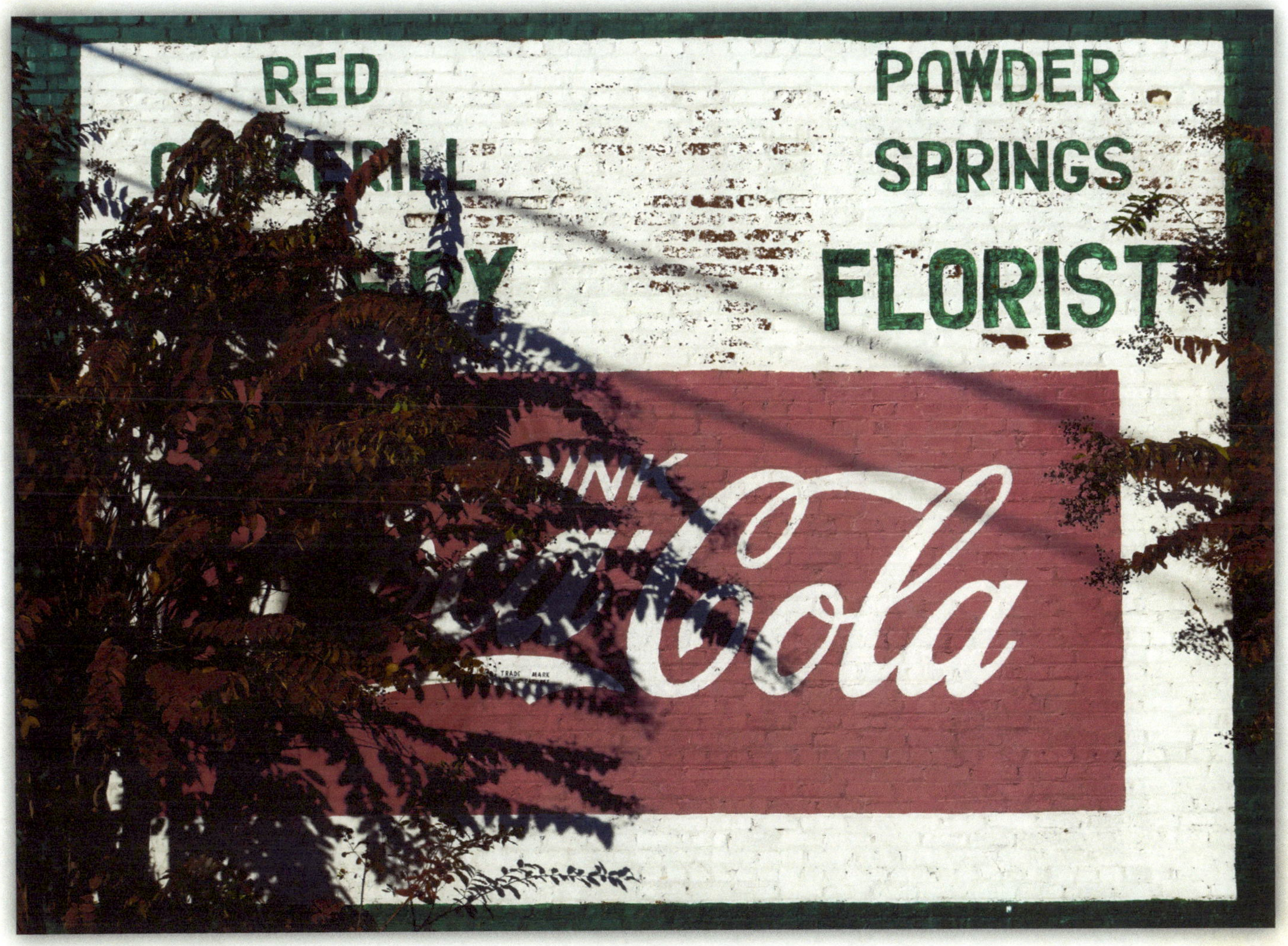

Rockmart

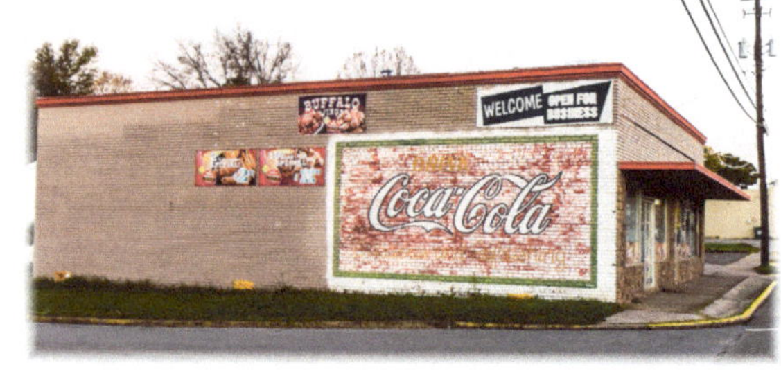

Corner of N Piedmont Avenue and Pearl Street
GPS 34°0'6" N 85°2'30" W

The Rockmart Coke wall sign, which Mike Martin originally painted in the early 1980s, was recently repainted. The building was Garners Cleaners at the time.

Alfred Barren, the owner of the Coke distributorship out of Rome, Georgia, had Mike paint it. Mike was taught how to paint truck letters as a child, and then later contracted to paint Coke signs.

The Coca-Cola white color was laid down first since it was the most stable. The red and other colors would be added on top of the white to produce the sign.

Since white fades the least, only the white lettering remains on so many ghost wall signs today.

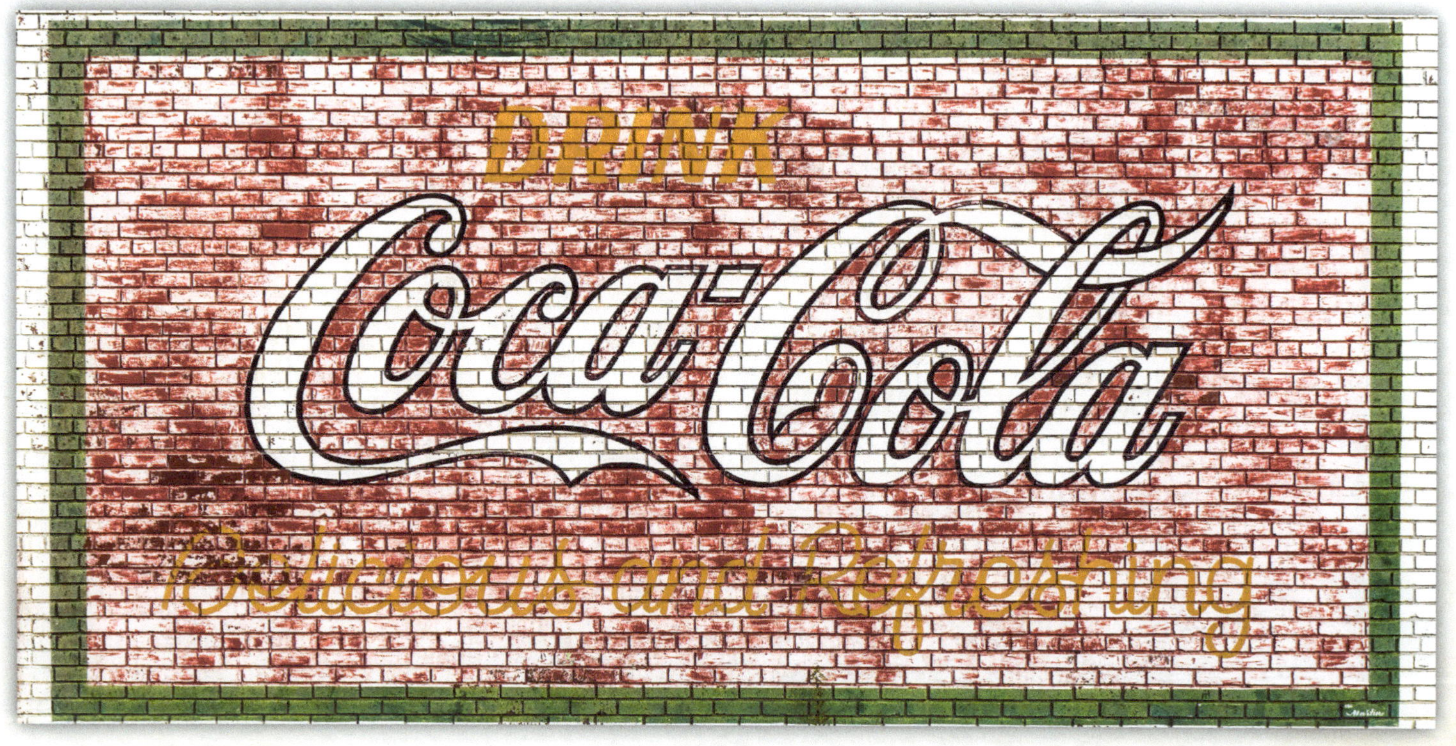

Delicious and Refreshing

Rome

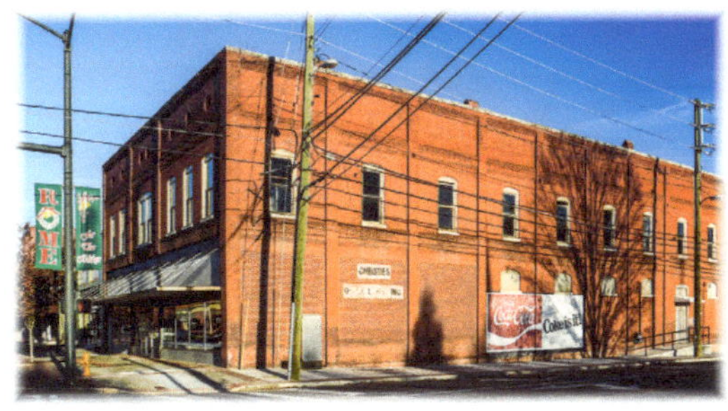

Corner of Broad Street and E 1st Avenue
GPS 34°15'6" N 85°10'31" W

While Rome, Georgia, wasn't the birthplace of Coca-Cola inventor John Pemberton, he spent most of his childhood there. This Rome sign was painted on the building in 1982 for Frank Barron, the sixth Coca-Cola bottler in the US.

While speaking with Frank, I learned that beginning in 1948, Rome was the "number-one per capita consumer of Coca-Cola in the world." That designation continued for quite some time.

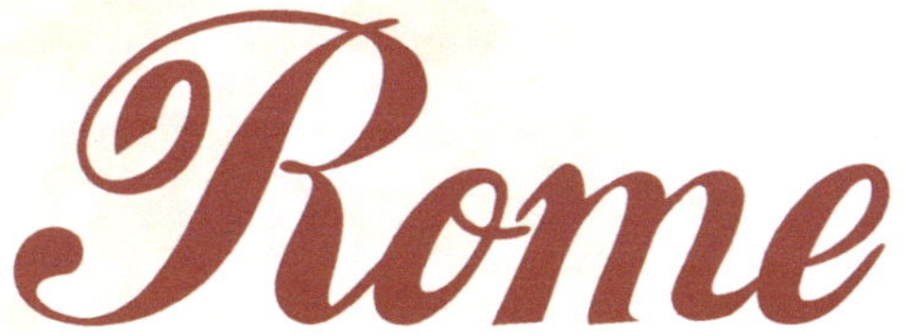

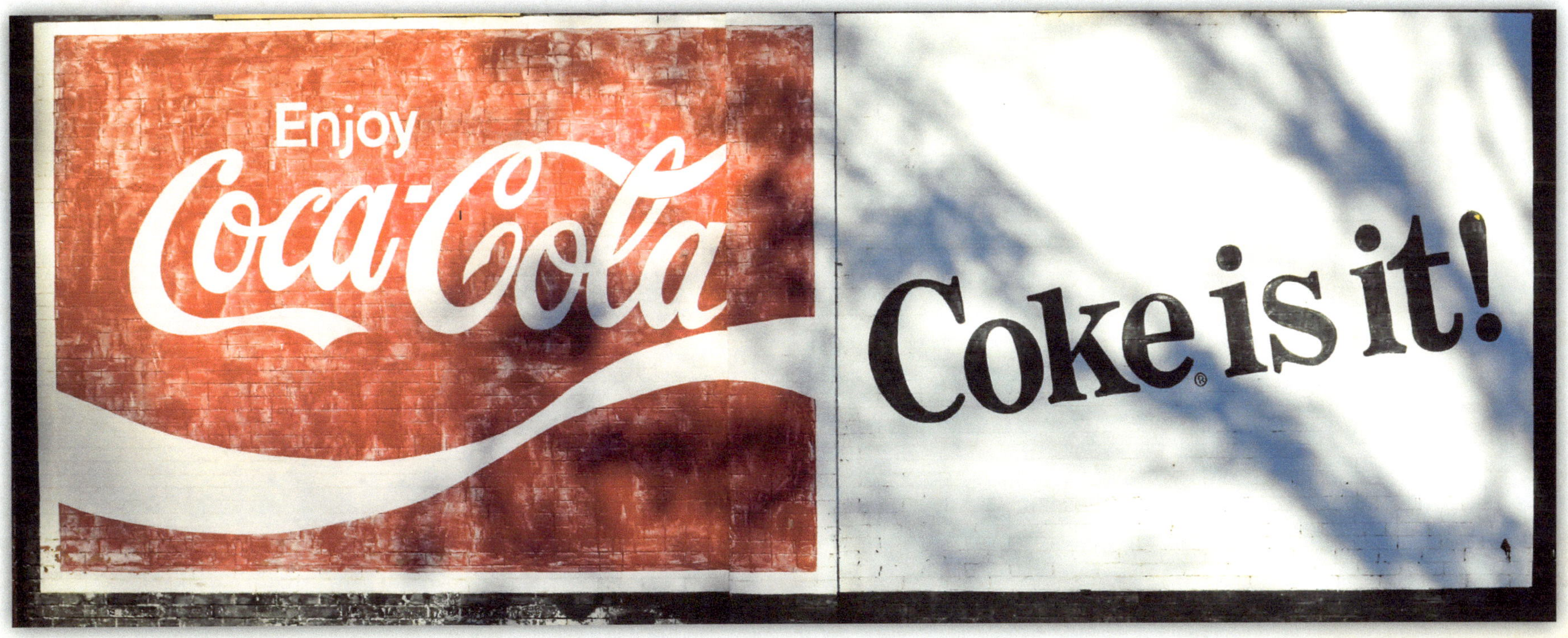

Roopville

**R.E. RINGER - On Martha Berry Highway/
GA 27 near Ringer Road**

GPS 33°29'51" N 85°5'2" W

Mike Miller painted this R.E. Ringer Merchandise store sign in the early 1980s.

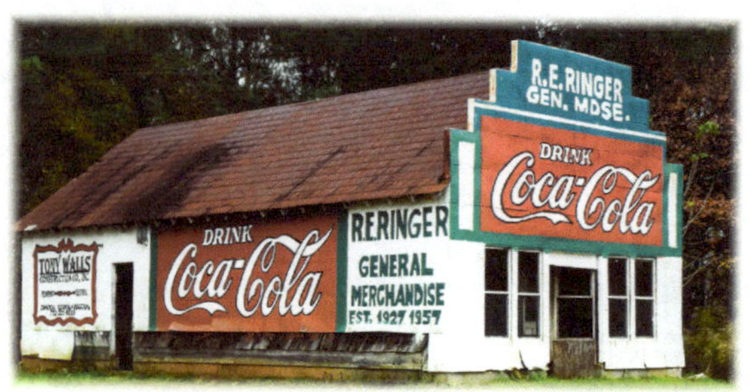

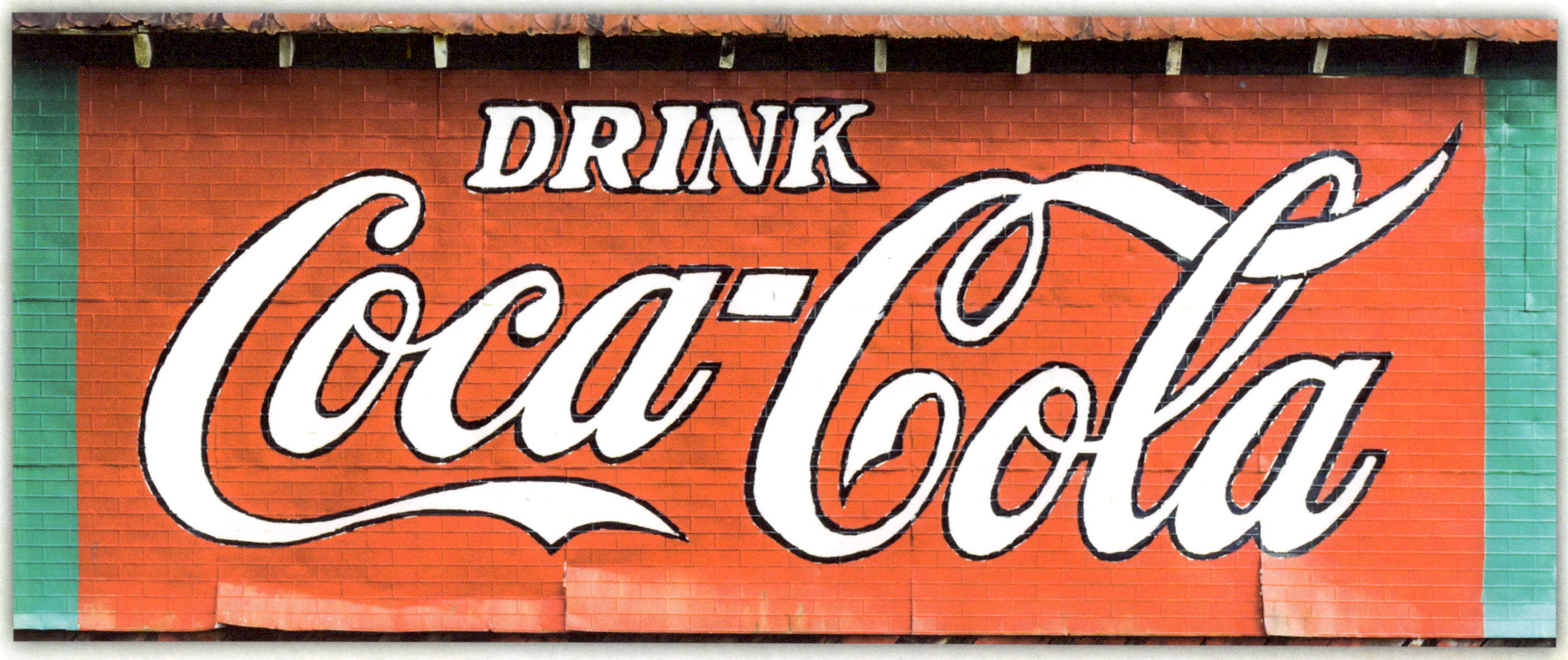

Delicious and Refreshing

W.E. JOHNSON'S - On Martha Berry Highway (Hwy. U.S. 27) near Roopville Road Baptist Church

GPS 33°28'29" N 85°6'37" W

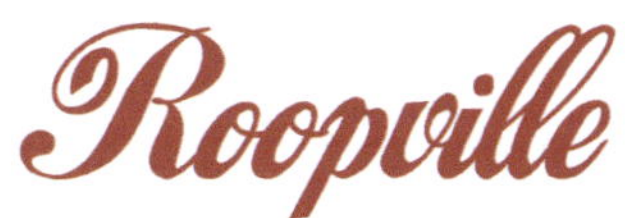

Alecia Searcy, great-granddaughter of Walter E. Johnson, shared that the curing house was built in the 1940s by Walter Johnson and his two sons, Horace and Wendell. It was used to heat up sweet potatoes, bringing out the sugars and making them sweeter.

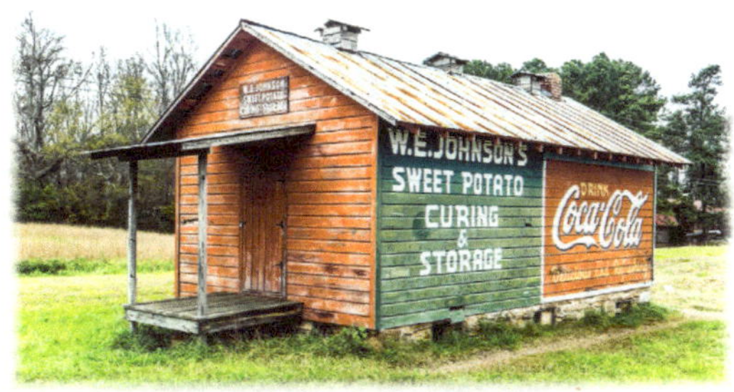

The curing house is found on U.S. 27, which at the time was the main road between Chattanooga and Carrollton. We think the Coca-Cola sign was painted on the curing house in the 1950s when it was also a bus stop.

Mike Miller knew that Henry Stone out of Rome, Georgia, painted the original sign.

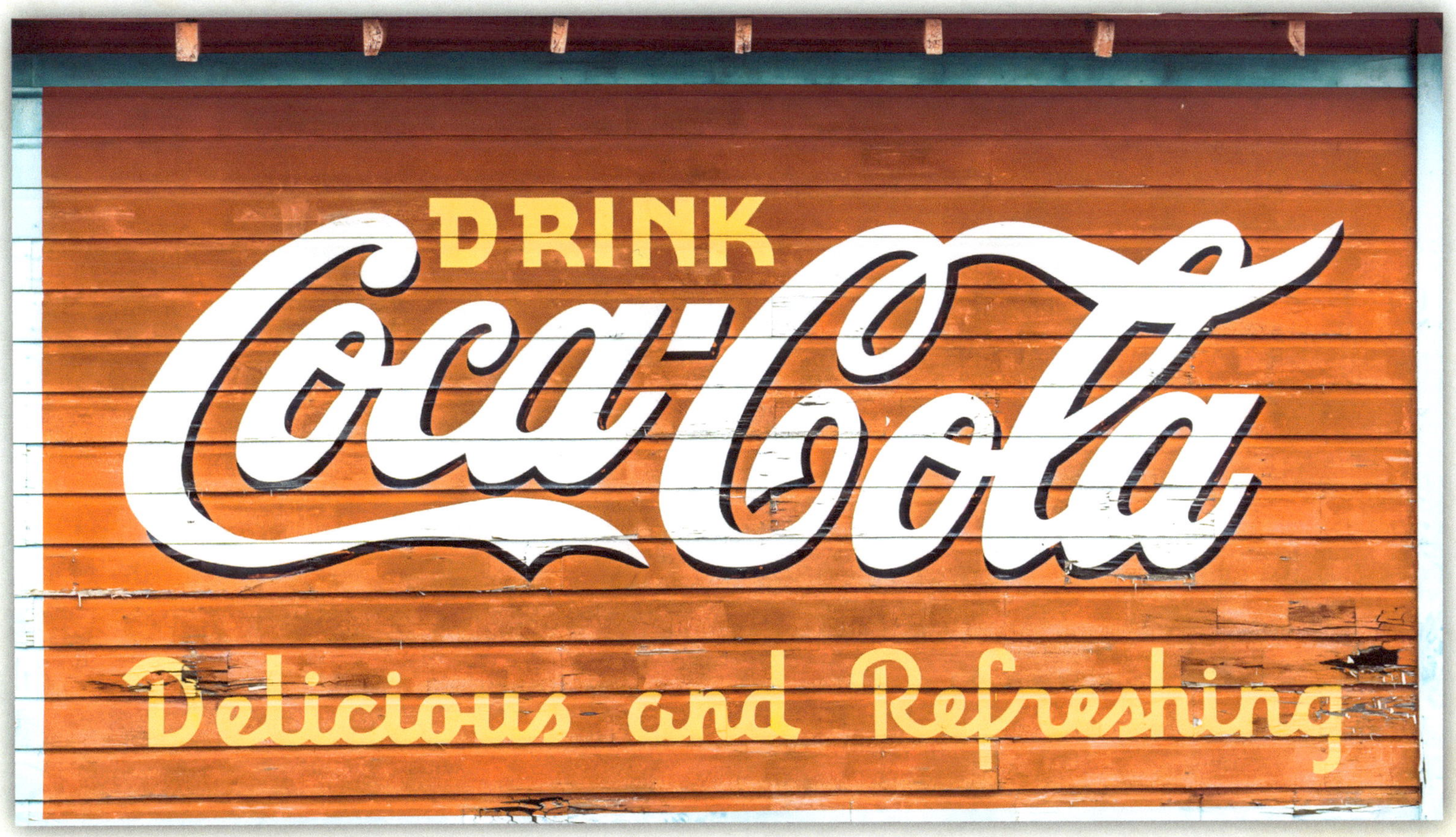

Sandersville

Sandersville Progress Buidling
on E Haynes Street
GPS 32°58'58" N 82°48'36" W

Dick Hudson's grandfather, O.L. Hudson, owned the Coke franchise from 1921 to 1986, and Dick remembers seeing this sign painted on the Haynes Cafe near the train tracks in the mid- to late 1930s.

The sign was painted with blue chalk, using the pounce bag technique. A cheesecloth bag filled with chalk was used to "pounce" over the full-sized pattern.

This sign was painted by Henry Collins using this then-new technique to make Coca-Cola wall signs more uniform.

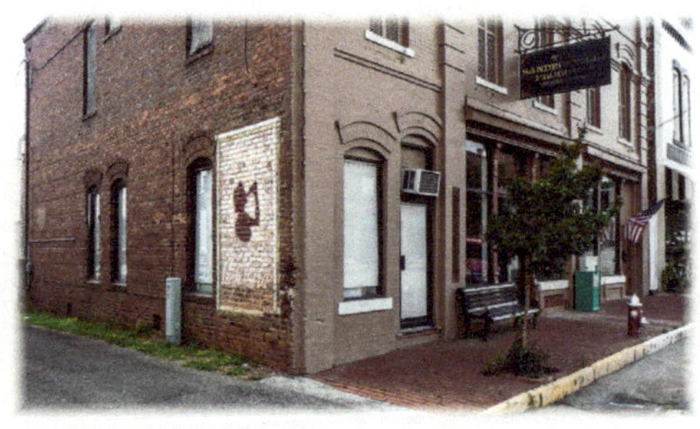

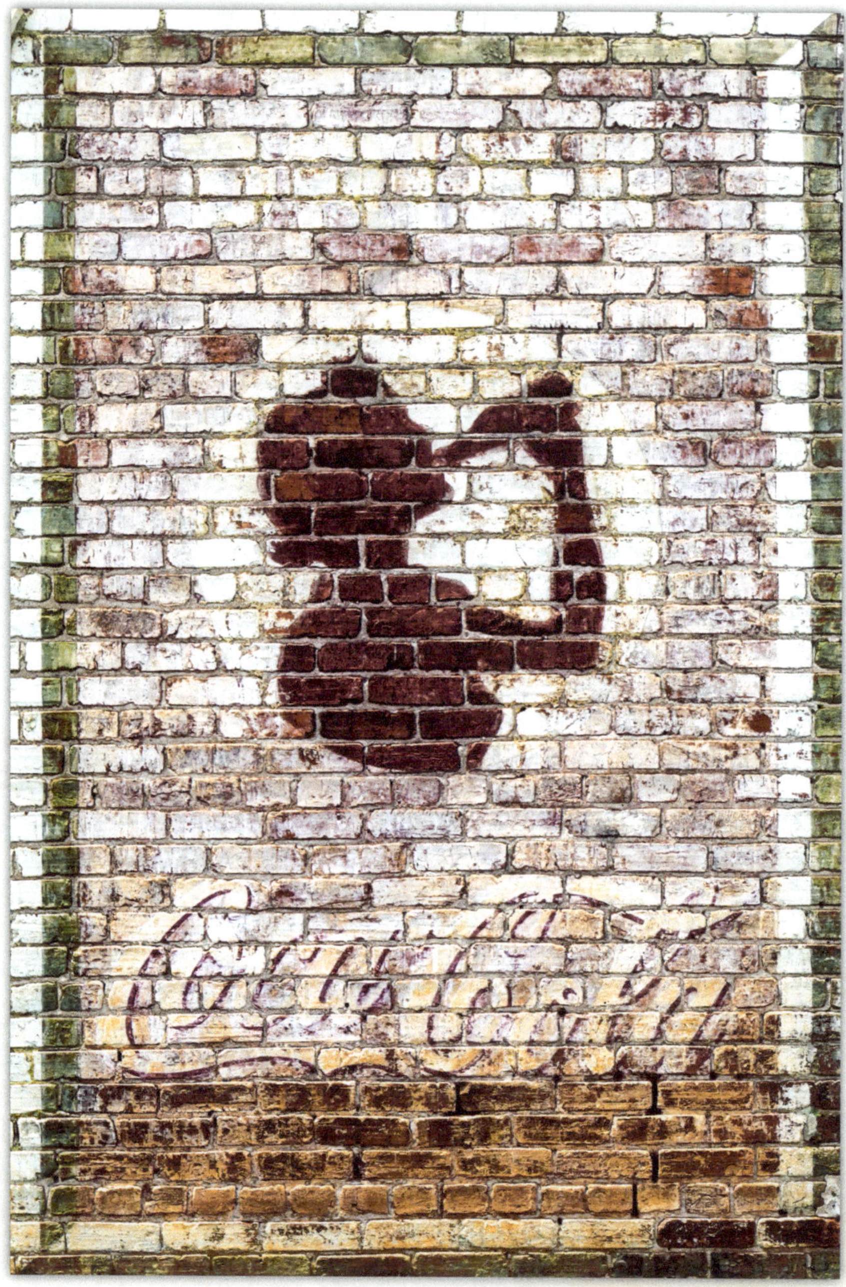

Delicious and Refreshing

Sasser

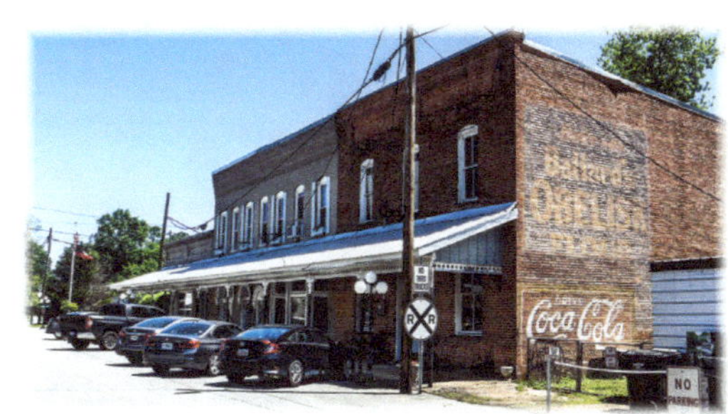

Corner of Albany Highway (GA 82) and Main Street W
GPS 31°43'10" N 84°20'54" W

This is the very first Coca-Cola sign I ever photographed. I could find little information about it.

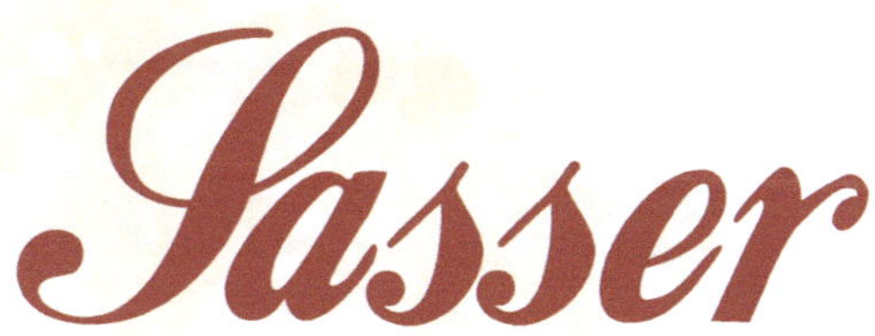

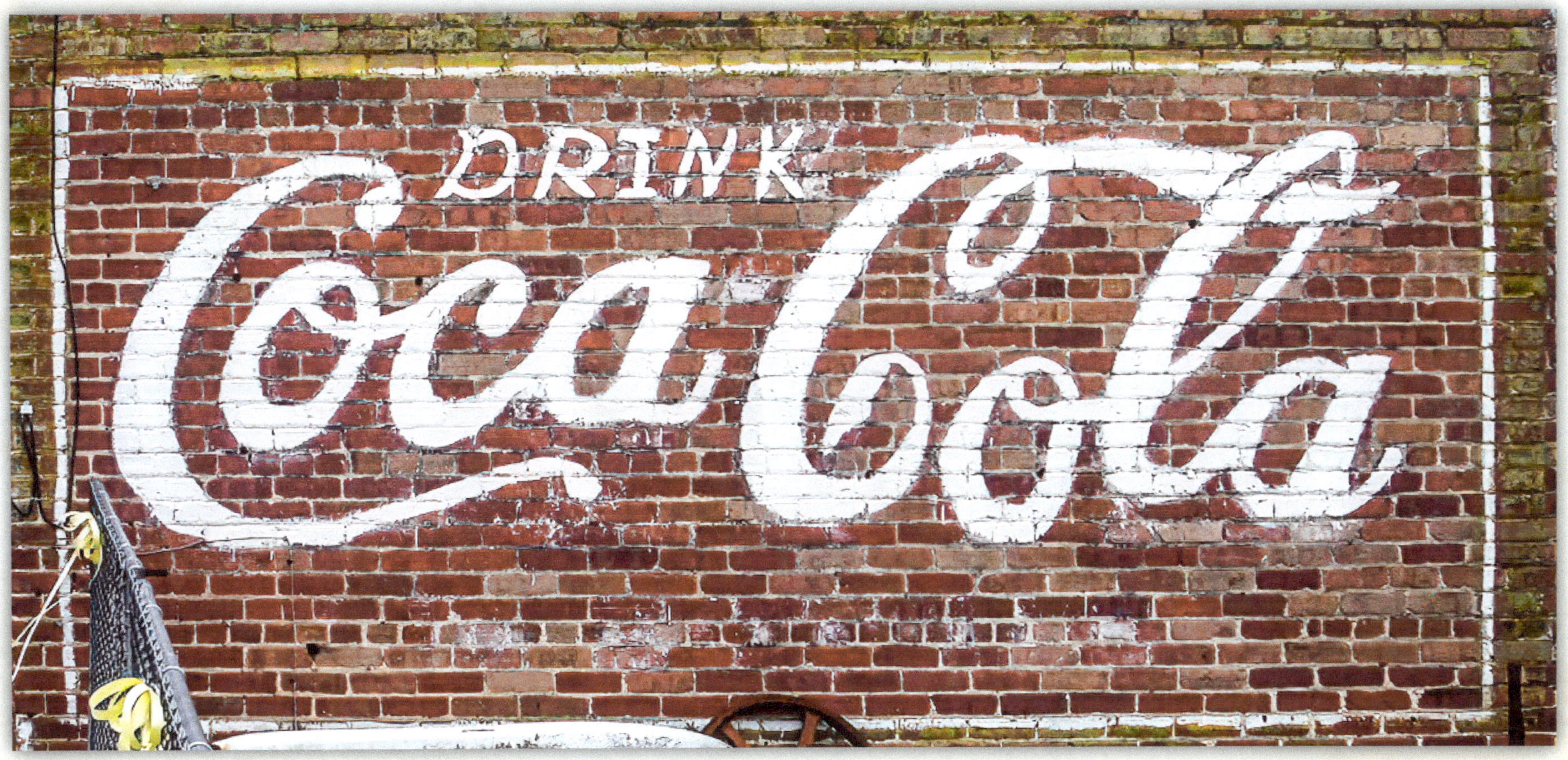

Sylvester

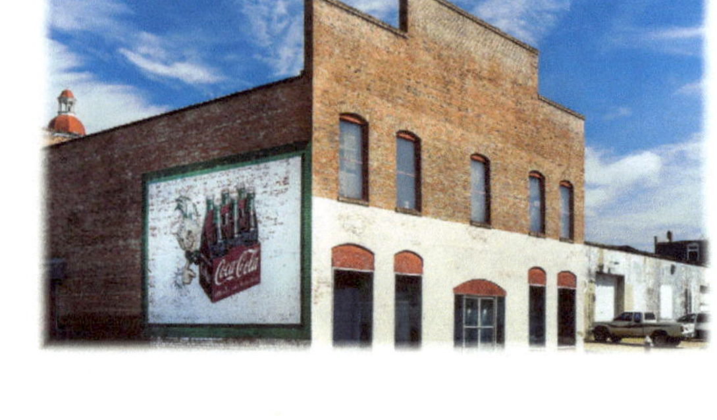

E Liberty Avenue between N Isabella Street/GA 112
and N Main Street
GPS 31°31'37" N 83°50'12" W

With the blessing of Coca-Cola, Jim Daniels commissioned the painting of this wall sign in 2000, using the original pounce-bag pattern.
Jim auctions and merchandises Coca-Cola memorabilia through Daniels Auction Company, so he wanted the iconic 1950s wall sign on his building.

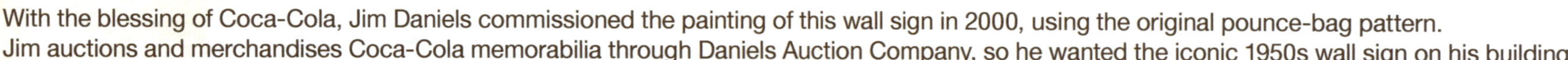

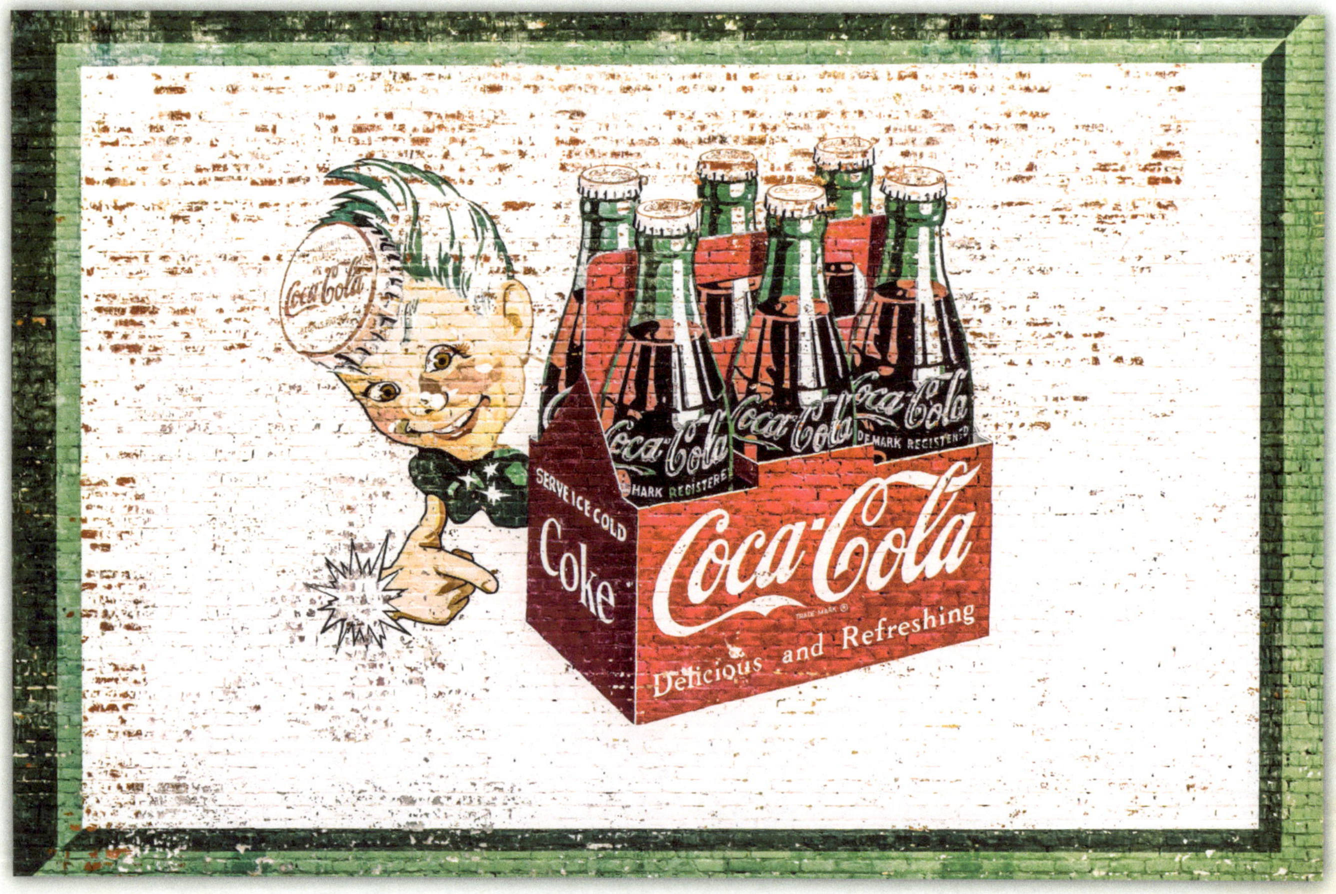

Delicious and Refreshing

Taylorsville

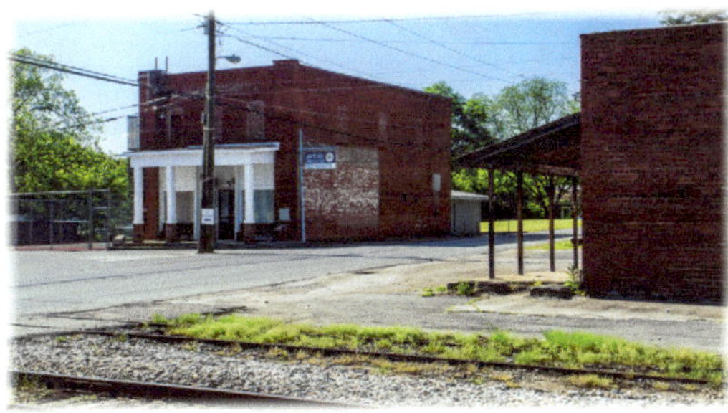

Corner of Euharlee Street and Mary Street
GPS 34°5'12" N 84°59'17" W

The Taylorsville Coca-Cola ghost sign is located across from the railroad tracks.
Details of the building and the sign could not be found.

The green bar above the sign and a "C" are still visible. On closer examination, a smaller Coca-Cola sign was painted over a larger one.

The original wall sign might have been painted between 1894 and 1940.

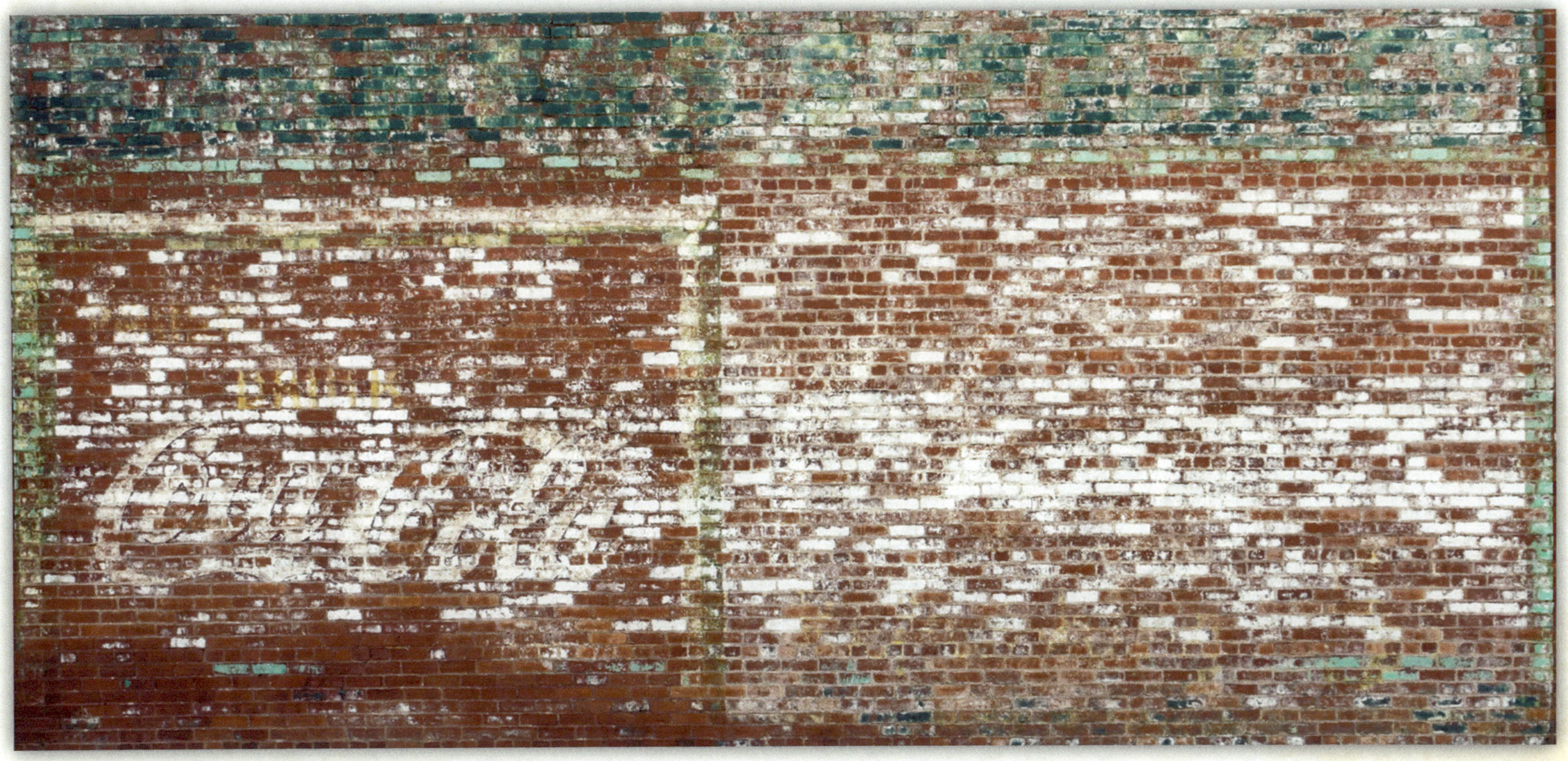

Tennille

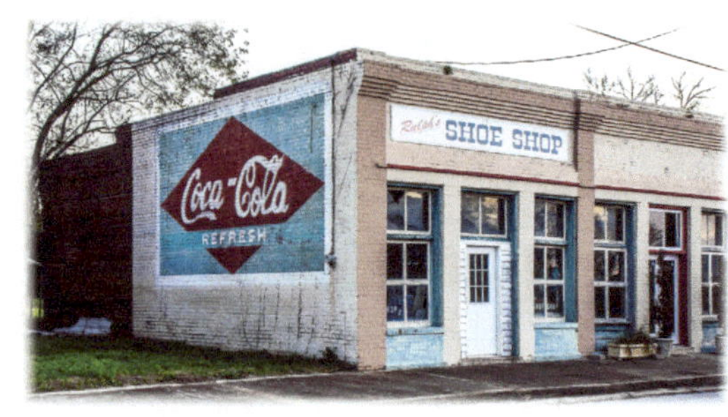

Corner of W South Central Avenue and S Main Street
GPS 32°56'8" N 82°48'43" W

Dick Hudson shared his recollections of the Tennille wall sign. It was originally painted on the side of a drugstore about 50 feet or so from the old railroad station. When the sign was restored is unknown, but its location near the railroad station dates the original sign between 1894 and 1940.

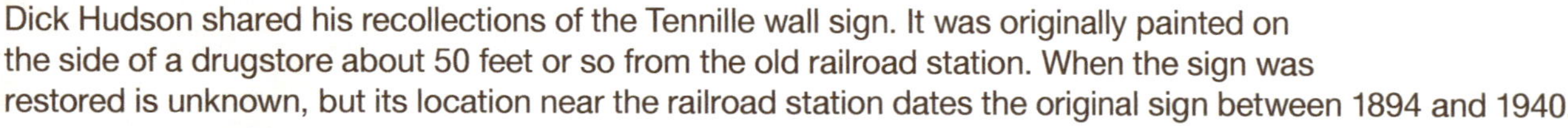

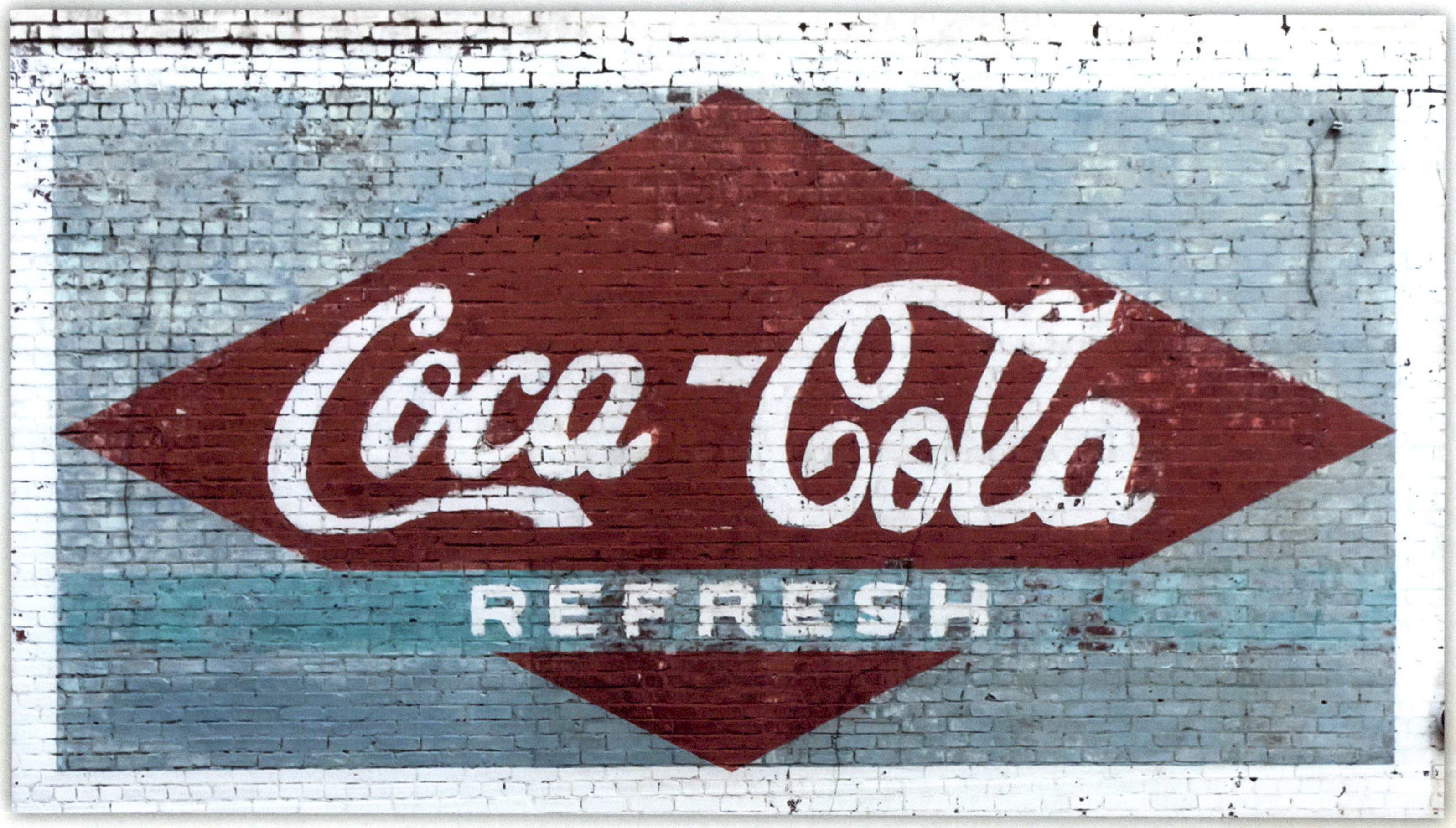

Delicious and Refreshing

Villa Rica

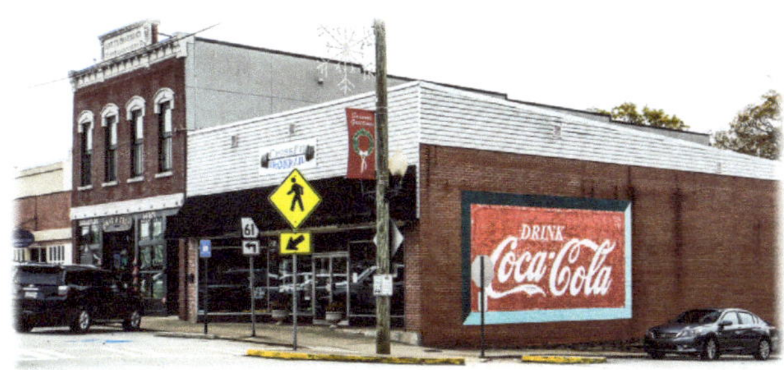

Corner of W Bankhead Highway and S Candler Street
GPS 33°43'54" N 84°55'11" W

Dr. Nancy Griffin Mims, chair of the Villa Rica Historic Preservation Commission, provided interesting town and sign history.

Asa Griggs Candler was born here on December 30, 1851. Asa purchased the floundering Coca-Cola Company from the inventor, John Pemberton, for $1,750.

Berry Pharmacy, built in 1895, was destroyed by an explosion in 1957. The destroyed buildings were rebuilt as they originally looked, along with the Coca-Cola wall sign.

The trademark location makes sense, as the original sign was probably painted between 1931 and 1941, again near the railroad tracks. Alan Kuykendall first restored the original sign, and it was restored more recently by Dianna Love Snell and Karl Snell, Art Productions, Inc.

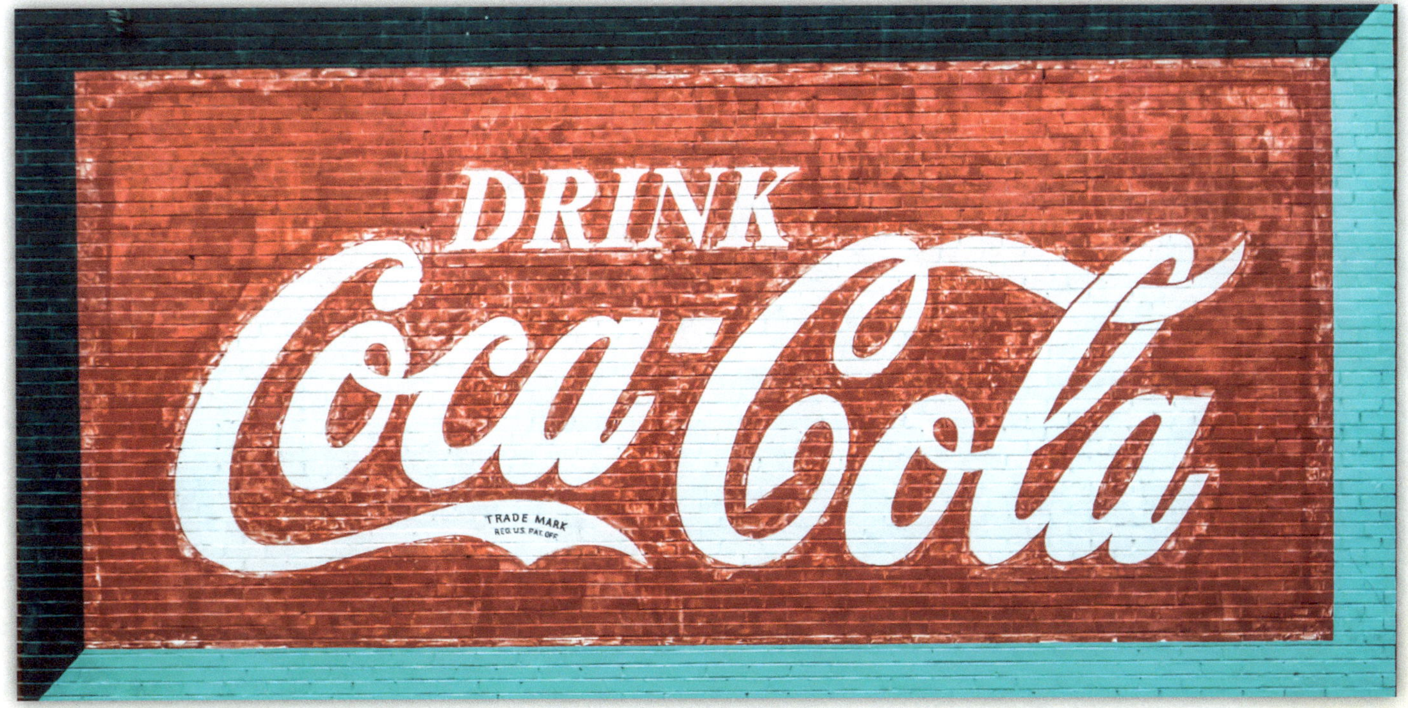

Warrenton

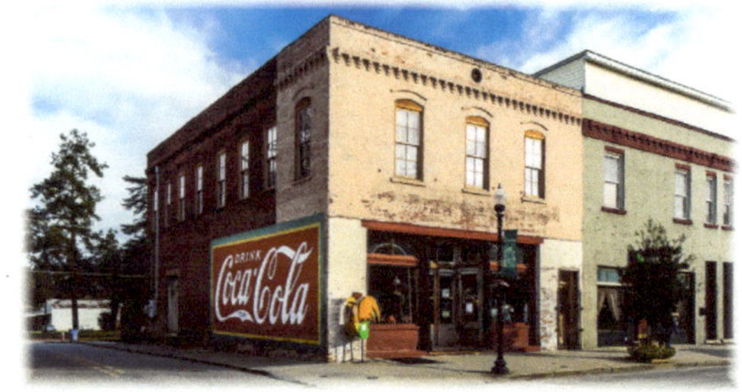

Corner of Depot Street and Main Street
GPS 33°24'25" N 82°39'44" W

In 2003, this beautiful Coca-Cola wall sign was repainted by Dianna Love Snell and Karl Snell of Art Productions, Inc., just as it originally appeared. Kimberly and CC Anderson own the building, which is home to Andersons Market.

Locals remember the sign as "always in town." The trademark information suggests it was originally painted between 1931 and 1941.

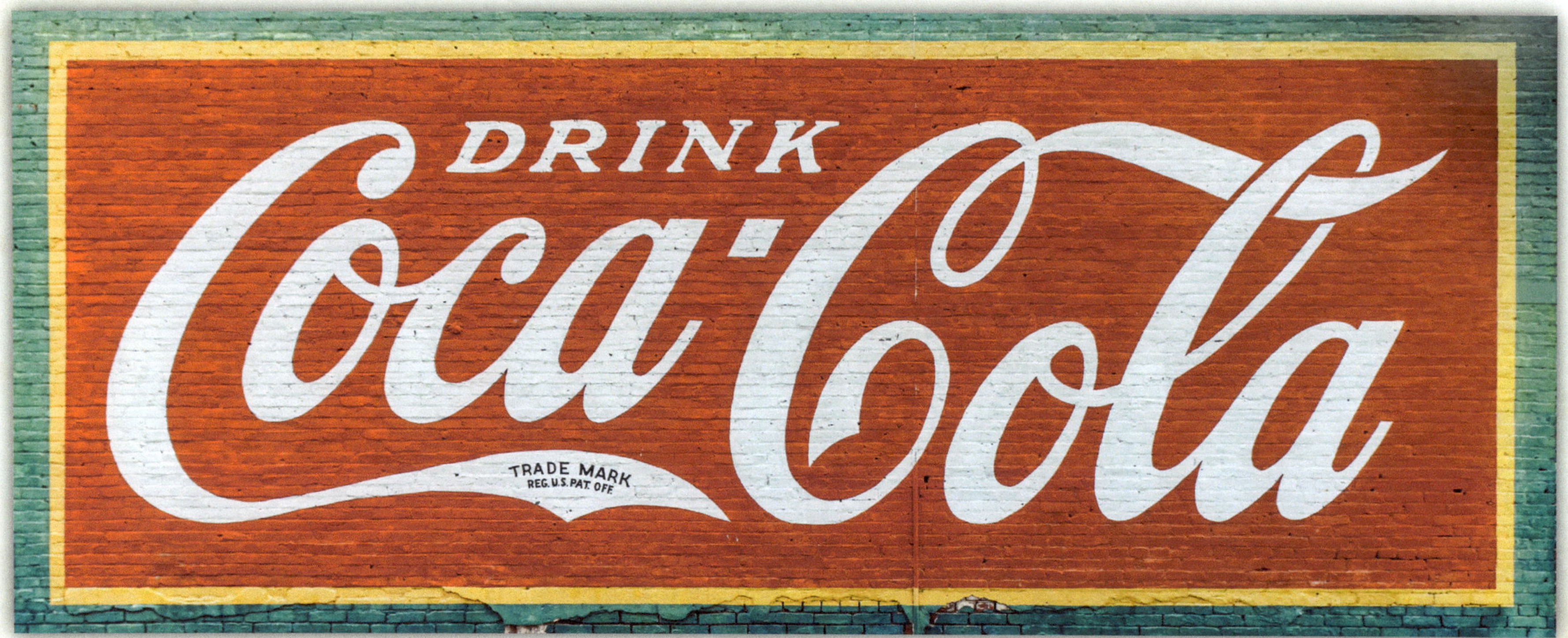

Delicious and Refreshing

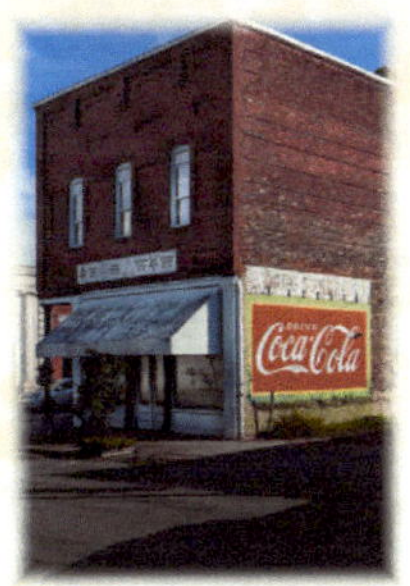

Masonic Lodge (Drug Sundries) -
Corner of W Gibson Street and Main Street
GPS 33°24'24" N 82°39'42" W

This sign was also repainted by Dianna Love Snell and Karl Snell of Art Productions Inc. in 2003, as it originally appeared. Little is known about this sign, but the fading building name is "Drug Sundries."

The copyright information suggests this sign was originally painted between 1931 and 1941.

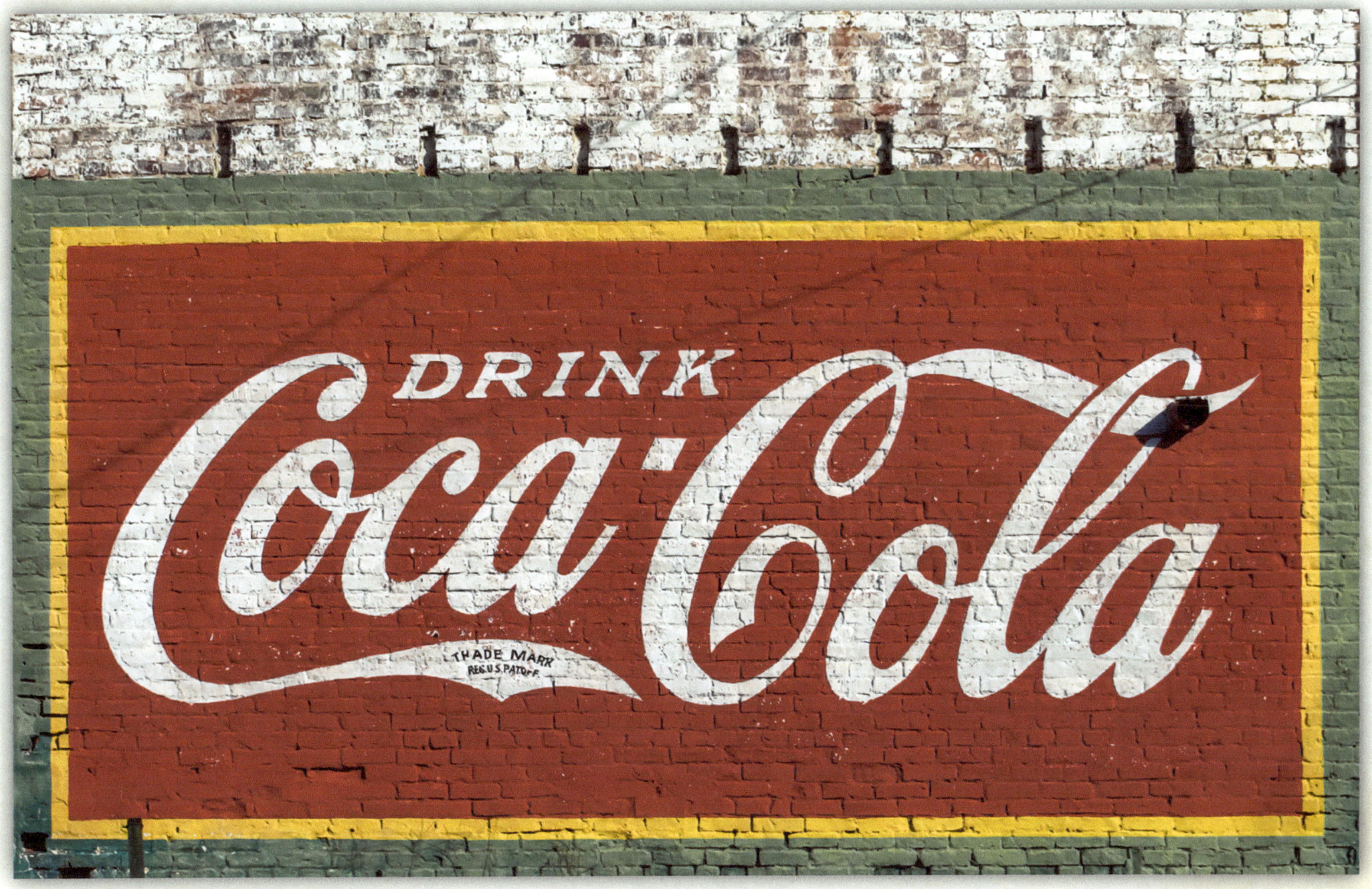

Warrenton

Depot Street across from Warren Street

GPS 33°24'27" N 82°39'45" W

Little could be found about this ghost sign on Depot St. The building is just up the road from the railroad tracks.

Just visible is the slogan "Delicious and Refreshing," which dates the sign after 1904.

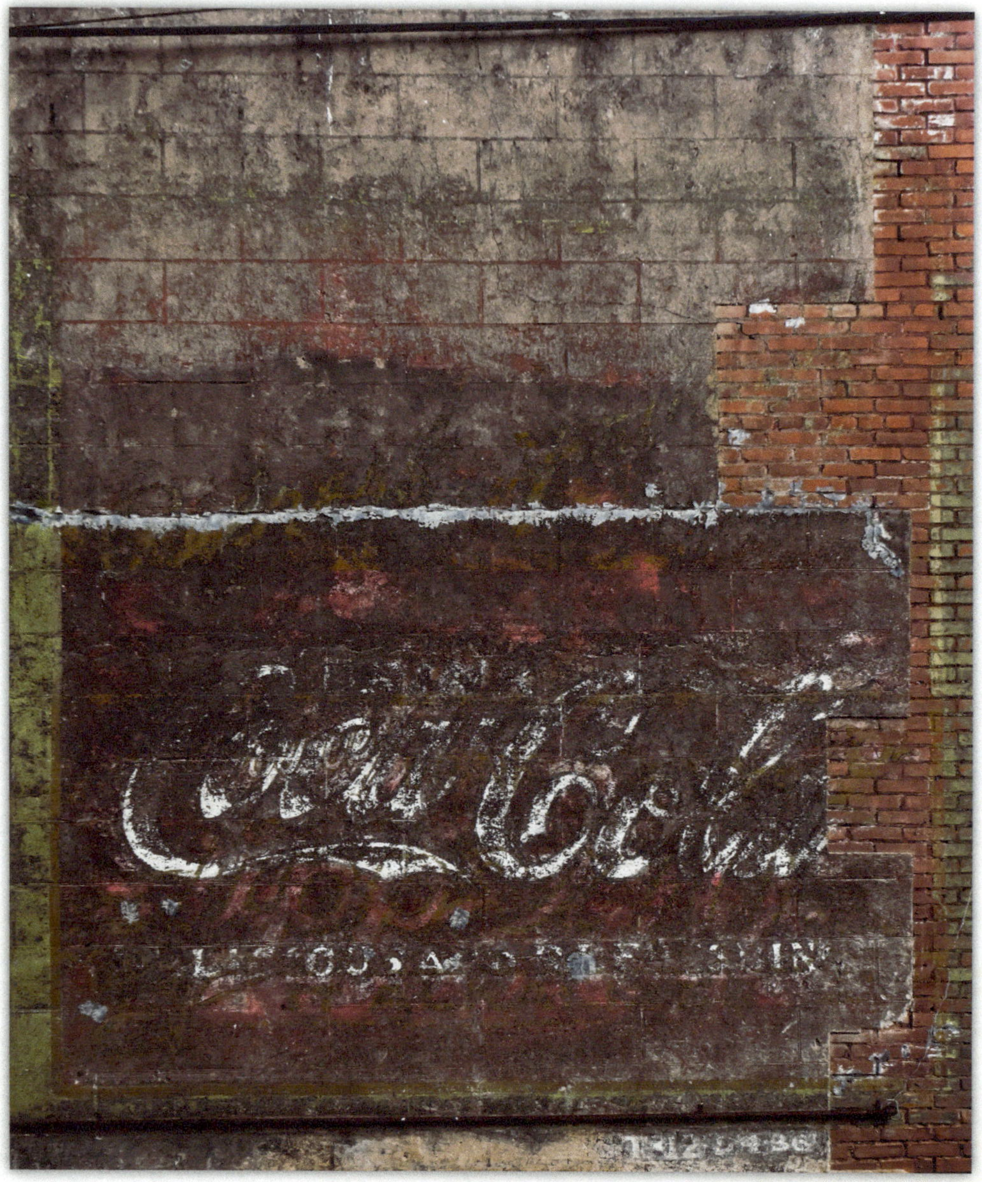

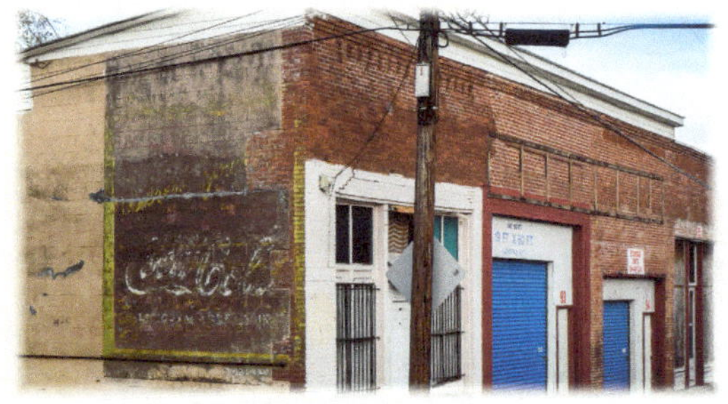

Woodbury

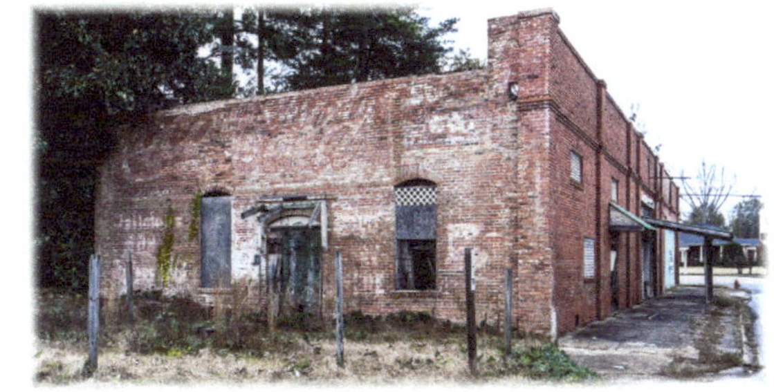

Corner of Bartee Street and Dromedary Street
GPS 32°59'0" N 84°34'60" W

According to building owner Vickey Matthews, who is interested in historic preservation, the building was constructed in 1913.

This Coca-Cola wall sign had the "Delicious and Refreshing" slogan on it.
These clues might date the original sign to 1913, when the building was home to Chun Supply Company.

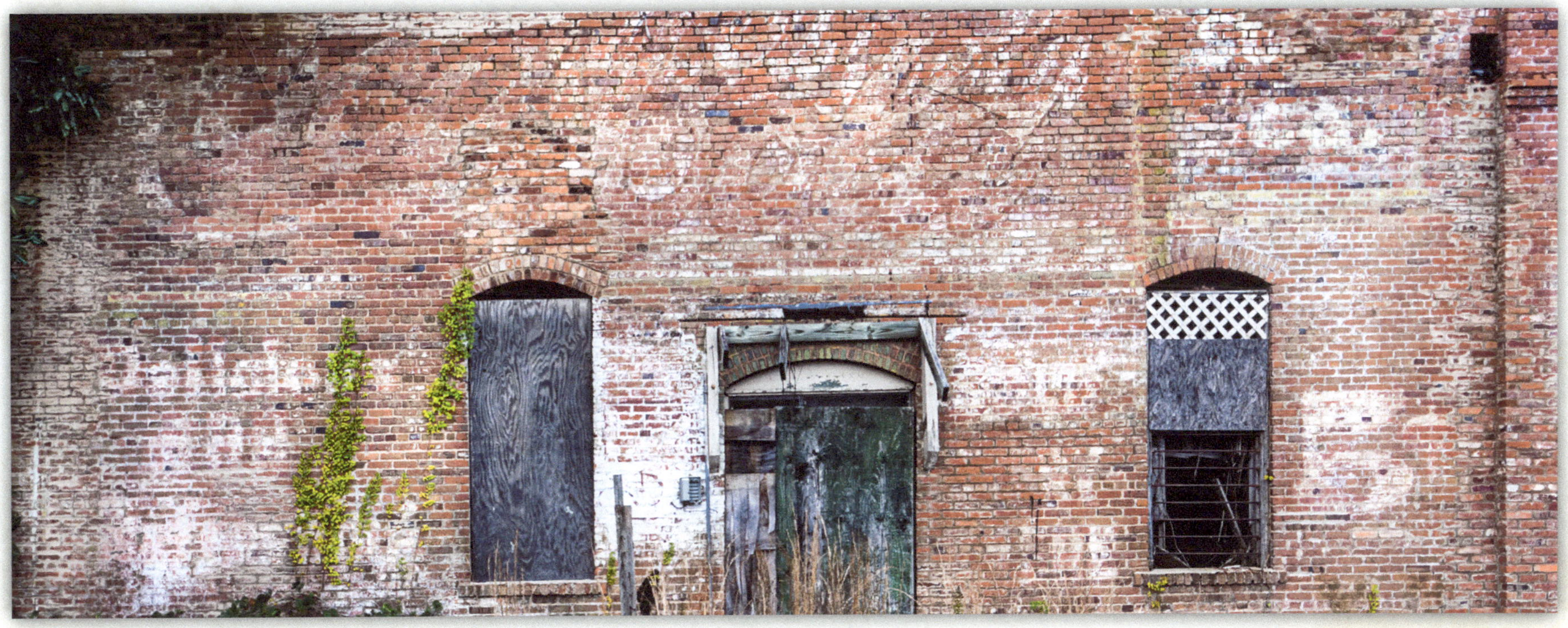

Wrightsville

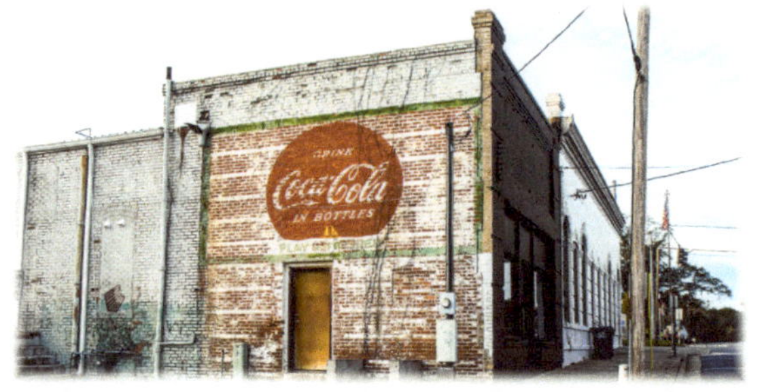

According to Leon Lovett, this wall sign was painted on the building when it was Clayton Lord's Country Store.
The store was built in the 1930s, so this indicates the sign might have been painted after 1942, when Coca-Cola
started advertising bottled Coke.

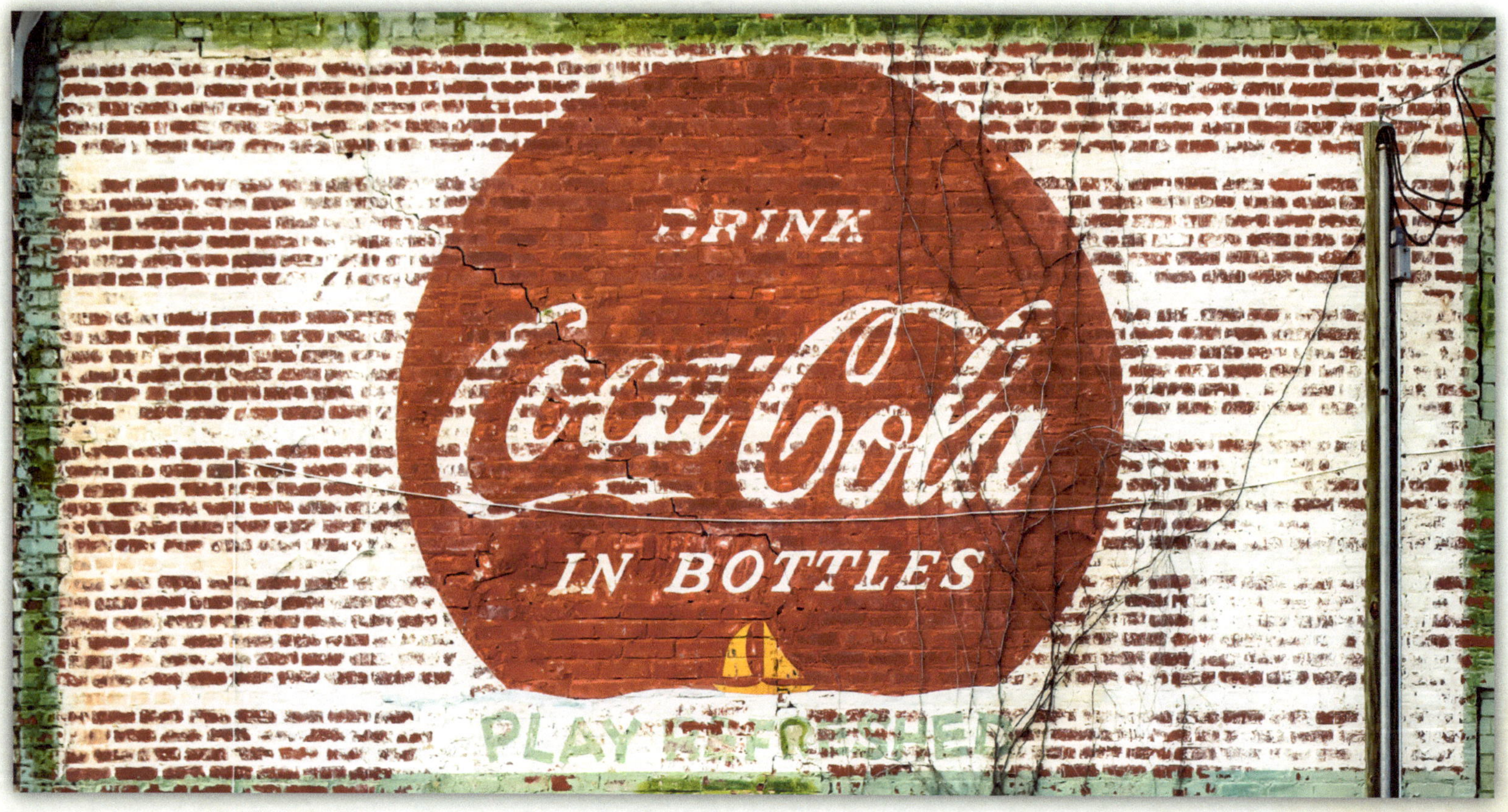

Delicious and Refreshing

I would like to thank all the people who allowed the use of their names, unique stories, and memories associated with historic Coca-Cola wall signs in their communities.

To the cities and Coke distributors that have refurbished the historic Coca-Cola wall signs: you are preserving a unique part of American history, part of the heritage and culture of our cities.

Many of the signs will fade into history, as some already have. These photographic images may be the only record of their presence.

To all the wall painters who shared their unique art and experiences refurbishing the fading ghost signs back to life again, thank you:

Karl and Dianna Love Snell	Alan Kuykendall
Bill Johnson	Mike Martin
Amber Thompson	Kim Wolfe
Ken Lynch	Ronald Fowler
Shannon Lake	Jack Fralin
Charlie Shepherd	John Christian

I apologize for Coca-Cola wall signs that I missed, or for which I have provided incorrect information. Please share corrections, new wall signs found, and personal stories through my website, rawillson.com.

I would also like to thank my friends Keith Ellington and Michael Kormanicki, who made the sacrifice of traveling with me on many miles of backcountry roads throughout Georgia. And finally I offer thanks to my wife, Diane, who is still dealing with my obsession to find another undiscovered Coca-Cola wall sign in every city we travel through.

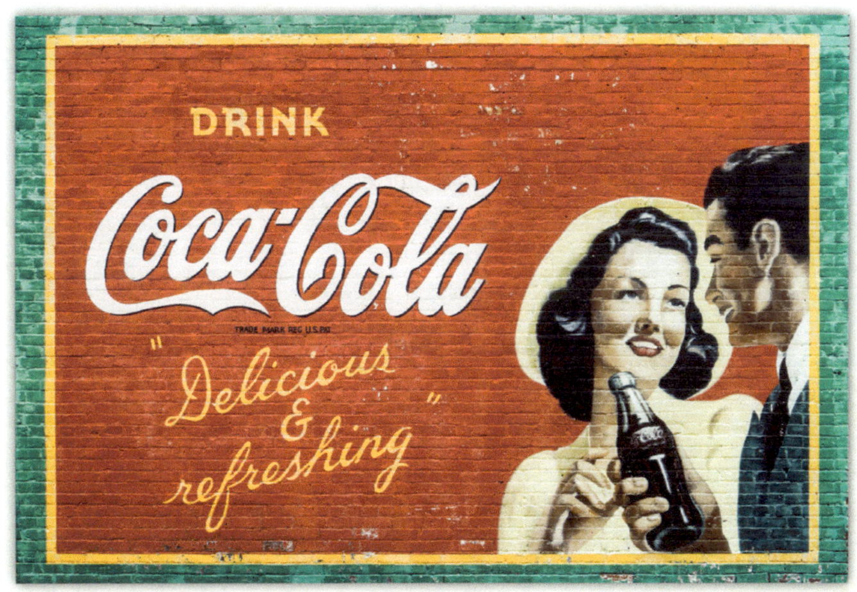

About the Author

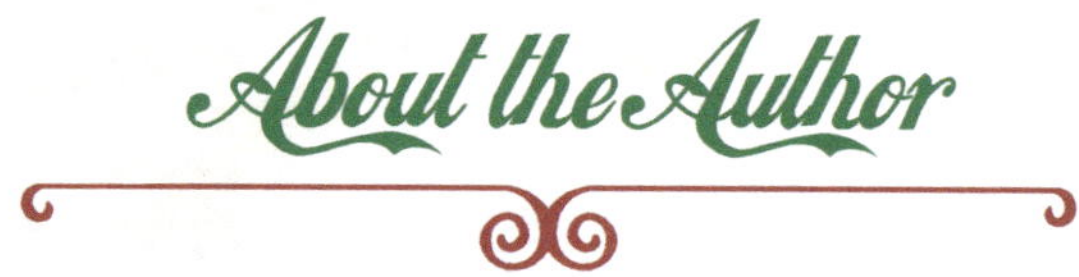

Robert Willson, OD, is a semi-retired optometric physician. His interest in photography started as a teenager with an Argus box camera. His high school graduation gift was a Nikon® F, and Nikons remain his favorite camera today. His interest in light, optics and a calling to serve others eventually led to a vocation in the field of optometry.

His photography education is a result of his college education, extensive reading, and course work at Crealde School of Art in Winter Park, Florida. Through photography teachers Peter Schreyer, Rick Lang, and Bob Learner his appreciation for documentary photography developed.

The Coca-Cola Wall Signs documentary is his first published body of work. You can purchase images or contact Bob Willson through his website at www.rawillson.com or CokeWallSigns@gmail.com.

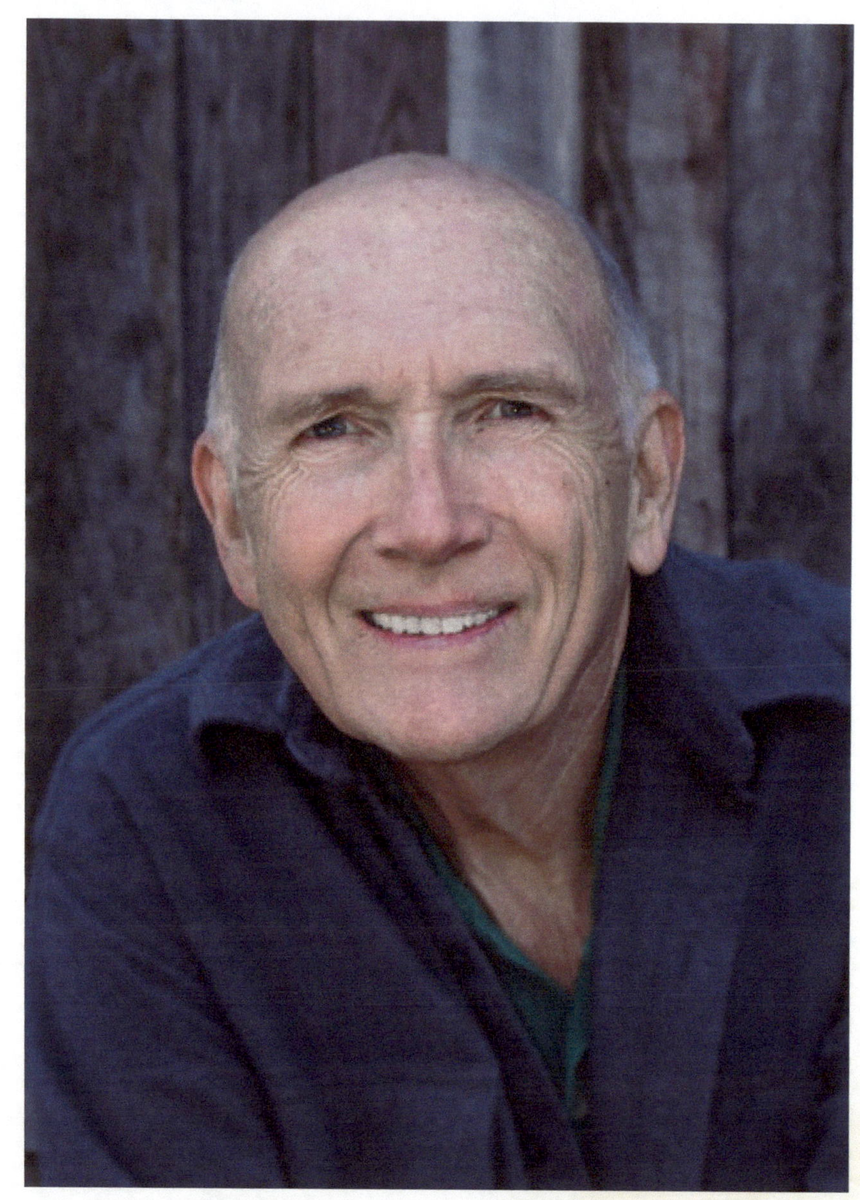

Delicious and Refreshing

This list of wall sign locations shares GPS coordinates of where the photos were taken (not of the wall signs themselves), and location cross streets at the time the photos were taken. Since the project started in 2015, some of the signs may no longer exist, and the names of some streets might have changed.

I credit the towns that have repainted the Coke signs as part of their town history and heritage that is slowly passing. As the signs fade into history they will always be remembered as a special part of people's lives.

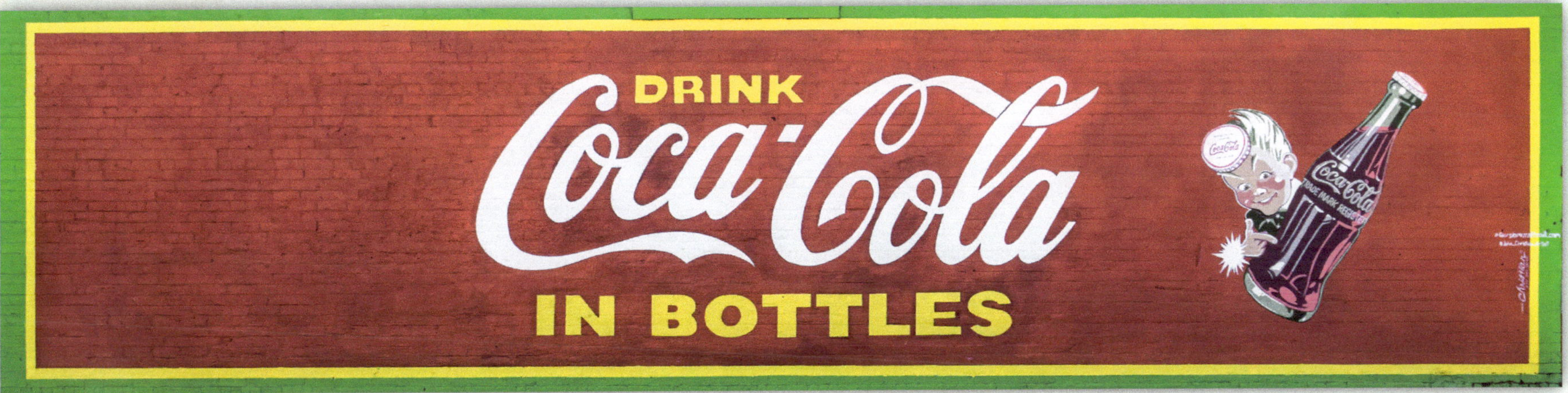

ACWORTH
GPS 34°3'58" N 84°40'40" W
Southside Dr. and pedestrian mall

GPS 34°3'60" N 84°40'39" W
Corner of South Main St/Old Hwy. 41 NW and Dallas St.

ALLENTOWN
GPS 32°35'34" N 83°13'33" W
Corner of Balls Ferry Rd. and Allen Ave.

APPLING
GPS 33°24'27" N 82°39'45" W
Cobbham Rd. near Mt. Carmel Church

ATHENS
GPS 33°57'36" N 83°22'57" W
Corner of Meigs St. and N Newton St.

ATLANTA
GPS 33°46'21" N 84°22'48" W
Mary Mac's - Corner of Ponce DeLeon Ave. and Myrtle St. NE

GPS 33°46'14" N 84°21'10" W
Manuel's Tavern - Corner of N. Highland Ave. NE and Williams Mill Rd. NE

GPS 33°44'1" N 84°22'25" W
Grant Park Coffee - Corner of Augusta Ave. SE and Cherokee Ave. SE

GPS 33°45'8" N 84°23'25" W
Underground Atlanta, Upper Alabama St.

ATTAPULGUS
GPS 30°44'56" N 84°29'3" W
Near the corner of Church St. and E Griffin Ave.Z

AUSTELL
GPS 33°48'48" N 84°38'5" W
Corner of Powder Springs Rd. and Broad St.

BAXLEY
GPS 31°46'39" N 82°20'56" W
Between NE Park Ave. and Washington St. on N Main St./U.S. Hwy. 1 N

BREMEN
GPS 33°43'17" N 85°8'50" W
Buchanan St. in the parking lot

BUCHANAN
GPS 33°48'8" N 85°11'21" W
Corner of Tallapoosa Rd. and Van Wert St.

BUENA VISTA
GPS 32°19'9" N 84°31'4" W
Corner of Forsyth St. and 4th Ave.

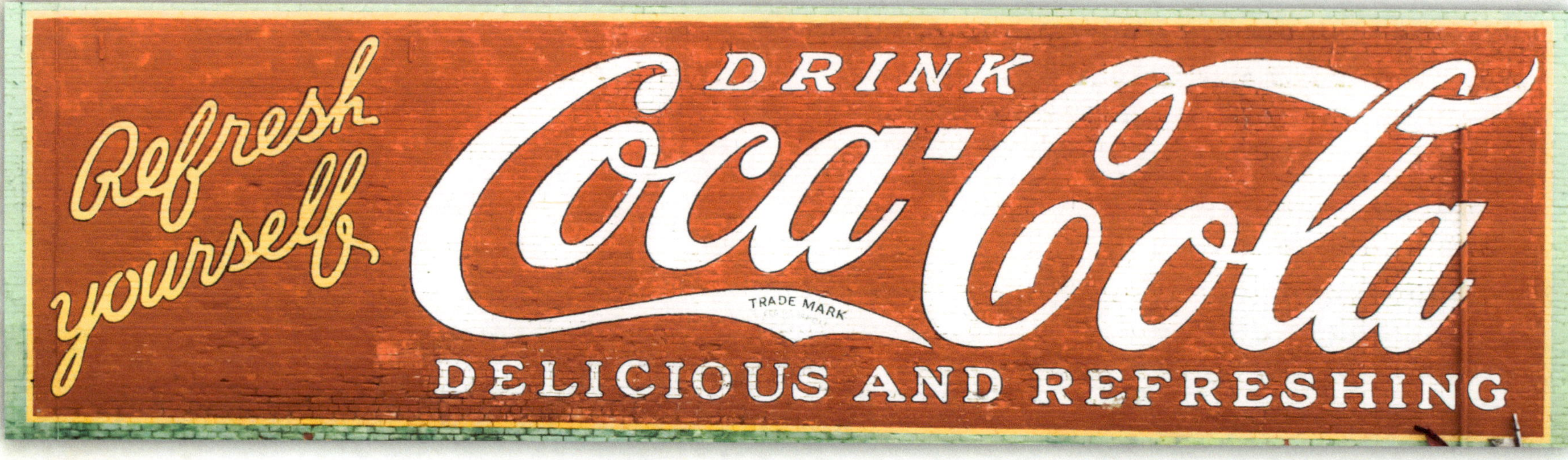

BUTLER
GPS 32°37'0" N 84°14'41" W
U.S. 19 near Garrett Rd.

CAMAK
GPS 33°27'11" N 82°38'46" W
Between Baker St. and Johnson St. on Railroad St.

CARROLLTON
GPS 33°34'48" N 85°4'24" W
Little Gem Barber Shop - Corner of Tanner St.
and State Rte. 166 Bus.

GPS 33°34'35" N 85°4'53" W
C.M. Tanner Grocery - Maple St.
where it crosses the railroad tracks

GPS 33°29'51" N 85°5'2" W
R.E. RINGER - On Martha Berry Hwy/GA 27
near Ringer Rd.

CARTERSVILLE
GPS 34°9'55" N 84°47'44" W
Corner of W Main St. and S Railroad St.

CAVE SPRING
GPS 34°6'28" N 85°20'14" W
Between Church St. and Broad St. on Hwy. 53

CEDARTOWN
GPS 34°0'44" N 85°15'18" W
Corner of Sterling Holloway Pl. and S Main St.

COLBERT
GPS 34°2'17" N 83°12'44" W
Corner of 4th Ave. and S 4th St.

COMMERCE
GPS 34°11'32" N 83°26'49" W
Corner of S Broad St. and Madison St.

CONYERS
GPS 33°39'57" N 84°1'2" W
The Pointe, at the junction of Railroad St. NW, Railroad St.,
and Warehouse St.

GPS 33°39'56" N 84°0'60" W
Walker-Owens Furniture Co, back of the same building in
the parking lot off Railroad St. NW

DOUGLAS
GPS 31°30'26" N 82°51'1" W
Corner of E Bryan St. and Peterson Ave. S, parking lot.

DOUGLASVILLE
GPS 33°28'29" N 85°6'37" W
W.E. Johnson's - On Martha Berry Hwy. (GA 27) near
Roopville Baptist Church

ELLIJAY
GPS 34°41'42" N 84°28'56" W
Old Hwy. 5 at the town square

FAIRMOUNT
GPS 34°26'6" N 84°42'2" W
Corner of South Ave. and Hwy. 53

FORT GAINES
GPS 31°36'20" N 85°2'57" W
Corner of E Carroll St. and Washington St.

GAINESVILLE
GPS 34°17'57" N 83°49'35" W
Corner of Bradford St. NE and Spring St. SE

GRANTVILLE
GPS 33°14'4" N 84°50'7" W
Near the train depot - corner of W Broad St. and
Church St.

GPS 33°14'1" N 84°50'4" W
Old shop at the junction of Church St. and Lone Oak St.

HAMPTON
GPS 33°23'12" N 84°16'58" W
End of Oak St and E. Main St. S

HAPEVILLE
GPS 33°39'32" N 84°24'32" W
Corner of N Central Ave. and N Fulton Ave.

HIRAM
GPS 33°52'30" N 84°45'41" W
On Main St. across railroad tracks and Beatty St.

Delicious and Refreshing

HOBOKEN
GPS 31°10'52" N 82°7'56" W
Corner of W Main St. and Palm St.

JASPER
GPS 34°28'6" N 84°25'47" W
Corner of Hwy. 53 and N Main St.

JEFFERSON
GPS 34°7'4" N 83°34'21" W
On GA 82 N/Sycamore St. across from College St.

LAKEMONT
GPS 34°47'1" N 83°25'1" W
On S. Main St./Old 441 S in the center of town

LAVONIA
GPS 34°26'7" N 83°6'22" W
Corner of W. Main St. and Grogan St.

GPS 34°26'9" N 83°6'20" W
Corner of E Main St. and Grogan St.

LINCOLNTON
GPS 33°47'38" N 82°28'39" W
Corner of N. Peachtree St. and School St.

GPS 33°47'35" N 82°28'38" W
N Peachtree St. and Ward Ave.

LUMBER CITY
GPS 31°55'54" N 82°40'58" W
Corner of Main St. and Central Ave.

MACON
GPS 32°50'8" N 83°38'3" W
Corner of Forsyth St. and Plum St.

MADISON
GPS 33°35'47" N 83°28'5" W
Corner of N 1st St. and W Jefferson St.

MAYSVILLE
GPS 34°14'53" N 83°33'30" W
Corner of Maysville Rd. and Grace St.

McDONOUGH
GPS 33°26'47" N 84°8'47" W
Corner of Macon St. and Sloan St.

MEANSVILLE
GPS 33°2'57" N 84°18'25" W
On Main St. across from Means St.

MILLEDGEVILLE
GPS 33°4'53" N 83°13'37" W
Corner of E Hancock St. and N Wayne St.

MOUNT VERNON
GPS 32°10'30" N 82°35'43" W
Corner of S. Railroad Ave. and Broad St.

MUSELLA
GPS 32°47'51" N 84°1'46" W
On Musella Rd. across from Post Office Rd.

NEWNAN
GPS 33°22'26" N 84°48'3" W
Corner of Spring St. and Lagrange St.

NORRISTOWN
GPS 32°30'26" N 82°29'40" W
Corner of Norristown Covena Rd. and U.S. 221 N Hwy.

PITTS
GPS 31°56'47" N 83°32'26 W
Corner of McDonald Ave. and 8th St. N

PLAINS
GPS 32°1'60" N 84°23'33" W
On S Bond St. between Main St. and Clark St.

POWDER SPRINGS
GPS 33°51'34" N 84°41'3" W
Corner of Marietta St. and Broad St.

GPS 33°51'34" N 84°41'0" W
Corner of Oakview Dr. and Marietta St.

ROCKMART
GPS 34°0'6" N 85°2'30" W
Corner of N Piedmont Ave. and Pearl St.

ROME
GPS 34°15'6" N 85°10'31" W
Corner of Broad St. and E 1st Ave.

ROOPVILLE
GPS 33°28'29" N 85°6'37" W
W.E. JOHNSON'S - On Martha Berry Hwy (Hwy. U.S. 27) near Roopville Road Baptist Church

SANDERSVILLE
GPS 32°58'58" N 82°48'36" W
Sandersville Progress Bldg. on E. Haynes St.

SASSER
GPS 31°43'10" N 84°20'54" W
Corner of Albany Hwy. (GA 82) and Main St. W

SYLVESTER
GPS 31°31'37" N 83°50'12" W
E Liberty Ave. between N Isabella St./GA 112 and N Main St.

GPS 34°5'12" N 84°59'17" W
Corner of Euharlee St. and Mary St.

TENNILLE
GPS 32°56'8" N 82°48'43" W
Corner of W South Central Ave. and S Main St.

VILLA RICA
GPS 33°43'54" N 84°55'11" W
Corner of W Bankhead Hwy. and S Candler St.

WARRENTON
GPS 33°24'25" N 82°39'44" W
Corner of Depot St. and Main St.

GPS 33°24'24" N 82°39'42" W
Masonic Lodge (Drug Sundries)
Corner of W Gibson St. and Main St.

GPS 33°24'27" N 82°39'45" W
Depot St. across from Warren St.

WOODBURY
GPS 32°59'0" N 84°34'60" W
Corner of Bartee St. and Dromedary St.

WRIGHTSVILLE
GPS 32°43'46" N 82°43'1" W
On N Bradford St. between E Elm St. and E College St./GA 57

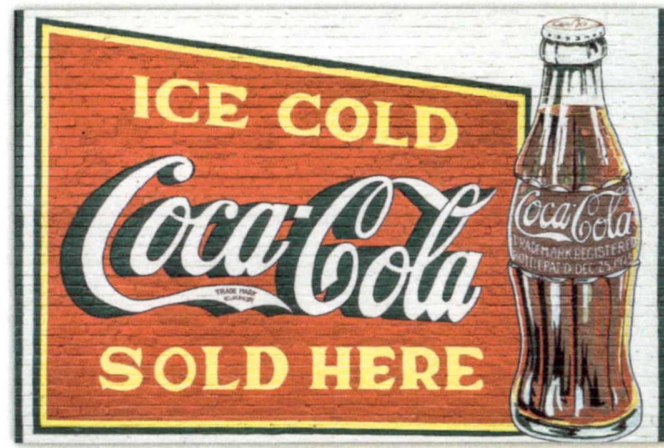

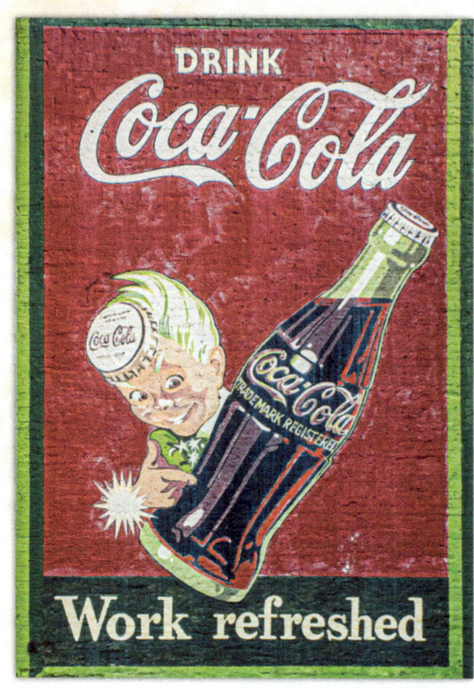

Signs were dated using the sign's location near established railroads and roads, the slogan appearing on the sign, the trademark on the sign, and/or the figure(s) that appear on the sign, like the Sprite Boy.

LEGEND

Regular font: Date of sign estimated using the slogan

Italic font: Date of sign estimated by trademark development

Bold font: Date of sign estimated using the figure(s) that appears in the sign

---

1886 - "Drink Coca-Cola"

1894 to 1940s - Signs Near Railroad Tracks

1893 to 1903 - TRADE MARK in Tail or Does Not Appear

1903 to 1931 - TRADE MARK REGISTERED or TRADE MRK REG in tail

1904 - "Delicious and Refreshing"

1905 - "Coca-Cola Revives and Sustains"

1906 - "The Great National Temperance Beverage"

1917 - "Three Million a Day"

1921 - "Thirst Knows No Season"

1923 - "Enjoy Thirst"

1924 - "Refresh Yourself"

1925 - "Six Million a Day"

1926 - "It Had to Be Good to Get Where It Is"

1927 - "Pure as Sunlight"

1927 - "Around the Corner from Everywhere"

1930 to 1941 - TRADE MARK PAT. REGISTERED, or just REGISTERED in tail

1932 - "Ice Cold Sunshine"

1936 - "The Pause that Refreshes"

1938 - "The Best Friend Thirst Ever Had"

1938 - Silhouette girl appears

1939 - "Thirst Asks Nothing More"

1939 - "Whoever You Are, Whatever You Do, Wherever You May Be, When You Think of Refreshment Think of Ice Cold Coca-Cola"

1940s to 1960s - Signs Near Historic Town Centers and Roads Leading into Town

1941 to 1962 - *TRADE MARK REG U.S. PAT or REG U.S. PAT OFF below tail*

1942 - "The Only Thing Like Coca-Cola is Coca-Cola Itself"

1942 - **Sprite Boy pointing at the Coke bottle**

1948 - "Where There's Coke There's Hospitality"

1948 - **Sprite Boy pointing to a case of Coke**

1949 - "Along the Highway to Anywhere"

1950 to Present - *TRADE MARK R or Trademark R below tail*

1952 - "What You Want is a Coke"

1950s - **Family holding Cokes**

1956 - "Coca-Cola…Makes Good Things Taste Better"

1957 - "Sign of Good Taste"

1958 - "The Cold, Crisp Taste of Coke"

1959 - "Be Really Refreshed"

1963 - "Things Go Better With Coke"

1969 - "It's the Real Thing"

1969 - ***Wave added; trademark R above the wave***

1971 - "I'd Like to Buy the World a Coke"

1975 - "Look Up America"

1976 - "Coke Adds Life"

1979 - "Have a Coke and a Smile"

1982 - "Coke Is It!"

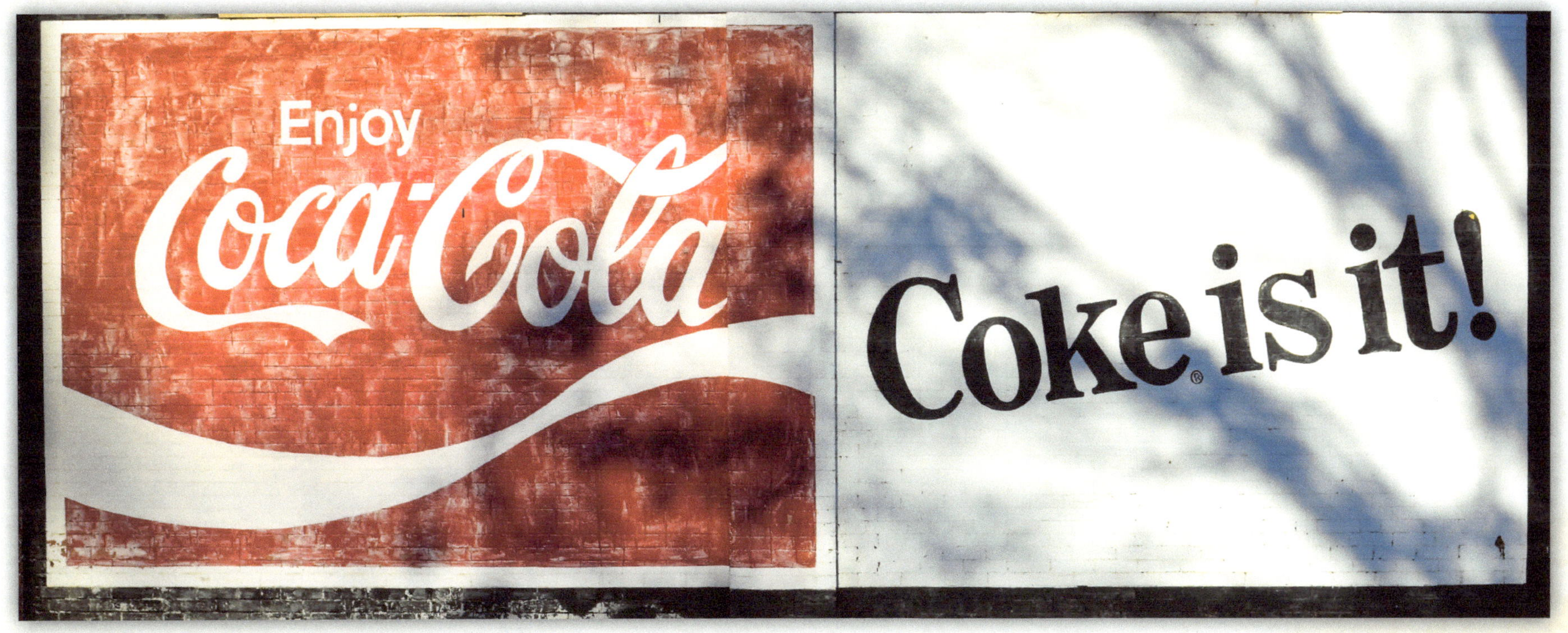

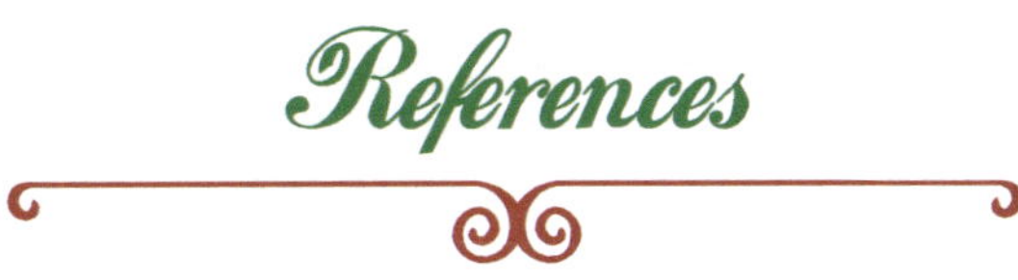

References

- Coca-Cola Company Archives Department: Atlanta, GA Ted Ryan, Phillip Mooney, Jay Moye, Justine Fletcher, Max Davis, and Coca-Cola company website, History section.

- The Coca-Cola Bottler, June 1926, pp 14. (Information on James Couden, beginning of sign painting, early Coke start-up.)

- Richmond Time-Dispatch, "First Coca-Cola Sign Uncovered," Tuesday 6, 1989. (Cartersville sign renovation.)

- The Coca-Cola Bottler, February 1950, pp 49. (Cartersville sign.)

- Coca-Cola Outdoor Paint, Confidential, The Coca-Cola Company, Atlanta, GA, pp 1-13. (Where signs would be painted, paint colors, location decisions, and how they were to be painted.)

- 1954 Wall Sign Manual, Designs for Painted Walls and Bulletins, The Coca-Cola Company, Atlanta, GA. (Updated information of painting and design of wall signs.)

- Randy S. Schaeffer and William E. Bateman, "Coca-Cola Painted Wall Signs," The Coca-Cola Collectors News, February 1988, pp 3-8, 14-15. (Main source of information on early Coke wall sign painting; information in the article came from Outdoor paint publication, use of early pounce patterns, timeline when certain copy on wall signs was used.)

- "Evolution of the Coca-Cola Trademark, 1880s to Present," supplied by Justin Fletcher, Coca-Cola Archives Department, Atlanta, GA. (Information used in trademark location and history section.)

- Heather Taylor, "Who Was the Coca-Cola Sprite Boy?," Huffington Post, Coca-Cola United, www.cocacolaunited.com, December 21, 2017. (Information on Sprite Boy.)

- "History of Coca-Cola Advertising Slogans, It's the Real Thing," Coca-Cola website, History, www.coca-colacompany.com. (History on slogans and their dates.)

- Gyvel Young-Witzel and Michael Karl Witzel, The Sparkling Story of Coca-Cola (Crestline, 2013), pp 14-48, 71-86.

- Ryan, Ted, Slogans for Coca-Cola from 1886 to 2006, Coca-Cola Archives Department, Atlanta, GA.

SIGN PAINTERS (WALL DOGS)

- Christian, John: Painted the Jasper and Cave Spring Coca-Cola signs. He is currently working on the Georgia Mural Trail (georgiamuraltrail.com).

- Cross, Jeff: Painted the Austell Coca-Cola wall sign.

- Fowler, Ronald: Recently painted the Cartersville Coca-Cola wall sign.

- Fralin, Jack, and Johnson, Bill: Painted the Manuel's Tavern Coca-Cola wall sign.

- Kuykendall, Alan: Painted the original Carrollton and Villa Rica Coca-Cola wall signs.

- Lake, Shannon: Painted the Hapeville and McDonough Coca-Cola wall signs.

- Lynch, Ken: Painted the Ellijay Coca-Cola wall sign.

- Shepherd, Charlie: Painted the Lumber City Coca-Cola wall sign.

- Snell, Dianna Love & Karl, Art Productions, Inc.: Painted Plains, Warrenton, Powder Springs, Villa Rica, Acworth, Milledgeville, Gainesville, Mary Mac's, Manuel Tavern, and Douglasville Coca-Cola wall signs.

- Thompson, Amber: Wall sign painter and resource contact.

- Wolfe, Kim: Painted Carrollton, Villa Rica, and Powder Springs Coca-Cola wall signs.

Local Resources

Amos, Bill: Butler – Owner of the McCants Mill Pond.

Anderson, CC: Warrenton – Contact with Andersons Market.

Anderson, Mary: Warrenton – Andersons Market.

Barnes, Mark: Baxley – Pharmacy owner and longtime family history in Baxley.

Barron, Frank: Rome – Rome Coca-Cola bottler.

Beers, Elizabeth: Newman – Resident who knew building's history.

Beggs, Kevin: Carrollton, Lincolnton – Owner of Beggs Funeral Home who has a wealth of information about Coke in the towns.

Belfield, Rachel: Atlanta – Current owner of Grant Park Coffeehouse.

Bishop, Je: Grantville, Newnan, Moreland – Director of Coweta County Genealogical Society.

Bodie, David: Appling – Runs the grocery store and friend of owner.

Bond, Judy: Conyers – Resident who was a great help with the history of Conyers.

Bookout, Kathy: Hiram – Owner of the downtown building.

Brown, Steve: Athens – University Archivist Emeritus, University of Georgia, Hargrett Rare Book and Manuscript Library.

Busby, Barbara: Lavonia – Welcome Center director who spoke with historical society.

Chase, Jeff: Acworth – Downtown Development Director.

Copeland, Billy: McDonough – Mayor of McDonough.

Corker, Ellen: Grantville – Works with Newnan-Coweta Historical Society.

Crawford, John: Carrollton – Owner of the Little Gem Barber Shop.

Daniel, Catherine: Maysville – Owner of the building.

Daniels, Jim: Sylvester – Owner of the building.

Davidson, Robert: Allentown - Mayor

Fletcher, Justine: Coca-Cola Company Archives Department, Atlanta, GA.

Flynn, Theresa: Athens – Vice President of the Athens Historical Society.

Gray, Doris: Attapulgus – Longtime resident of Attapulgus.

Griffin, Brittany: Rome – City staff over historic preservation.

Gumby, John: Lincolnton – Owner of the Hobby Corner.

Henderson, Linda: Hoboken – Longtime resident.

Hudson, Dick: Sandersville, Tennille – Grandfather had Coke franchise for these towns.

King, Wilton: Pitts – City clerk.

Kidd, Culver "Rusty": Milledgeville – Georgia House of Representatives and building owner.

Klear, Karen: Fort Gaines – Contact through city hall who found everything she could about the sign.

Kocher, Ken: Madison – Preservation Planner for Madison.

Loudermilk, Jim: Lakemont – Resident.

Lovett, Leon: Wrightsville – Resident who knew sign history.

Maloof, Brian: Atlanta – Current owner of Manuel's Tavern.

Martin, Mike: Rockmart – Retired wall painter who painted the sign.

Mathis, Pete: Cave Spring – Longtime town resident.

Matthews, Vicky: Woodbury – Owner of the building.

McDaniel, Dale: Soperton – Longtime resident.

Milby, Lee: Meansville – City historian.

Mims, Dr. Nancy: Villa Rica – Chairman of the Villa Rica Historic Preservation Commission.

Moon, Britt: Buena Vista – Owner of Swamp Fox Distilling Co.

Morris, Daniel: Cedartown – Family started the Coke Museum; vice president of operations at The Cedarstream Co, Inc.

Morris, Jamie: Cedartown – Family started the Coke Museum; president of The Cedarstream Co, Inc.

Peterson, Hugh: Mount Vernon – Father owned the *Montgomery Monitor.*

Presley, Richard: Maysville – Mayor of Maysville.

Pinion, Margaret: Camak – Longtime resident.

Redding, Randall: Bremen – President of R. K. Redding Construction, Inc.

Searcy, Alecia: Roopville – Owner of the sweet potato curing house.

Shepherd, Tom: Soperton – Worked at city hall.

Siebert, Shelli: Conyers – Executive director of the Conyers-Rockdale Council for the Arts.

Smith, Lisa: Rome – Contact in city hall.

Stinson, Craig: Lumber City – Owner of the building.

Tanner, Johnny: Carrollton – Owner of Tanner Grocery.

Tatum, William: Cartersville – Owner of Young Brothers Pharmacy.

Thompson Matt: Atlanta – Current owner of Mary Mac's Tea Room.

Trinrud, Ellyn and Carl : Colbert – Owners doing restoration of the building.

Wainwright, Vicky: Butler – Butler city clerk.

Watts, Calvin: Fairmount – Mayor of Fairmount who knew town history.

Williams, Al: Plains – Owned the warehouse across the street.

Williams, Denise: Damascus – Longtime Damascus resident.

Wilson-Edwards, Shauna: Powder Springs – Special projects coordinator for zoning and plan review, City of Powder Springs.

Worthy, Peter & Joan: Roopville, Carrollton – Residents with knowledge of the area.